# Praise for *The Global Education Toolkit for Elementary Learners*

*We all seem to agree that the globalized world needs globally competent citizens, but how to cultivate global competence in our traditionally isolated schools and increasingly narrowed curriculum presents a daunting challenge to our already overworked teachers. In this well-written book, Homa Sabet Tavangar and Becky Mladic-Morales provide numerous practical and inspiring ideas for creating opportunities to foster global competency. A must-have for both experienced and beginning educators who care about their children's future.*

Yong Zhao, Presidential Chair
University of Oregon
Eugene, OR

The Global Education Toolkit for Elementary Learners *is an invaluable how-to guide for educators and parents who want to better prepare children for work and citizenship in the 21st century. Filled with practical suggestions, it is an essential resource for teaching and parenting in today's interdependent world.*

Tony Wagner
Author of *The Global Achievement Gap and Creating Innovators*
Innovation Education Fellow
Harvard University

*I've been deeply concerned as I travel around the country by how little attention is being paid to the global competence of our nation's young people. In the 21st century we need global citizens and students capable of thriving in the global economy. Fortunately, Homa Sabet Tavangar and Becky Mladic-Morales have written a tremendous new resource for educators who want a comprehensive guide to how to bring global competence to their students. Not only do their students need these global competencies, they are anxiously waiting to be taught in these contexts. Don't wait another minute to construct them!*

Ken Kay, CEO
EdLeader 21
Co-author, *The Leader's Guide to 21st Century Education*
Tucson, AZ

*We have been wading around for a number of years talking about global-ready graduates, but unable to marry the desire we have for our students to obtain global competency skills with the realities of preparing students for standardized tests. Now we can.*

*One only need to look inside the cover at the ten ways the book can be used to know that a long-awaited answer to desperately needed curricular and pedagogical changes in the new global world order has arrived. Thank you.*

*Tavangar and Morales nail it by offering clever, economical, and practical suggestions to merge traditional academic content with desperately needed global competency skills in our curriculum. Not a book to be read, pondered, then shelved, but rather a manual to be open on the teacher's desk at all times. I need this now.*

Robert M. Hollister, EdD
Superintendent
Eastern Lancaster County School District
Lancaster, PA

The Global Education Toolkit for Elementary Learners *engaged, empowered and educated me deeper as an elementary educator. It encouraged me to continue building that global learning community in my classroom. The ideas and activities provide opportunities for differentiated instruction and support the state standards across the curriculum. This book is the next best thing to actually taking your students on a long field trip around the world!*

Luke Merchlewitz
Elementary Educator
Winona Area Public Schools
National Education Association, Senior Global Learning Fellow
2011 MN—Teacher of Excellence

The Global Education Toolkit for Elementary Learners *is a gift to educators with heartfelt, rigorous, and creative strategies to make the shift from the last century to the now. Tavangar and Morales have shaped an organized, dynamic, and thoughtful series of both classic and digital approaches to personalizing the global for our learners.*

Dr. Heidi Hayes Jacobs
Editor and author of Leading the New Literacies: Digital, Media, and Global, Solution-Tree
President, Curriculum Designers
Rye, NY

*Joy and skill! That's what this compendium of insights, innovations and practical wisdom ultimately delivers! Homa Tavangar and Becky Morales open up a true 21st century toolkit for teachers and parents alike. This work uses the engine of a child's wonder to spark a revolution in "learning tools" for helping children express their deepest joy.*

John Hunter
President and Founder
World Peace Game Foundation
Charlottesville, VA

*This book is very timely. With tighter budgets and increased demands, educators need simple, yet effective ways to cultivate a global perspective. The focus on integrating technology and showing how ideas and activities can be seamlessly integrated into the Common Core are especially helpful.*

Jennifer McMahon
Assistant Principal
Brockport Central School District
Brockport, NY

*This is a book that I would add to my professional library and use as a required textbook in a methods or differentiation course for teachers (pre and in service).*

Yolanda Abel
Assistant Professor
Johns Hopkins University
Baltimore, MD

*This book takes a very practical approach, as seen in the name "Toolkit" and the concrete suggestions and resources that are provided to facilitate global activities that can start slowly and organically from dedicated parents or other individual school staff. I think K-5 parents, teachers, administrators, and staff would find the book useful given the specific resources that are provided in the book, the easy-to-follow personal stories, and the concrete but manageable suggestions provided by the authors.*

Margaret Powers
Lower School Technology Coordinator
The Episcopal Academy
Newtown Square, PA

*This is a great resource for K-6 teachers. Because it integrates global learning into different disciplines, I think it would be very useful. Since I teach math I was very interested in the section that discussed integrating global learning in mathematics. I really liked the hands-on and project based learning activities; they were well presented and easy to follow.*

Sandra Burvikovs
K–5 Gifted Specialist
May Whitney Elementary School
Lake Zurich, IL

*I would definitely buy this book. It is well written and organized and, as a teacher, I would have welcomed this resource. It supports the move in education toward 21st Century skills, including working with diversity and being an effective team member. Greater understanding of diversity reduces student conflict and bullying.*

Jim Gibbons
Senior Education Advisor
Alberta School Boards Association
Alberta, Canada

*This toolkit allows teachers to expand their learning as well as the learning of their students and the entire school community.*

Gustava Cooper-Baker, Ed.D.
Retired Principal
Kansas City, MO

*Homa Sabet Tavangar and Becky Mladic-Morales have created a masterful collection of resources and practical strategies for building global competency in young learners. At a time when it has never been more critical to ensure that young people develop the knowledge, skills, and dispositions to thrive in our interconnected, diverse global society, this book is a road map for educators looking to globalize their approach.*

Dana Mortenson
Cofounder and Executive Director
World Savvy

THE
# Global Education Toolkit

FOR
# ELEMENTARY LEARNERS

**CORWIN**
A SAGE Company

THE
# Global Education Toolkit
FOR
## ELEMENTARY LEARNERS

Homa Sabet Tavangar

Becky Mladic-Morales

**CORWIN**
A SAGE Company

**CORWIN**
A SAGE Company

FOR INFORMATION:

Corwin
A SAGE Company
2455 Teller Road
Thousand Oaks, California 91320
(800) 233–9936
www.corwin.com

SAGE Publications Ltd.
1 Oliver's Yard
55 City Road
London EC1Y 1SP
United Kingdom

SAGE Publications India Pvt. Ltd.
B 1/I 1 Mohan Cooperative Industrial Area
Mathura Road, New Delhi 110 044
India

SAGE Publications Asia-Pacific Pte. Ltd.
3 Church Street
#10-04 Samsung Hub
Singapore 049483

Managing Editor:   Arnis Burvikovs
Associate Editor:   Desirée A. Bartlett
Editorial Assistant:   Ariel Price
Production Editor:   Amy Schroller
Typesetter:   C&M Digitals (P) Ltd.
Proofreader:   Pam Suwinsky
Indexer:   Rick Hurd
Cover and Interior Designer:   Janet Kiesel

Printed in the United States of America

A catalog record of this book is available from the Library of Congress.

ISBN 978-1-4833-4418-8

This book is printed on acid-free paper.

SUSTAINABLE FORESTRY INITIATIVE
Certified Chain of Custody
Promoting Sustainable Forestry
www.sfiprogram.org
SFI-01268

SFI label applies to text stock

14 15 16 17 18 10 9 8 7 6 5 4 3 2 1

# Contents

## CHAPTER 1

### How to Get Started: Planning Considerations for Bringing the Global to Your School   1

## CHAPTER 2

### Things to Do: Look at All the Places We Can Go!   21

# CHAPTER 3

Infusing Global Learning Into Academic Subject Areas (With Special Consideration for Aligning Common Core Standards)    67

# CHAPTER 4

Technology Tools to Connect With the World: Unlocking Global Education 2.0 113

# CHAPTER 5

## Charitable Giving and Service: Ready, Set, Make a Difference!     157

# ADDITIONAL RESOURCES  191

www.corwin.com/globaledtoolkit

# Thank You.
# Merci. Gracias.
# Xie Xie.

This book began as a kernel of an idea to share resources and tips to organize a successful international event or week, and through our collaboration, as well as the input and encouragement of too many people to mention individually, grew into a much more ambitious project. Every example from a school, organization, teacher, parent, or child you read about in this Toolkit represents someone that we likely tracked down, were inspired by, and who graciously went back and forth with us to get their story right. If you read about them in these pages, please know that we admire and thank them. Their real, and often courageous, patient, even visionary experiences form the backbone of the *Global Education Toolkit*—without them, we couldn't encourage our readers to try so many creative, new ideas.

We've been fortunate to work with a great team at Corwin, namely Executive Editor Arnis Burvikovs, Senior Associate Editor Desiree Bartlett, and ever-helpful Editorial Assistant Ariel Price. They embraced the concept right away and have been incredibly responsive, thoughtful, and enthusiastic. We became an instant team.

Our collective Sabet-Tavangar and Mladic-Morales families stand as the stars between every line in this book. Between the two of us, we have seven children, a supportive husband each, six siblings (a special thanks to Emily Mladic), their spouses, and our four parents and in-laws who stepped in for crucial advising, cheerleading, babysitting, and feeding. Our "global kids" say and do and bring home from school so many awesome things, stay relentlessly curious, and have inspired our journeys in developing global education resources; we wouldn't be doing this without them. Our friends, neighbors, and readers from the *Growing Up Global* and Kid World Citizen communities also served as continual sources of ideas, challenges, and encouragement. What a gift to have support that transcends every boundary.

We learn that to be globally competent, effective communication is crucial and takes diverse forms. So this is just one layer of saying "thank you," but please know that if you helped illuminate in some way the path to building or completing this book, we still have many more "thank-yous" to express. Thanks also in advance to those of you who believe in bringing global learning to all children, even in the face of tight resources and academic and professional pressure. We hope opportunities from our Toolkit can reach every child so they truly see themselves as global citizens ready to make their mark on our ever-more-connected planet.

# About the Authors

 **Homa Sabet Tavangar** is the author of *Growing Up Global: Raising Children to Be at Home in the World* (Random House/Ballantine Press), hailed by national education and business leaders and media ranging from Dr. Jane Goodall to the BBC, NBC, ABC, *Washington Post, Chicago Tribune and Sun-Times, Boston Globe,* PBS, Scholastic, *Parents* magazine, Rodale, and many more.

Her work is sparking initiatives to help audiences from CEOs to kindergartners learn and thrive in a global context—and have fun along the way. She serves as education advisor to the Pulitzer Center on Crisis Reporting and has been a visiting scholar at the University of Pennsylvania. She is a contributor to the *Huffington Post,* PBS, SproutTV, Momsrising, GOOD, Ashoka's Start Empathy initiative, and Edutopia, among other media, and is a sought-after speaker and trainer around global citizenship, parenting, globalizing curriculum, empathy, and inclusion. She is the author of "Growing Up in a Global Classroom" in the anthology *Mastering Global Literacies,* edited by Heidi Hayes-Jacobs (Solution Tree Press, 2013).

Homa has 20 years of experience in global competitiveness and organizational, business, and international development with hundreds of businesses, nonprofit agencies, governments, and international organizations. She has lived on three continents and is a graduate of UCLA and Princeton University's Woodrow Wilson School of Public and International Affairs. She speaks four languages and her religious heritage includes four of the world's major faiths. She has served on various nonprofit boards, including the Board of Directors of the Tahirih Justice Center, a national leader protecting immigrant women and girls fleeing violence. She is married and the mother of three.

 **Becky Mladic-Morales** is the founder of KidWorldCitizen.org, offering parents and educators activities that help young minds go global. Her work has been featured by Scholastic, the U.S. Department of Education, NBC Latino, MSN, and PBSKids, among others. She is a teacher, teacher-trainer, speaker, and educational consultant. She has worked with different foreign exchange programs, including the setup of the International Club at her local elementary school. Becky holds an MA in teaching ESL, concentrating on cross-cultural communication, from the University of Illinois in Urbana-Champaign and an MA in school counseling with a focus on immigrants in schools from Roosevelt University in Chicago. For the past 15 years, she has taught ESL and Spanish in different settings ranging from high school to college-level courses. Her expertise encompasses global education, geo-literacy, service-learning, educational technology aiming to connect students worldwide, as well as setting up cultural exchange programs. Becky currently resides in Houston with her husband and four children, whose curiosity, compassion, and energy are her perpetual inspiration.

# Introduction and What You Can Get Out of This Book

*"We need to learn to live in this global world,*
*to manage the events of the global world. So far,*
*we have not yet learned how to do it well."*

—Mikhail Gorbachev, April 23, 2012,
speaking to students in Chicago Public Schools

## Why This Book?

Recall a moment, after a really good day at school, when your child steps into your arms and conveys an enthusiasm that can barely be contained by your embrace. Perhaps he figured out a math concept without stumbling, got to mix elements that created a surprise chemical reaction, played his favorite game in gym class, created a piece of art in a style that opened new frontiers in his imagination, watched a performance that inspired him, learned a phrase in a foreign language that delightfully rolled off his tongue, or made a new friend. While it's hard to avoid reading anything about education today that doesn't sound the warnings of a highly competitive, globally connected, technology-driven knowledge economy requiring "21st-century skills," when it comes down to the child into whose eyes you lovingly gaze, what you really care about is for him to come home happy and look forward to going back to school the next day.

This book is about bridging that gap between the pure joy that accompanies childhood discovery and the realities of learning for a changing, interconnected world our children will inherit. Whether you are a parent or a teacher (or both) reading this, the intersection between the joy and the skills is the crucial—and often elusive—sweet spot you might spend years seeking to find and nurture.

Our children's success depends more than ever on their ability to communicate and work effectively across cultures, to adapt to rapid changes in the ways complex problems must be solved, and to realize that not everyone thinks like they do. The sooner they start thinking about the wider world, the better they'll do—not because they are motivated by panic or competition but because they enjoy interacting with new friends around the world, discovering new interests, and imagining doing big things in it. This positive approach can help them to flourish in life.[1]

For today's children—tomorrow's leaders—solutions to challenges around health, the environment, natural resources, the economy, global security, and even ideological coexistence and the cultivation of creative arts will be among the most urgent questions they will face.[2] The answers can't be contained within one city's, let alone one country's borders. Though yet to be invented, we know that effective approaches to these increasingly complex and interconnected issues will be centered around a whole new category of skills like *global collaboration, empathy, creativity, and effective communication.* These also happen to be the skills most needed for peace building and living a happy, meaningful life. As big and elusive as realizing these outcomes may be, the small steps we take at home and at school to launch meaningful connections with the wider world can make the most lasting impact.

The need for a straightforward "how-to" guide, or toolkit, for K–5 learners to connect with the world led us to team up and write this book. Over the past few years, terrific global tools have proliferated, a #globaled (global education) community is sharing ideas on social media, and adults are taking more initiative to bring the world into their schools. But wading through so many resources can be unwieldy, offering content that is inappropriate for younger learners, and volunteers and professionals can feel isolated or overwhelmed by the effort.

In our work around global learning and raising global citizens, we were continually asked which specific resources and tips would encourage creative, empathic, effective global citizens and learners as well as help to build more inclusive elementary school communities. Resources for secondary school students seem to have proliferated, but adapting these for younger students often doesn't work, limiting in-depth global learning and authentic engagement in elementary schools. This book is our attempt to share in one easy-to-use guide our own experiences and research, as well as hundreds of excellent outside resources we have personally used—to enrich and enliven the global learning experience for K–5 students and the adults who care about them.

## Ten Reasons You Should Use This Book

This book can assist you if want to do the following:

1. You would like to seamlessly integrate global lessons into existing curriculum.
2. You are considering organizing special events around global awareness at your school.
3. You already are planning an International Day, Week, Month, or Year and want to infuse some fresh ideas and best practices.
4. You would like to involve more parent and community volunteers and organizations in the life of your school.
5. Your elementary school is planning on holding after-school clubs with a global theme, from foreign language classes to art and sports activities.
6. You would like to use educational technology to connect with students in other locations and participate in global collaboration projects.
7. You are looking for fresh ideas for your classroom teaching.
8. You would like to incorporate global themes and activities into your lessons meeting Common Core Standards.
9. You are looking for fodder and feedback on global projects with your Personal Learning Networks.
10. You care about the world and hope the children in your life grow up to get along with each other and with the wider world!

Whether your school is based in a cosmopolitan city or a rural town, with ample or very limited resources, *The Global Education Toolkit for Elementary Learners* offers numerous exercises and tools for incorporating global awareness into the curriculum and outside class time. Building intercultural skills does not happen in a vacuum of a single lesson or a single week but rather through meaningful exchanges and activities taking place throughout the academic year.

We start from the position that schools do not need to add an extra class for teaching global studies. Instead, when they take an interdisciplinary approach to integrate multicultural lessons into their classes across grade levels and content areas—personalizing the global—they will begin to realize what global citizenship looks and feels like, and this contributes to a process of cultivating lifelong learners. Children begin to see diversity as an advantage and a natural part of their lives; they are less likely to view differences as a threat, and they will approach international experiences with greater know-how and enthusiasm.

## Considerations for an International Fair

We recognize that every school will be at a different place in realizing global education goals. Some may not be ready to integrate global resources and perspectives throughout the curriculum but could benefit greatly from a special focus like a "Global Awareness Week," "Culture Day," or "International Fair." An annual celebration allows students to experience many different cultures in a concentrated time frame. This is not the same as holding a single, isolated international activity while ignoring global studies the rest of the year.

An effective "International Fair" can meet distinct needs:

1. as a culminating showcase of students' projects from the year

2. to highlight and celebrate the diverse cultures represented in the school, fostering an increasingly inclusive community

3. to encourage curiosity and learning about various cultures and countries

4. to build enthusiasm for new global initiatives just starting out

5. as an entry point for a topic to be studied more in depth, possibly across age and grade levels (such as folktales, water resources, or where food comes from).

## How to Use This Toolkit

Whether you want to integrate international lessons throughout the year or would like to start an International Night at your school, this guide provides the tools for practical, effective, and fun activities that will advance global awareness in your K–5 students—and beyond. Many teachers are interested in increasing their students' knowledge about the world but haven't found the right activities to incorporate into their existing lessons. The age-appropriate ideas and resources we have collected here can be used on their own for individual lessons, in homeschooling, in after-school clubs, in Scouts, for special celebrations, or to tie into an entire year's theme. Teachers, parents, and volunteers can use the simple and clear instructions, low- or no-cost ideas, while students will thrive with experiential learning.

The following chapters contain numerous activities that can be used on their own or altogether. There is no required sequence or recipe that calls for anyone to follow the sections step by step.

*Chapter 1—How to Get Started: Planning Considerations for Bringing the Global to Your School.* The information in this chapter helps teachers, staff, and volunteers take the first steps, ask the right questions to determine the scope of their efforts, determine themes, and build support.

*Chapter 2—Things to Do: Look at All the Places We Can Go!* This is a stand-alone resource of over 50 globally inspired ideas that you could implement immediately, in any setting.

*Chapter 3—Infusing Global Learning Into Academic Subject Areas (With Special Consideration for Aligning Common Core Standards).* This chapter offers a breakdown by subject areas, so global learning can be plugged right into various academic subjects and themes. It also showcases examples of lessons that meet Common Core Standards.

*Chapter 4—Technology Tools to Connect With the World: Unlocking Global Education 2.0.* Tap into some of the best and simplest interactive, digital tools to build relationships with people, places, and ideas in the wider world, as well as enhance your own professional development.

*Chapter 5—Charitable Giving and Service: Ready, Set, Make a Difference!* Develop your school, club, or classroom's plan for making a difference—near or far. Get inspired by—and learn from—dozens of examples shared in this chapter, of elementary school–aged kids engaging in philanthropic giving and service, to start your own initiative.

Whether you dedicate a day, week, month, or entire year to an international theme or you decide to intersperse global activities and learning across disciplines, special activities, or community building, a thoughtful execution of global education resources, themes, and technology can help build a foundation of awareness that can change the school's culture and shape the way students will react to the world around them, for many years to come. We hope that the resources contained in the following chapters will help you along a path of discovery and encourage lifelong learning.

## Note From the Publisher

All of the resources in this Toolkit have been collated by the authors and are available through a companion website: www.corwin.com/globaledtoolkit. On the website, you will find links to all of the resources **bolded in blue** throughout the book, organized by chapter and section in which the links appear. Also, the Additional Resources are available on the website to be downloaded and printed. Please note that there are no live links in this book.

Links provided on the companion website may provide access to websites that are not maintained, sponsored, endorsed, or controlled by Corwin. Your use of these third-party websites will be subject to the terms and conditions posted on such websites. Corwin takes no responsibility and assumes no liability for your use of any third-party website, nor does Corwin approve, sponsor, endorse, verify, or certify information available at any third-party website.

## Author's Note From Homa

When I made a career and lifestyle switch to research and write *Growing Up Global: Raising Children to Be at Home in the World*, the sheer amount of resources available to help expose our children to the wider world overwhelmed me. Like a game of Whack-a-Mole, each time I thought I'd gotten a topic under control, more initiatives and perspectives would pop up, and the "game" could never be won or done. I resolved that issue when it became clear that my goal needed to be to help *share a mind-set that would lay a foundation for a lifelong journey of connecting* with a dynamic, fascinating, perplexing, surprising, beautiful world. Though many practical resources and recommendations were included in *Growing Up Global*, I found the secret sauce was more about the vision than the "stuff." But the need for turn-key solutions for lesson plans and a global education toolkit never went away.

As I traveled to dozens of communities across North America with *Growing Up Global*, teachers and parents continued to ask for more specifics, and I would often write the name of an organization or tool that had just come to my attention on a blackboard, piece of scrap paper, or included in a PowerPoint presentation. A more systematic process clearly was needed. Thanks to the power of social media, Becky Morales and I met virtually. We admired each other's work, and it seemed to converge around a much-needed tool for elementary school–aged children, where we saw the biggest gap. Collaboration seemed to come naturally, and I'm so happy to share the result of our partnership—this resource. I'm sure the Whack-a-Mole feeling won't go away, as innovation continues—and that's a great thing.

I hope this book can serve as a strong beginning for anyone who wishes to instill a love of global learning in children who will certainly inherit a world whose future connections we can dimly anticipate. As this is a labor of love, we know the process isn't over, and we look forward to sharing this journey of learning and discovery with all who care to join us.

# Author's Note From Becky

Years ago, when I began to teach Spanish in a local high school, I was shocked at the lack of geography skills and basic cultural awareness I witnessed. Pointing to a map of Europe and Africa, I had been talking about the Islamic architecture in southern Spain and the influence of Arabic on certain Spanish words. I was about to explain how the Moors had come up across the Strait of Gibraltar. As I pointed to Morocco and North Africa, I asked the students to name the continent. In class after class—and even at another school when I changed jobs—students incorrectly answered "South America." *National Geographic* confirms that geography is taught by less than 9% of K–12 social studies teachers and not even one quarter of high school students graduate with a geography class.

A few years later, I brought in my sister-in-law, visiting us from Mexico City, to class as a guest speaker. In the Spanish 1 classes, students were to interview her in Spanish, about her life as a teenager in Mexico. Imagine my embarrassment as my students asked her (coming from one of the most populous cities in the world) if she had ever seen an apple, a car, or a computer before. They simply had not been exposed to many people outside of their local community. How would this deficiency—this lack of global awareness—stand in the way of their future?

In my Spanish classes, I did my best to weave together language, culture, and geography lessons, and guide my students to discover the richness of Spain and Latin America. I wanted my students to graduate from high school with a global mind-set, a friendly attitude toward people of different backgrounds, and an awareness beyond their immediate community. Nonetheless, I understood that these lessons of our interconnectedness should begin much earlier and should be an integral part of all of their subjects. Teachers and parents of elementary-aged kids can—and should—take the initiative to give them the opportunity to see issues from different perspectives and communicate with and learn from peers around the world. In this book, our aim is to help educators to do so, offering very practical tools.

As we raise our own four young children, my husband and I seek out activities, festivals, and experiences that will expose them to the world and to other cultures. We have quite the international family: My husband is from Mexico City, we have two biological daughters, one son adopted from China, and another son adopted from Ethiopia. As their parents, we feel it is our responsibility to not only teach them about our family's cultures and traditions and to instill pride in their heritage but also to demonstrate respect toward all people regardless of race or ethnicity.

Developing global awareness in children is not only important for multicultural families such as ours: The world is more interrelated today than ever before, and parents, schools, and businesses are pushing to change the way schools teach and prepare our students for the 21st century. Are we preparing today's youth for the international challenges they will face tomorrow? How can we start building a global foundation for our younger students? I think children are never too young to begin learning about the world, especially when the activities are fun and interactive.

# NOTES

1. Pioneer in positive psychology Dr. Martin Seligman posits that to flourish is the goal in measuring "well-being," which goes further than the attainment of happiness. Flourishing realizes ever-increasing "*Positive* emotion, *Engagement*, *Meaning*, Positive *Relationships*, and *Accomplishment*," or PERMA. This also can be considered as "thriving." From: Seligman, M. E. P. (2011). *Flourish: A visionary new understanding of happiness and well-being.* New York, NY: Free Press.

2. These findings have emerged from numerous studies such as: Committee for Economic Development. (2006). *Education for Global Leadership: The Importance of International Studies and Foreign Language Education for U.S. Economic and National Security.* Washington, DC: Author. Retrieved from http://files.eric.ed.gov/fulltext/ED502294.pdf

www.corwin.com/globaledtoolkit

# How to Get Started Planning Considerations for Bringing the Global to Your School

So you've made the decision to include more global activities in your classroom, curriculum, or club, or possibly to host an international event for your school. How should you start? Where should you look for ideas on activities that excite and engage the students? What types of events and activities should you include? What can parents do to help? How can you involve the entire school community in some way? Will you be happy with taking "baby steps," or are you looking to shift the whole school culture toward a global orientation?

The planning steps might seem overwhelming, but it doesn't need to feel that way. Use the organizational tools offered here, and tap into some of the great resources available (referenced throughout this book) in order to successfully engage your students in experiential and cultural learning opportunities—whatever your budget, infrastructure, location, level of expertise, or aspirations. In this chapter we try to break down some of the key planning steps to create a more systematic, inclusive, and fulfilling process.

## Assess Your Starting Point

Before plunging into execution and recruitment details, understand your starting point. Take a step back and look at where you are, what you have to work with, and who will work with you. For example, has there been any previous experience with global learning and activities? What is already happening? Are there any funds available for new programming? What other resources can you tap into? Who are your natural allies, and how can you bring on more supporters? It may sound obvious to ask, "Where are we starting from?" (Answer: "The beginning!") But the reality is that this first step could take a few minutes or a few weeks and should help to avoid reinventing the wheel; it can help you to learn from past experiences and offer the vision to build a thoughtful, lasting process for quality global learning and multicultural experiences.

One tool used specifically for assessing engagement with global citizenship asks the following questions (among many more follow-up questions):

- Is your school an institution actively promoting global citizenship?

- Does it encourage a global perspective?

- Are children and the whole school community aware of their responsibilities as global citizens?

- Do they realize what actions they can take to become more active global citizens?

To establish your baseline, calculate your school's score to see how well your school is actively promoting global citizenship using the **Global Footprint quiz.**

## To Move Forward, Try Backward Planning

Backward planning is a strategy in which you visualize your goal(s) as already having been achieved and work backward to your current point to determine the steps you would need to have taken to achieve the goal(s) and ideal benchmarks. In other words, start with a concrete vision of the end. Take as many small steps as you can to realistically reach milestones, and if needed, break those milestones down into smaller accomplishments.

Here are some questions you can ask: What do you hope to accomplish that benefits the children? What do you hope to accomplish that benefits the school? (These are your end goals.) How does this fit into overall learning or strategic goals for the grade or the school? How long will you need to accomplish the goals? How long will it take to secure volunteers and establish a strong team? How long will teachers need to plan and prepare to engage their class and work in some of the resources or initiatives into their class planning? What funds will be needed and how to secure those? How long will it take to raise the money for the activity or the charity?

---

## Backward Planning for Classroom Instruction

Rebecca Alber, consulting online editor at Edutopia.org and instructor at UCLA's Graduate School of Education, set out these useful steps for conducting backward planning for lesson design. These guiding points also can inform planning outside-of-class activities and considering these in the context of school climate or other benchmarks. You can replace your own learning or experiential goals for the standards mentioned in Step 1 to tailor planning for your specific purposes.

1. Look at standard(s). (Adapt this: What are your strategic, community, or academic goals?)

2. Make a list of the skills, concepts, and knowledge kids need to learn.

3. Next, design the final assessment/project where students will demonstrate understanding to mastery of these skills, concepts, and knowledge.

4. Then, create a set of lessons that lead up to that end.

5. Once you've done this, reflect on the set of lessons, making sure all the skills, concepts, and knowledge for student success with the end assessment are being taught.

*Source:* http://www.edutopia.org/blog/backwards-planning-thinking-ahead-rebecca-alber.

## Ten Questions for Starting to Plan Global-Themed Events

Throughout this Toolkit, we will share information and resources that straddle two distinct strands: (1) how to include meaningful global lessons throughout the regular curriculum for various disciplines and (2) how to hold a special international festival or event, for a day or night, a week, a month, or more.

Chapter 3 contains many ideas for academic integration, and Chapter 2 shares dozens of things to do throughout the classroom or school for global events or themed activities. If you decide to go with an international festival or event—perhaps as a stepping stone to more in-depth curricular integration—consider the following questions. As you determine your approach and answers to the questions, you'll inevitably come up with more points to be answered, but we have found these to be a good starting point for filling in details and getting a program off the ground.

1. Will your school dedicate a month, a week, or a day for your international event?
2. Which schoolwide activities will take place on which days? (See Chapter 2: Things to Do.)
3. Will you have a global theme for the event? Will each grade be in charge of a geographic region? (See the next section for examples of themes.)
4. Who will be in charge of planning the event (e.g., teachers, International Club, parent volunteers)? How much contribution of time and resources do you expect from each group?
5. How can you create conditions so a wider circle of staff and volunteers gets involved in the planning and execution? (More on this topic later in this chapter.)
6. Will you have any/some/most activities at night to include parents who work during the day?
7. Does your school district have restrictions on serving/preparing food?
8. Do you have a budget for outside entertainers/experts? For food? For arts and craft supplies? What other plans require funds?
9. Do you need to fundraise to realize goals for the program? How far in advance do you need to begin fundraising?
10. Is there a way to involve the wider community (e.g., university, cultural groups, experts) in your events? (More on this topic later in this chapter.)

## Theme Ideas for an International Day, Week, Month, or Year

Picking a relevant and interesting global theme can create much excitement and support for your program. When you want to get beyond a general world theme, this idea can be broken down into so many subgroups and variations. Themes can reflect interests in diverse cultures, countries, arts, hobbies, and sciences. Below we share some examples.

When you are ready to start planning, you'll see that you can cross over and combine various themes. For instance, each grade level can pick a country, then within that look at the country's natural environment, major holidays, and musical traditions and possibly even do some sort of service activity benefitting that country or its immigrant population locally, cutting across many categories. There really is no limit to the combination and creativity strong themes can present. Here are some diverse themes around several key ideas:

- *Travel and geography.* Each grade level can choose a city, country, continent, iconic landmarks, buildings, "wonders of the world," or series of destinations and highlight what's special about those places. Theme titles might include "Visit (Name of Place)," "Travel the Globe," "Passport to Learning," "Adventures Around the World," "Our World," "One World," and "World of Wonders," as well as the specific choices reflecting various geographies.

- *Holidays and celebrations.* Celebrate each season or focus on one with autumn/winter/spring/summer celebrations around the world, birthday traditions around the world, New Year's around the world (can highlight Lunar, Gregorian, Persian, Jewish, new school year in the northern versus southern hemisphere—these cover almost every season), and "Celebration Foods" with a culmination community potluck.

- *Science, natural resources, and physical spaces.* Integrate science class with the global themes. Some themes might include "Water, Water, Everywhere" examining water availability, scarcity, pollution, uses, and sources around the world; "Energy Sources," "A Green World," "Innovation and Inventions From Around the World," "Native Plants and Foods," "Native Animals and Wildlife," "Endangered Species," "Houses and Homes," and "Making a Difference—Service Projects."

- *Arts and culture.* Themes highlighting arts and culture can stay general, like "Embracing Our Diversity," "Families Around the World," and "Cultural Traditions," or get more specific, like "Active Kids Around the World" (a variation on "Favorite Sports and Games"), "A Journey of Folktales," "Favorite Books From Around the World" (different grade levels can pick particular countries/continents or themes, like books about animals, families, adventures, and landmarks), and "Exploring the Arts" (or "Music," "Dance," "Textiles," "Movies"). These themes also lend themselves to a culmination celebration like a Global Arts Talent Show.

# Gain Support From Key Stakeholders

The support and buy-in from administrators, teachers, parents, and other community members can mean the difference between a small, one-time, low-impact experience and exactly the opposite. Each group will play a key role, from the decision to hold an event or plan a program in the first place, to carrying out detailed execution steps. The greater unity and shared understanding that can be built around the goals and activities of the program, the more success will be ensured.

Given how important diverse buy-in is for lasting impact and school-wide participation, early efforts at gaining support will be worth the extra time that might be needed. Don't rush or skimp on this vital foundational work. Spend a fair amount of time *listening* to interests, experiences, and concerns. Make time for face-to-face meetings and for additional communication via e-mail, letters, and phone calls, and expect that responses might take longer than you think they should. Everyone has a lot on their plate and their own priorities. As you work on gaining buy-in, consider each of these key players and their specific roles:

## Administration

Ideally, school administrators (e.g., principal, vice principal) get on board at the start of the process. They probably need to approve the projects, theme, outside guests, and other elements. Their positive opinion will be pivotal because the administrators may use this initial event as a pilot program to determine future events, and they have a sense of the bigger, strategic picture of learning goals, future curricular and staff changes, scheduling demands, and other factors behind the scenes. At the same time, administrators can use the results of a successful event to promote the school in the media and within the district.

Organizers work with the administrative team to determine the dates, length, and scope that works well with your school's curriculum and calendar. Administrators understand district policies (such as food restrictions), building limitations (such as fire code hazards), budget constraints (from additional janitorial services for example), and calendar conflicts (such as the buildup to state assessments). An informed administrator is able to balance the district and school calendar and help determine the logistics of an international event, while keeping student learning a top priority. In addition, administrators will be approving or denying all activities on school grounds, ensuring that academics and special events run smoothly. Keeping in regular contact with a point person from among your administrators is vital, and scheduling regular meetings will keep him or her up to date with the planning and details.

## Teachers and Staff

Parents may wish to share their cultural experiences, and administration may sign off on a vision of global learning or an international fair, but curricular adjustments are not possible without support and involvement from the teachers, and extra activities planned by parents won't get reinforcement in class activities or discussion without a shared understanding of global learning experiences among the teaching staff. Teachers understand their students' abilities and the necessary annual standards to be reached, and may be able to design lessons with a global component that complement their curriculum. An excited team of teachers will spread their enthusiasm and can change the attitudes of those working at the school—sharing lessons and ideas with each other to spread the global activities across grade levels. We have seen over and over again how sometimes it might just take one trained or visionary teacher to ignite a spark of global learning and demonstrate this to her colleagues.

When starting out, try including one teacher from each grade level at the planning meetings. Invite them to communicate their class needs and wishes, and then ask them to share the information with their grade- (or subject-) level colleagues. Teachers are most familiar with their grade's curriculum and how lessons must tie into state standards; they've mapped out their year and have planned their lessons, so they understand best what projects would work with their students, at what time of year, and where to locate talents and enthusiasm that might be just under-the-radar.

At one school in Naperville, Illinois, the third-grade curriculum already included a month study on different Japanese communities as part of their social studies class. Planning the international fair after the completion of this unit would allow the third graders to showcase their final projects at the event. Taking into account the completion of special grade-level projects that might be displayed during the event is important when choosing the dates.

In addition to timing the event to coincide with existing curriculum and projects, including teachers also offers an opportunity to showcase the talents and experiences of teachers and other school staff which may not be highlighted during the traditional program. You could create a simple survey (you can make one on **SurveyMonkey**, for example) to uncover interests and skills.

Surveys, with language like that included in the sample below, can highlight many interests and talents, including so many global possibilities from media, library, and technology specialists as well as art, music, and P.E. teachers. Distribute surveys to teachers, and don't overlook other members of the school staff community. For example, cafeteria workers may be able to plan special menus during the time frame to reflect a variety of cultures, and it could serve as an opportunity to showcase cuisines they grew up with, beyond standard school fare. Similarly, custodial staff may have emigrated from many countries or know your local community thoroughly, with fascinating histories and talents that are rarely displayed. An International Fair might not only offer them an opportunity to share but expand the children's relationships with people they might come in contact with daily but not truly "see" until this opportunity. The experience can showcase diversity already at your school, expand into cross-curricular lessons, and unite the school toward one goal, one vision, and deeper friendships.

---

## Example of language for a survey to teachers and staff (remember to include particular questions unique to your community!)

---

Dear Teachers and School Staff,

Thank you so much for taking a few minutes to complete this survey about global interests and expertise. We are hoping to organize an International Fair/ Theme Week/Global Night (or other title of your choice) and hope to showcase as many talents as we can from our own community. (OPTIONAL: Include more information here, like when, where, special guests already confirmed, any other known elements that will be included.)

We also hope to get a better picture of global learning that might already be going on at our school. Please share your ongoing efforts in the corresponding questions below. In order for this short survey to not burden you, you only need to complete the questions that are relevant to you and your interests.

THANKS AGAIN!!

1. Do you have a particular culture of interest/experience? Yes _____ No _____

2. If yes, which one(s)? (This can include local culture, too!) _____
   _____

3. Have you ever lived outside the United States (or whatever home country you are in)? Yes _____ No _____

4. If yes, where? _____

5. Do you speak a language other than English? Yes _____ No _____

6. If yes, what? _____

7. Do you have a particular talent, interest, or hobby you'd like to share? Yes _____ No _____

8. If yes, what? (This can be anything from cooking, storytelling, performing arts, fine arts, organizing games, crafts, movies, music, literature selections, and much more!) _____

9. Do you have cultural items you'd like to bring in for display or demonstration? Yes _____ No _____

10. If yes, what sorts of items? _____

11. Do you have suggestions for how to incorporate global concepts and lessons into your grade- or subject-level curriculum? Yes _____ No _____

12. If yes, could you share here? _____

13. Do you need support/assistance for implementation? Yes _____ No _____

14. What kind of support could you use? _____

15. Are you already teaching lessons with a global component? Yes _____ No _____

16. If yes, what? _____

17. Do you know of a school or classroom in another city or country that might be able to communicate with our school via video chat (like Skype or Google Hangout)?

18. Do you have any suggestions of local community members with experience in another culture who might be willing to visit our school or share their knowledge, a collection, or other talents?

19. If yes, do you think there will be any expense associated with their participation?

20. Please share any other thoughts you may have about our proposed [International Fair—insert specific name or type of event you propose here].

Thank you so much for completing this survey! If you have any questions or concerns, please contact [POINT PERSON'S NAME], [PHONE NUMBER], [E-MAIL ADDRESS].

# Parents

At some of the highest functioning schools, parents put in hundreds of volunteer hours a year, working at schools to help support and enhance their children's education. In some cases, working parents or parents from other countries are unsure how to get involved or feel that they are unwanted or redundant to existing efforts. Organizers need to work consciously to figure out ways that *all parents* have the opportunity to support the international efforts. Parent volunteers are a key resource that schools can tap into to get cultural and global experience, fill in human resource shortages, or add expertise where it might not even have been planned.

We have found the best recruitment of parent volunteers takes a multifaceted approach to reach parents who stay at home as well as those who work outside the home and travel or work nontraditional shifts, those parents who prefer a flyer on paper; and those who read everything online. One common element among parents is the fact that it seems everyone is too busy today, so multiple communications also help reinforce, remind, and renew commitment. Some parents grew up in a culture of significant volunteer involvement, and to others, this concept is totally new. So whatever you do, try, try, and try again.

### Parent Involvement at Becky's Children's School

In order to reach a large percentage of parents at Becky's school, on the very first Meet-the-Teacher day, parent volunteers from the International Club set up a table for parents to sign up to help throughout the year. To lure families to visit the booth, they had a huge sign that asked, "Can you say 'friend' in another language?" Not only did they gather many ways to say "friend" (and then used these to create a school display), they also gathered e-mails, explained the function of the International Club, and recruited new members. The coordinator invited working parents to participate during after-school hours, such as helping to do culture booths at the International Night or preparing a dish for the international potluck. As the year went on, organizers were pleasantly surprised when different groups of parents stepped up to sponsor country tables at International Night. New volunteers included parents who emigrated from other countries, parents who had adopted children from around the world, and also parents who had lived around the globe as expats.

As more parents joined the International Club, members were encouraged to reach out to others who had never volunteered at school. Oftentimes, mothers who were not quite fluent in English felt intimidated to volunteer at school. The International Club served as the gateway into the school for them, as there were often people who could help translate, or at least were sympathetic to the feelings of newness. Because many of the families were immigrants to the United States, their International Club meetings became one of their first experiences at school. In addition to flyers, newsletters, and e-mails, oftentimes the meetings were advertised through word of mouth in different ethnic communities, offering a more personal connection and warm welcome for newcomers.

The International Club became a team of parents who wanted their children to learn about the world, whether the parents had just arrived in the United States or had lived in the same state their entire lives. Sharing the common goal of preparing their children for the 21st century, they used each others' skills and experiences to work together. Collaborating for International Night turned into an ideal way to channel volunteer energy. The committee's plan for creating Show-and-Touch Tables for the kids (see Chapter 2, Section 4 for more details) offered a chance for many volunteers to participate by bringing in objects from home.

One mother from India contacted her friends to donate bangles to be handed out at the India table. Another mom from China rounded up Chinese parents to showcase toys, books, and games from China and had someone writing the kids' names in Mandarin. A group of Mexican parents brought in Mexican candy to give out during the event, which turned out to be extremely popular with the kids. Several parents from Palestine, Jordan, and Saudi Arabia and a family who had lived as expatriates in United Arab Emirates joined together to make a Middle Eastern table complete with baskets of traditional clothes—the kids loved playing dress-up and seeing their parents and teachers dress up as well. IT experts helped to set up videos and PowerPoint slideshows, and a graphic designer helped to make flyers.

The International Night was successful because diverse groups of parents stepped in and offered their know-how or their treasures—beautiful objects they had brought from their home countries or from their travels. Sharing these authentic experiences helps initiatives like this grow every year.

# Communication Tools for Working With Diverse Parties

With the myriad communication tools available today, it's unrealistic to think that one size fits all, especially when trying to recruit busy parents for volunteer jobs. For greatest effectiveness of communications, we recommend mixing and matching between at least two methods listed below and having a dedicated volunteer focus on communications, if you can. In some cases, jobs can be broken down further, with one person focused just on social media, another taking care of the e-newsletter, and so on. Here are a few tools to try:

- *Facebook group.* To involve parent volunteers and try to garner higher attendance at larger events, a Facebook group that's "by invitation only" can serve as an efficient way to frequently communicate with parents (not so much for school staff) while maintaining privacy and not broadcasting to those outside your school community. This is effective if you live in an area with a wide adoption of Facebook among parents.

- *Twitter list.* You can set up a protected list of all parents on Twitter to send out quick reminders or links to website posts. We would suggest this as a supplemental, not primary, communication tool. Too many parents we have met are not using Twitter as a regular communication tool for matters relating to their children.

- *E-newsletter.* Create a simple, eye-catching format that allows for periodic updates and reminders efficiently sent to a large group. Constant Contact and MailChimp are popular platforms for e-newsletters.

- *Yahoo Groups, Google Groups.* Set up a group e-mail list so that everyone gets the same e-mail message with just one address distributing to the whole group.

- *E-mail.* Whatever methods of communications you pick, simple, "old-fashioned" e-mails to parents remain among the most read, effective channels. This can be your stand-alone communication, or more effective is usually supplementing with others listed here. Be careful that e-mails convey necessary and not superfluous information, as a long e-mail can defeat the effectiveness of your communication!

- *Printed flyers/letters.* Like e-mail, this really "old-fashioned" method still works. It might increase clutter at home, but kids can remind their parents when a physical note comes home, and paper might reinforce electronic communications that flood inboxes.

- *Phone chain.* Create a chain of parents who will call 3–4 parents and have each of those responsible for calling 2–3 more families. At the end of each chain, make sure the last person on the chain calls back the starting point person to ensure the phone chain didn't break. This is one of the oldest methods but serves as a nice way for many people to get informed, feel more invested, and may be less intimidating than electronic communications for some. Alternately, for very high-tech communities, this also might serve as a welcome change.

> - *Voice (or text) message broadcasts.* Numerous services offer a low cost per call to send out a broadcast message to a large group. Political campaigns are notorious for using these services; school districts also use them to announce closures, emergencies, and, less commonly, reminders of schoolwide activities. If your community is more comfortable with phone and voicemail than electronic communications and your population is too large for a phone chain, then this might be worth investigating.

*One Parent Volunteer—Passionate About Global Learning*

The experience of one outstanding volunteer, Sharon Deol, of Laurel Mountain Elementary in Austin, Texas, shows what a difference one parent can make in a school. She started off volunteering for her PTA's Inclusiveness Committee; soon after joining this committee, she conducted focus groups to learn what parents representing diverse demographics were thinking about the school and what their hopes were for their children. It was during these sessions that Sharon and the school principal discovered that many parents wanted their children to know about other places and cultures around the world.

This led Sharon to start researching how to incorporate geography and cultural learning at the school. In collaboration between the principal and the PTA, they launched Holidays Around the World to teach students about the history and customs of holidays. Sharon describes the event:

> *We worked with an entire grade—six classes—and once per week for 3 weeks, we spent an hour with students. I enlisted four volunteers to develop and deliver the class materials. We also worked with the school's music teacher to teach the kids songs in different languages. This activity culminated with a Holidays Around the World evening event where these students performed their songs and many families showcased holidays that are special to their cultures.*

To reach the entire student population, Sharon and another parent volunteer brainstormed with their principal and came up with a monthly Holidays Around the World bulletin board located prominently in the school. (See more on this in Chapter 2.) She also began leading the school's Geography Club after school. This club had been solely focused on preparation for the annual National Geographic Bee, but she helped it evolve into a year-round program, as well as starting Geography Stars, which also is described in Chapter 2.

By her third year of engagement in global and geographic education, she teamed up with another like-minded parent to develop a year-round global-learning environment they called Growing Up Global, with the blessing of their principal. (They also sought permission from Homa to use her book's title, *Growing Up Global,* and this is how we originally got acquainted.) Their Growing Up Global program encourages teachers to incorporate global learning into their classrooms, provides tools for teachers to conduct monthly United Nations Days, offers Geography Club and Geography Stars, strengthens the annual Global Fest, and has established a committee made up of school staff, teachers, and parent volunteers who collaborate and implement the programs and will continue the rich, new traditions at Laurel Mountain. The year's culmination takes place at the school's annual Pride Night with a global spin, including a Global Village hosted by parent volunteers and a world music dance party.

Of course, not every school can organize such extensive programs. We have met volunteers from many schools around the world who wanted to instill global citizenship and friendship at their school, often starting with just one of the examples included in this Toolkit. They might have enjoyed organizing a cultural cuisine night, a Skype discussion between two faraway schools, or initiated a service activity with a global component. In each case, the most successful programs had volunteers or staff who started off doing what they loved, what they were most interested in. This way the initiative felt less like homework and more like friend making: joyful, mutually beneficial, and involving authentic growth and discovery.

## Community

The community at large represents the final essential resource that shouldn't be ignored (but often is). Research by Joyce Epstein and the Center on School, Family, and Community Partnerships at Johns Hopkins University has found that family, school, and community represent the three major contexts in which students grow and develop,[1] and global activities offer an ideal vehicle for this overlap and learning to occur, giving an opportunity for contact between the school and family to be on positive terms instead of focused on problems.

Furthermore, the larger community represents an often untapped treasury of knowledge and talent, which is eager to share their experience in educational settings. Look for businesses that employ parents in the school, for those with a global clientele or human resource base, nonprofit agencies, and any local cultural groups that can volunteer to perform or educate students such as martial arts schools, ethnic dancers and musicians, and university student groups and faculty. Many more ideas for tapping into the talents and resources of the wider community are expanded on concretely in upcoming chapters.

## Sample Timeline for Planning an International Event

The following timeline can be thought of as a general checklist as much as a guide for timing. We have found that advance planning ideas might be as culturally diverse as which foods to serve at the celebration. For example, in some schools, starting the planning 2–6 months in advance might offer plenty of time to put a program together, whereas at others, if the process doesn't begin at least a year ahead, it cannot get off the ground. In general, when initiating a new program, consider planning 12–15 months ahead of time; start small, and try to think of the program beyond a one-time surge of activity. As seasoned volunteers have shared with us, a 3-year game plan for what you hope the program will become can offer a very useful guide.

In light of how subjective the timing and specifics might be, we offer the following points as a simple guideline to which you should add your specifics and tweak as much as you need for this to be useful.

12+ Months Before:

☐ Begin with an e-mail, phone call, meeting, or meal with a few "champions"—those who share your ideals to bring an international event to the school. These fellow champions could be friends, like-minded teachers, families who have relocated from overseas, those who have hosted exchange students or share an interest in the wider world or in great experiences for children. Among each other, share some broad ideas or goals you hope to realize. It's best not to fixate on specifics like theme, date, duration, or logistics at this point. The response from your potential champions will help delineate how ambitious to make the program (i.e., enthusiasm and commitment from most people you contact can lead to a larger program).

□ Gain support of the PTA (or whatever your parents' association is known as), so that it is included among their plans for next year.

□ Contact school administration with the general idea. Offer your idea in writing (probably via e-mail, if this is how your school operates) so it can be used as a reference point for the meeting you propose to have with administrators and champions, if you have them.

8–12 Months Before:

□ Arrive at an agreement/gain approval from administration. Points to include are as follows: program dates and duration, who will be involved (the entire school, one grade, a club?), timing (during school, after school, evening, weekend?), whether or not food will be served, and any resources (financial, human, publicity, supplies) the school will commit to the program.

□ Once you've set a few details with administration, announce the broad program to the school community and begin to recruit parent volunteers. Encourage announcements in PTA and principal's communications.

□ Coordinate with teachers at each grade level, discussing participation and crossover with regular curriculum and projects.

□ Schedule events with building maintenance teams to reserve rooms and request equipment.

6–9 Months Before:

□ Decide on and finalize a theme.

□ Determine which activities will happen on which days or times.

□ Contact and firm up outside groups such as speakers and performers. (Note that many outside speakers and performers require a year in advance to secure booking.)

□ Delegate tasks such as communications and outreach, liaison with teachers, set-up/clean-up, talent and food coordinators, decorations, tickets, and so on to different parents. (Note that this responsibility calls for attention to detail and needs to be very carefully thought through, especially when dealing with outside performers, vendors, etc.)

3–6 Months Before:

☐ Hold a meeting with all participants to explain duties and expectations; this is a great time to bring in an example Show-and-Touch Table or display for participants.

☐ Check in with teachers and administration, including staff that are not grade-level teachers.

☐ Coordinate with the librarian and/or IT specialist to ensure the technology needed is available (or can be loaned from another school) and any books or other resources will be ordered.

1–3 Months Before:

☐ Communicate and advertise the event (via flyers, posters, e-mails, newsletters—whatever works for your school) for parents and the student population. Ideally, begin with teasers possibly 2 months ahead; another 1 month ahead, then weekly leading up to the event.

☐ Confirm details of visits from outside groups. Have any and all contracts finalized.

☐ Confirm volunteers and their teams have clear plans. Clarify any questions.

1 Month–1 Week Before:

☐ About 3 weeks before the event, send home any projects (like decorating flags, cultural dolls, or map activities like the printable World Map Activity in the Additional Resources at the end of this book) that children will work on for school decorations. Ask for them to be returned 1 to 2 weeks before the event so there is time to assemble all of them.

☐ During morning (daily) announcements, build students' excitement for the upcoming program. This can be through asking trivia questions, encouraging wearing special clothing on the day(s) of the program, multilingual announcements, songs, and more.

☐ E-mail teachers updated program schedules and ask that they share with their classes.

☐ Take a final volunteer roll call: Make contact with all volunteers (or committee leaders) and clarify any questions.

☐ Test all technology (for example, a test Skype call or Google Hangout) to ensure that all microphones, cameras, speakers, and projectors are working properly.

The Night Before:

☐ Get a great night's sleep so that you are able to enjoy the fruits of your labor!

Day(s) of Event:

☐ Distribute a list of key features of the program and who is responsible for each, as well as where they need to be and any supplies or set up they need, to all key volunteers/organizers. This way, when new volunteers, performers, guests, food service workers, or others arrive, multiple people can offer good information and help get things going.

☐ Have water and simple snacks available for performers, volunteers, and other participants as needed.

☐ Save special parking space(s) for performers and guests to use. If possible, create a sign like "Reserved for Ballet Folklórico de Guadalajara" so that the name of the guest or group in the parking lot offers yet another festive indication of the program, as well as providing a courtesy to guests.

Within 1 Month Following Program:

☐ Have a debrief and thank-you session, inviting volunteers, staff, and engaged administrators. Discuss lessons learned and ways to have an even better program next year while saving time for socializing among new friends and fellow volunteers.

## Concluding Reflection

Each person who goes through some of the planning exercises in this chapter will experience the process differently—even if you are serving at the same school or have received almost identical professional development. Relationships with various stakeholders will vary, as will experiences with diverse cultures, global topics, organizational inclinations, energy levels for introducing new initiatives, and of course, preferences around themes that speak more or less to you. Take a few minutes to reflect on your personal preferences which emerge from the planning exercises in this chapter; then, if you have a colleague or fellow volunteer who shares your interest in global education, share some of your reflection with that person in order to widen your perspective of possibilities that can come from planning as well as start to build collaborative opportunities.

Complete the sentence: "Global education is important because
_____." Return periodically to your answer in order
to remember some of the ideas you held when you started reading this
Toolkit.

After reflecting on the planning, communicating, and recruiting
exercises in this chapter, jot down a few concepts you'd like to implement. What could you do that is well within your reach (e.g., what's one
thing you could start tomorrow)? What would be a stretch goal, but one
that could make true impact on your school community? Beyond its
effect on students and the community, how could it benefit you personally or professionally? Where would you like to be with these efforts in
one year? Three years?

Remember, this process sticks when it begins with interests and
capacities you already possess, personally or as a community. So start
with what you love.

Here's to breaking down the barriers!

---

## A Sample Letter to Solicit Parent Volunteers

---

### Calling All Families! We Need You for:

#### *International Week*

The International Club parent volunteers are excited to announce that we will
be celebrating our diverse cultures at International Week on _____!
We are in the process of planning a week of events to involve all grade
levels in learning about world cultures. Throughout the week, the
teachers have international learning experiences planned during
their classes. Here are the schoolwide activities that require parent
volunteers. Please consider lending your time or talents to make this an
unforgettable experience!

**MONDAY** Flag Day! Let's make flags from our various heritages.

**TUESDAY** Diversity Quilt: Each student makes a quilt square representing their
families' holidays, food, values, traditions, etc.

**WEDNESDAY** Show-and-Touch Tables: These are organized by country and are
run by parent volunteers.

**THURSDAY** International Bread Day: Share a bread (pita, tortilla, naan, injera,
arepas, etc.) from around the world with your class.

**FRIDAY** National Clothes Parade: Wear your national costume or other traditional clothing from your cultural heritage and share with your friends in a schoolwide parade. Parents are invited to come!

**We need volunteers!**

_____

_____

_____

Help us celebrate International Week! Please check your interest and return to school as soon as possible.

☐ I can help hang up the flags on Monday.

☐ I can help to display the Diversity Quilts on Tuesday.

☐ I would like to participate in the Show-and-Touch Tables by loaning some items from _____ (country)

☐ I would like to volunteer to supervise one of the country tables: _____
_____

☐ I can write children's names in another language: _____
_____

☐ I am available to help in any way needed on the following days/times: _____
_____

**Questions? Contact** Name: _____ Phone #: _____
E-mail: _____

## NOTE

1. Joyce Epstein and Associates. (2009). *School, family and community partnerships: Your handbook for action.* Thousand Oaks, CA: Corwin.

www.corwin.com/globaledtoolkit

# Things to Do
## Look at All the Places We Can Go!

This chapter is dedicated to highlighting and demonstrating simple, terrific ideas that can almost literally take your school or club to a new culture or country, while spotlighting local talents and interests. We've sifted through some of the best ideas we've tried at our own schools, those we've shared and found around the Internet, and activities that have been tested by new and old friends from other schools around the world. You can fill a week's, month's, or year's worth of special days with these, and we'd love to hear how they work for you. Specific activity ideas fall under the following five categories:

- Section 1: Schoolwide Crafts and Displays

- Section 2: Incorporating Food

- Section 3: Music, Movement, Sports, and Play

- Section 4: Global Fair/International Festival Activities

- Section 5: Integrating Global Perspectives Into the School Environment Throughout the Year

Use the following table as a checklist of 50 ideas; details on each activity are contained in the following pages.

## Schoolwide Crafts and Displays

☐ Diversity Quilt

☐ Multicultural Paper Dolls

☐ Flags

☐ "Where in the World Is . . . ?"

☐ Traveling Mascot Display

☐ Multicultural Art Gallery

☐ Our Student Population on the Map

☐ Postcard Roundup

☐ Halls of Fame

☐ Peace Display

☐ Holidays Around the World Map and Calendar Bulletin Board

☐ Rotating Multimedia Display (books, movies, music, links in e-newsletters)

## Incorporating Food

☐ Friendship Salad

☐ Global Cookbook

☐ International Bread Day

☐ International Potluck

☐ Oxfam World Meal

☐ Community Garden

☐ Lunchtime Around the World

☐ Accompany Themes With Food

☐ Fill (and Make!) Empty Bowls

## Music, Movement, Sports, and Play

☐ Schoolwide World Cup

☐ International Game Day

☐ Student Performances

☐ Performances by Outside Groups

☐ Friday Music From Around the World

☐ Drumming Workshop

## Global Fair/International Festival Activities

☐ Country Displays

☐ Cultural Fashion Show or Parade

☐ Passports/Stamps

☐ World Friend Bingo

☐ Movies for Classroom Discovery and Family Film Fun Events

☐ 25 Favorite Foreign Films for K–5!

☐ Show-and-Touch Tables

☐ Guess the Flag Game

☐ Exploring a Country Through the Five Senses

☐ Passport Day

## Integrating Global Perspectives Into the School Environment Throughout the Year

☐ Video Chat With a Sister School

☐ Worldwide Culture Swap Boxes

☐ Pen Pal Program

☐ Language Lessons

## Everyday Foreign Language Exposure

☐ "My Place in the World" Projects

☐ Map the Settings of Books Read

☐ Daily Geography Trivia

☐ Exchange Student Panel

☐ Speakers From Around the World

☐ Multilingual Announcements

☐ Incorporating Google Earth Into Lessons

☐ Take a Google Lit Trip

☐ Geography Stars

☐ Instill Meaning Through Service and Giving

**See Chapter 3 for Interdisciplinary Global Lessons for Classrooms and Clubs**

# Section 1: Schoolwide Crafts and Displays

Schoolwide displays can offer a wonderful addition to your international curriculum. Our approach to teaching kids about the world is to reach them from as many different classes, lessons, and disciplines as possible. In creating this global environment, one activity that unifies schools might be collaborative art projects that can be displayed for the whole school to enjoy. Another benefit is that children in every grade can participate in creating crafts and displays, while they enjoy viewing them, too.

In some of the more engaged schools we've interacted with, the International Club (run by parents) works with the school and asks their volunteers to put up and change out the displays throughout the year. In other schools, a specific staff member is assigned either as part of their job description or through their own personal commitment to coordinate schoolwide displays or activities. You can choose one or two ideas from the list that can stay on display for a month or entire marking period (semester). Once you've successfully completed a schoolwide craft, you may be inspired to try even more the following year. Let's get started!

## Diversity Quilt

Using photographs, drawings, and text, every student creates a paper quilt square that embodies their characteristics, cultural heritage, traditions, and celebrations of their family. One year, for the International Week at Becky's school, a square of colored construction paper was sent home to all of the students with the instructions to *"share something about your family's culture: something you celebrate together, something you enjoy to do together, something that represents you and your family."* The teachers heard a lot of positive feedback because many children worked with their parents to come up with what they thought represented their family—making this project meaningful on more than one level.

Each class was given a different color and then put the squares from the four to five classes in a grade together to make a quilt. The quilts were hung at the end of each grade's hallway. From far away the colorful squares created bright patterns; as viewers got closer to the quilt, they could appreciate the details representing individual families.

The resulting patchwork quilt is a representation of the school's diverse and unique population and how they come together to make one unified school with many strengths. **Kid World Citizen has one example of a school's diversity quilts.**

## Multicultural Paper Dolls

Clothes reflect our identity, help us express our personality, and can say much about our cultural background. Students can make **International Paper Dolls** based on traditional clothes worn in their families' native countries or from cultures in which students have an interest. Teachers or volunteers can show some examples of dolls and traditional clothing to view, and the students can work on the project at home with their families using cloth and textiles, ribbons, buttons, or any other tactile materials they can find.

This creates a wonderful collaboration, as parents (or teachers, or after-school clubs) can answer questions and provide materials (different textiles, media) for their kids. The multicultural paper dolls can then be presented in class as a conversation prompt about the use of different colors, materials, climate, symbols in different cultures, languages, or any other "clues" that the dolls and their costumes might offer. Teachers can discuss and compare traditional clothes to modern clothes, dress-up clothes to what kids wear to school or outside to play, or clothing used for religious celebrations to family parties. Becky smiled one time when a new student from Sierra Leone commented that all of the students in the United States make jeans and t-shirts look like a uniform because of their ever-present appearance in schools!

## Flags

Students can be invited to create a flag that represents their ancestry, and then the flags can be displayed in the hallways. The older children could research the meaning behind the choice of colors and symbols and share it with the class. While Becky helped to hang the 600+ flags created at her elementary school, she was so impressed by the diversity: from U.S. flags to Texas flags, to a couple of American Indian nation flags, plus many of the countries of the world. Immediately as volunteers were hanging up the flags they heard the students commenting, "There's another Brazil flag!" "What is that green-and-white one everywhere?" (Pakistan).

To add an element of collective engagement here, try a flag ceremony or parade, similar to the Olympics Opening Ceremony, where each country's representatives are announced, they proudly walk out, and join at the end to combine with other countries in a display of friendship and sharing. In its simplest form, this can plant a sense of possible cooperation between nations among children who have great potential to envision peace. When students have a personal experience in such a flag ceremony, they become more engaged and interested when they watch an Olympics or other larger-scale flag ceremony.

Making flags and learning various countries' flags can also serve as a foundational activity for many other global activities you might try from throughout this book. See the **CIA's World Factbook** for up-to-date depictions of flags of the world.

## "Where in the World Is . . . ?"

If you live in a community where children or their parents travel, throughout the year ask students who travel abroad (or to another state) to take a picture of themselves in a typical setting in that place or in front of a landmark. Have your students bring in this picture of themselves to be used in a hallway display. Using these, teachers or parent volunteers can create a bulletin board asking students to guess where the student is and also display the past as puzzles and answers. Not only is it exciting for kids to see their vacation picture, it's fun for everyone to try to guess where their schoolmates have traveled. For more fun, have the teachers and staff participate as well!

## Traveling Mascot Display

The "traveling mascot" display is very similar to the above project, except the photos include a surprise appearance by the school mascot. Most schools have some sort of mascot, such as an animal, bird, or character. Make 15–20 laminated copies of a picture of the mascot, and students can then check out a mascot from the front office before making a trip with their families. While on their trip, the children can take photographs of the mascot in front of famous places or cultural icons. Upon return, the students can write up a description and it can be included in a display of where the mascots have traveled (similar to a Flat Stanley project). The mascots should be available to check out especially during school holidays and the summer, when most families travel. This dynamic display starts conversations, piques students' interests, and is a source of pride for the students.

To start generating ideas around where the mascot might travel (even if the children aren't going on long journeys), consider friends you've made through classroom collaborative projects; contacts that parents and community members might reach out to through their friends, family, or colleagues; or write to schools, clubs, or other organizations you find online (and screen initially by the adults in charge) with interesting missions, locations, or activities to join in your traveling mascot display.

If logistics become complicated for sending the mascot, they could simply send a photo of themselves playing a sport, doing homework in their kitchen, engaging in a classroom activity, holding or buying a common object the classroom chooses, or some other unifying "action" shot. Especially for children, seeing these environments through a personal project such as these helps them connect globally in a more tangible way, even if they haven't personally visited.

## Multicultural Art Gallery

Many schools already do lots of multicultural art. One way to display the art is to choose a few excellent examples of each project and showcase it with a labeled description about the country/culture of origin (similar to a real museum gallery). Students can learn techniques and materials that artists use in different regions of the world and then integrate geography by locating the country and learning more about the people who produce the art.

Before the teacher begins the art project, do research about the cultural origins, purposes, and original techniques and uses. YouTube has many videos that demonstrate specific art techniques in the country of origin that can be used as an introduction for students. For example, try searching for videos or pictures that demonstrate paper marbling techniques such as **Turkish** *ebru*, **Japanese** *suminagashi*, **Guatemalan or Ecuadoran weaving**, or **Malian** *bògòlanfini* (mud cloths). After seeing short clips of authentic artists producing unique art, students feel more connected to doing the art project themselves.

Creating art is universally human. Children can learn that since the beginning of time, humans around the world have used art to creatively express themselves. Hanging multicultural art projects in the hallway—as a museum would, with short descriptions and explanations of their origins—allows students from the whole school to enjoy and appreciate the creations of their fellow classmates.

## Our Student Population on the Map

Either as a class or as a school, have students pin their birthplace (or family's origins) onto a world map. In a visual, live graphic, it is exciting to see the places on Earth from which the school community has come. At Becky's school's International Night, parents and students alike crowded around the map to absorb—and "ooh" and "aah"—the diversity of their population. "There's another family from Angola?! Where are they, we have to meet them!" It was interesting to see the number of families from other states as well as other countries. Teachers can incorporate math skills by graphing the school census either by continent or on a global scale. In addition to showing the "resources" of the school, an added benefit comes when a new student learns there is another family from their corner of the world.

## Postcard Roundup

Kids love to get mail! Students are invited to ask family and friends who live outside of the community (in another state or abroad) to send them a postcard, addressed to the school. The postcards themselves tell a story with their often iconic pictures on the front, the handwritten message on the back, and even the stamps needed for postage. Teachers can hang the postcards around the map and use string to connect the postcards to their geographical locations. Students are able to visualize their origins with this concrete example and enjoy seeing from how many places they can attain postcards, which traveled the farthest, which postcard comes from which continent, which has the most interesting pictures on the front, and so on.

If you search online for "elementary school postcard exchange," every year there are new groups starting with elementary classes from around the world promising to mail each other postcards from their home cities. It is a great way to practice reading, writing, geography, and friend building in one fun activity. One example, called **Post Crossing**, is an ongoing project that allows anyone to send and receive postcards (real ones, not electronic) from around the world.

Allow plenty of time for mail delivery and responses so students are not disappointed when it's time for culmination of this project. To be safe, we suggest 4 to 8 weeks' lead time, depending on reliability of mail systems in the country of correspondence and how well you know adults in charge of the class with which you are corresponding. For example, are they quick to respond? Do they juggle multiple priorities with ease or difficulty? Do they have plenty of supplies and resources to send letters back to your students?

## Halls of Fame

Schools often display African American heroes and role models for Black History Month or famous women during Women's History Month. This idea for a Global Hall of Fame expands on the idea by showcasing diverse people from around the world who have done extraordinary things. Students can work in teams to create a poster or other displays that highlight their famous person or people. Think of using one of the following unifying themes for your hall of fame:

- Nobel Peace Prize winners

- Outstanding inventors or scientists

- Athletes such as soccer players from around the world, Olympic medalists, stars from other sports popular in your community

- Authors

- Musicians

- Painters and other fine artists

- Leaders, activists, or other outstanding individuals that come from a variety of countries represented by the school population.

Some worthy possibilities might not be well known or in the mainstream, but you can learn about them by soliciting parents, faculty, and staff for examples of whom they admire from diverse parts of the country or world.

## Peace Display

Collecting how to say "peace" (or "friend" or "love" or any word you choose!) in different world languages can either be done as a homework assignment for older kids or can happen as a result of asking a diverse student population how they say peace in their native language. Either way, the final display can be a reminder that around the world cultures work toward peace and that the school environment is in fact an accepting and peaceful place for students regardless of nationality, ethnicity, or native language. As kids walk down the hallway, you will find them trying to pronounce the different words for peace and even trying out their new vocabulary with native speakers. One of Becky's favorite moments was minutes after hanging their peace display, a shy child smiled and pointed at the Urdu sign and said, "That one is mine! I say it like that!"

Take your peace display a step further and join as many as 100 million+ participants from all over the world to celebrate the United Nations International Day of Peace, or Peace Day, commemorated in the week of September 21 each year. **Peace One Day** serves as a clearing-house organization, where creative ventures, like the film of the same name, service activities and Skype discussions are shared. Local chapters have been formed, too. For example, **Peace Day Philly** has spurred initiatives in city and suburban public and independent schools, from planting **Peace Poles** and peace gardens, to simply taking a moment of silence at noon on September 21 to envision peace—personally, locally, and globally. At Homa's daughter's elementary school, thanks to the initiative of one teacher enthusiastic about Peace Day, a full day's program dedicated to thoughts and actions around peace became a fond tradition soon after it was introduced to the school community.

## Holidays Around the World Map and Calendar Bulletin Board

Think outside of Valentine's Day and Halloween by dedicating a hallway display of the many holidays around the world. Sharon Deol, a parent volunteer in Austin, Texas, created a bulletin board highlighting holidays celebrated by diverse faiths, cultures, and countries during the particular month or season the board was displayed. Teachers found that the bulletin board led to rich classroom discussions of various holidays, spurred by inspiration they got simply by walking by and noticing the wall display. Children whose family backgrounds were different or less known from the mainstream felt validated in their traditions and shared from their firsthand experience, and knowledge of cultures became personal and exciting for all students. Even information on Christmas, which Americans might assume is ubiquitous and well known, was worthwhile. Children of immigrants from countries that either celebrate Christmas differently or don't celebrate it at all learned about the deeper meaning of an important holiday, beyond the commercial elements they are bombarded with in stores and on television.

To enhance the learning, teachers were e-mailed a PowerPoint version of the board's contents by parent volunteers so they could share the information within their classrooms. Morning announcements, run by students, included a mention and description of the holidays as they occurred, which comprised not only religious and cultural holidays but also national holidays and historical events from around the world.

One simple tool—a hallway bulletin board that changed at different times throughout the year—became a cherished fixture impacting the culture of the entire school. Families may be invited to loan cultural items for the display or to share their knowledge and pictures with the school. This also can serve as a positive way to involve new and diverse families, who may not be as visible in other school activities.

Kid World Citizen's **2014 Diversity Calendar** can be found online; also see the excellent multicultural calendars from the **University of Rochester** and the **University of Kansas Medical Center** and the multifaith calendar from **PBS's Religion and Ethics Newsweekly**. The calendars include holidays from many of the world's major religions and ethnic groups. Once you learn about an upcoming holiday, look for a corresponding lesson plan online, such as this extensive lesson plan from Harvard's Center of Middle Eastern Studies about the **Persian holiday of Nowruz** which occurs on the spring equinox.

## Rotating Multimedia Display (books, movies, music, links in e-newsletters)

Librarians, or more accurately, media professionals, are natural partners or leaders in any international effort school staff or volunteers undertake. They can be involved from the beginning of planning, as they are apprised of the newest resources, know the catalogues of various publishers, and what books, films, and websites their colleagues around the country are excited about. Display themes can rotate across countries, continents, character themes (e.g., perseverance, courage, service), necessities (e.g., water, shelter, clothing, food, family), or other themes from the curriculum, cultural arts programming, or your particular community.

Displays can remain in the library or take a more prominent place at the front of the school. E-newsletters distributed to the parents can highlight a few favorite links relating to the display theme so that families can easily click hyperlinks and go directly to resources high-lighted at school. When the displays and themes, and overall expertise of media professionals, are integrated into the work undertaken in the various grades, a process of collaborative, creative, constructive learning is launched.

# Section 2: Incorporating Food

Incorporating food into global learning offers a simple, fun, natural starting point. These ideas take kids beyond the books and computer to begin experiential learning and a multisensory experience. They also can offer a portal for including new people in schoolwide initiatives, like parents with limited English fluency, food service staff, grandparents, and community members.

## Friendship Salad

Friendships salads are common bonding and team-building activities among Scouts and other groups. This **simple recipe for a Friendship Salad** requires no artistic or culinary skill.

Each child is invited to bring in a different fruit, and when the diverse ingredients are mixed together, the resulting salad is harmonious and bursting with flavors. Like the fruit, we each bring unique attributes to the classroom or group and work together to form a cohesive team. In some examples of Friendship Salad, the teacher will take out a rotten banana and attempt to add it to the salad—to the shock and dismay of the students. Their cries of "Stop! It will ruin the salad" introduce the idea that unfriendly behaviors will also taint the classroom. Teachers can globalize the lesson by introducing ideas of compassion: Negative stereotypes and discrimination destroy the unity of the group and are not welcome, while diversity of fruit type, color, texture, taste, and geographic origin enhances the salad.

For another learning activity, talk about and map the origins of the fruits and discuss how they have traveled from many different countries to come together to make one fruit salad.

## Global Cookbook

Collecting recipes from around the world and compiling a cookbook can combine with an assignment in reading, writing, diverse ecosystems, computer applications, and a glimpse into popular flavors from around the world. Even more meaningful is when cookbooks are made in classes where the diverse population shares their home recipes for their favorite ethnic foods. These recipes might shed light on new uses of locally grown vegetables, uniting concepts that come from near and far. Classes can make their global cookbooks into a fundraiser for their favorite charity or for a need the school has. At one school, the ESL (English as a second language) classes wrote and published the cookbooks and used the money to make a scholarship for students wanting to take summer school. Other schools use their International Festivals to sell their cookbooks in order to benefit their International Club.

## International Bread Day

"This was my favorite day EVER in school!" (overheard by a fourth grader at a recent International Bread Day). When Becky's school held an International Bread Day, it was wildly successful. Kids were asked to bring in a sample of bread that their family typically ate or a special bread representative of their heritage. The participation was astounding: Kids brought in pitas, naan, tortillas, injera, soda bread, bagels, pan dulce, pandesal, challah, rice buns—even a loaf of gluten-free bread. Most classes made a "bread buffet" at the front of the classroom, and each student could talk about the bread they brought in: if it was eaten at a special time of year, what accompanied the bread, if they would make it or buy it, what type of flour it was made of, and so on. Students and teachers alike enjoyed the activity and begged to repeat it the next year. Even if your school doesn't boast such diversity, a trip to most local grocery stores or markets can begin to highlight diverse breads that are easily accessible.

A wonderful children's book to accompany the bread day is *Everybody Bakes Bread* **by Norah Dooley**. This activity offers an example of how students can look at something so common and widespread to get a more personal view of the world's rich diversity. Similar activities (perhaps for subsequent years?) can take place around pasta/noodles or foods that are wrapped, like dumplings, pierogies, samosas, and tacos/enchiladas/quesadillas.

## International Potluck

This extremely popular activity serves as a delicious way to eat your way around the world. Families bring in an ethnic dish to share, and everyone enjoys tasting authentic dishes from a variety of countries. One teacher outside of Calgary, Alberta, Canada, told us:

> *Who doesn't love to eat? And who doesn't love to show off their mom's great cooking? Having kids bring in their favorite dishes, to share with one another and their teachers, is our favorite way to help kids expand their knowledge about the world and try something outside of their everyday routine. Oftentimes kids surprise themselves by loving a dish that began as unfamiliar.*

It might be helpful to have students bring in a small note card with their dish to share. The card can contain information about the dish: country of origin, main ingredients, whether it is vegetarian or contains meat, and any other details you'd like them to include. By having this information presented for every dish, tasters are more informed about their meal and might be willing to try something new.

One important conversation to have with the students before tasting the new foods should include reminders of being polite when refusing food, being mindful of our facial gestures, and trying at least one bite. While certain textures or spices are common in one culture, they might be unheard of to others. Children should be careful not to offend their friends if they don't enjoy something.

## Oxfam World Meal

Mainly used with older children (fifth grade and up), the **Oxfam America Hunger Banquet** offers a tangible way to build compassion since "the place where you sit, and the meal that you eat, are determined by the luck of the draw—just as in real life some of us are born into relative prosperity and others into poverty." This can be an emotionally intense experience, so it is recommended for a more mature group. Participants are randomly assigned to high-, middle-, or low-income groups, based on actual proportions of people living at those levels. Because these proportions usually are quite imbalanced, a few people might eat a full, balanced meal including meat and vegetables, where others could eat plain rice and water. This firsthand experience helps broaden minds to gain a new perspective on hunger, poverty, abundance, and justice; leaves participants with much to talk about afterward; and often motivates participants to do something to make a difference.

One simpler variation on the World Meal can be achieved by packing brown lunch bags; this works well for Grades 3 and up. Each bag looks the same on the outside. For the wealthiest 15%, you can include a bottle of water, a granola bar, and a few pieces of wrapped, favorite candy; for the "middle" class, or 35% of the population, include water and a granola bar, but no candy; and for the poor, which make up 50% of the world's population, include just a package of saltines. This is simple to pack, with a stark message about who really gets what in the world.

Be sure to leave time for reflection and processing of the experience for children, especially since it will take longer for younger children to digest what just took place and is certain to leave a powerful, lasting impression.

## Community Garden

Community gardens, or local school gardens, are growing in popularity around the world. These not only offer a closer connection with our food and can instill a healthier diet but also demonstrate a greater appreciation for the bounties of the Earth. Eating in season and understanding what grows locally helps put food from around the world in perspective. Kids get a sense of what local versus faraway food looks, feels, smells, and tastes like. All can be appreciated, but a sense of near and far can be gained by participating in growing, harvesting, or collecting one's own food.

Kolter Elementary, in Houston, Texas, notes that their school garden provides endless lessons in botany, charting in math, writing about it in English, and gives a sense of community as families work on certain Saturdays to take care of it. When they harvest their large crop of sweet potatoes, families are invited to make any dish they'd like that uses sweet potatoes as a main ingredient and bring the dishes to school. Coming full circle, the classes share these incredibly diverse dishes and enjoy the sweet potatoes that they planted and took care of.

Teachers and parents might be surprised when otherwise picky eaters are more likely to taste food that they have grown, especially when their peers are all enjoying it! The experience of a community garden can serve as a nice conversation starter if you have a partner school in another country that your students communicate with. Many online organizations can help schools get started, including the **School Garden Wizard** site, which has a wonderful collection of resources and lessons "created for America's K–12 school community through a partnership between the United States Botanic Garden and Chicago Botanic Garden."

## Lunchtime Around the World

The school cafeteria can serve as a terrific partner for your international activities. Decorate walls with posters of foods and markets from around the world. Serve variations on traditional lunches with a global theme, helping suggest new ideas for weekly menus or for individual items to be inserted into traditional lunch menus. Display words like "Thank You" or "Fork" in multiple languages around the tables (e.g., table tents, centerpiece displays) or on walls, and even hand out utensils like chopsticks for a class that's won a contest around one of the global themes, or offer them as an alternative to Western silverware once a critical mass of children have mastered chopstick use.

Learn what kids around the world eat for lunch. Look at photos showing typical school lunches from various countries, which can be found on websites like these 30 examples of **School Meals From Around the World** and these **11 Schools Lunches From Around the World** from TripBase. Allow time for young minds to have the images sink in before saying anything that would influence their impressions. Interesting discussions can follow from those slideshows:

- Which lunch would you like to try?
- What do most of the lunches have in common? Why do you think that is the case?
- Are there common ingredients among the lunches?
- Are there foods you have never heard of or have never eaten before?
- What looks delicious, and why or why not?
- Based on the lunches, is there a particular country you'd like to visit? Find it on the map or globe, learn what languages they speak there, learn about the climate, and more.

Author of *French Kids Eat Everything*, **Karen Le Billon** posts French school lunch menus on her blog that offer some great ideas for introducing new twists on some relatively common ingredients, like parsley-topped potatoes and grated celery with apples, as well as more ambitious recipes with less common items, like roast guinea fowl and trussed veal. The lovely blog **Global Table Adventure** by Sasha Martin documents one American family's adventure cooking 195 meals from 195 countries over 195 days. Sasha's own young daughter transitions from being a picky eater to "eating the world." All of these can stimulate ideas for new meals and activities to engage the cafeteria and possibly can spill over at home and in the classroom, with kids feeling inspired to eat new foods, encouraging their families to do so, and cooking for themselves.

## Accompany Themes With Food

Enhance the sensory experience of academic units with corresponding foods that reflect the theme, whether you are studying revolutions, colonial times, immigration, the rainforest, master painters, composers, oceans, or it's a celebration in math on Pi Day (perhaps there are infinite ways to make pie!). This also works well for pairing films from other countries (see the Foreign Films section later in this chapter for recommendations) with corresponding snacks from that culture. The memory of a book or a movie is enhanced when the senses of taste and smell are awakened and accompany what is processed by the eyes and brain.

## Fill (and Make!) Empty Bowls

The **Empty Bowls project** offers a wonderful means to engage with food as an entry point for learning about the wider world, for creating something beautiful and useful, and for building stronger community ties. Students will learn about food insecurity near or far as a complement to the process of creating decorative clay bowls (to be filled with soup!) that they can take pride in and unite parents, teachers, and the wider community for a vital cause as they share a simple, healthy soup meal. Empty Bowls events take place in hundreds of schools around North America. Elise Smith, a parent volunteer at Stratford Road Elementary School in Plainview, New York, on Long Island, shared with us their overwhelmingly positive schoolwide experience with Empty Bowls.

As of this writing, their school had presented Empty Bowls events for 3 years in a row with the hope that it will continue as a schoolwide tradition. Initiated by one of the third-grade teachers, Mrs. Myra Brand, she brought the idea to the school administration, which supported it; then the PTA got involved and completely embraced it.

In school, the students prepare for the Empty Bowls event by decorating paper shopping bags that will carry nonperishable food donations (a side project of the event); third and fourth graders work with the art teacher by creating and decorating the clay bowls, which she then fires in the kiln and completes with the help of volunteer teachers and parents; and issues of hunger take on heightened importance as awareness grows among students. For the younger children, the focus is on local food insecurity, and the hope is that as students get to upper elementary and middle school, global hunger issues may be introduced and responded to through events like Empty Bowls. Elise notices how the children really put in their best work to decorate the bowls, since this is linked with important issues affecting their community.

The culminating event which takes place in the school cafeteria has become the most loved event of the year. At Stratford, no entry or dinner fee is charged, but people can make donations if they wish (at some other participating schools around the country they might charge a fee). Kids talk about it among themselves, and this "buzz" spreads to parents and many more around town. Demonstrating the idea that "world peace begins at the dinner table," the Stratford Road Elementary event also brings together parents from very diverse cultural backgrounds for meaningful discussion and socializing over bowls of soup and bread, strengthening bonds of friendship. The soup reflects the ethnic heritage of diverse parents and the offerings of restaurants in the community.

Although the couple of hundred people per year who come to the event are primarily students, parents, and teachers, the effort creates clear ripple effects as it generates some larger donations for hunger alleviation, including from local residents, patrons of the participating restaurants who hear about the effort and want to get involved, and business people who may or may not have kids in the school yet drop by or remotely make a donation because of the positive message around the program. In the lobby on the night of the event, there are also raffle baskets and literature and donation forms for Island Harvest, Long Island's largest food bank and recipient of all proceeds.

# Section 3: Music, Movement, Sports, and Play

Through music, movement, sports, and play, a wider circle of children is brought into the excitement of global discovery. The kinesthetic learner—or the kids that might not be as stimulated by arts, crafts, or literature—can find a niche that introduces an active connection with the world. Don't limit these experiences to music or physical education (P.E.) classes—integrating them into the regular classroom as well will help reach and meet the needs of a range of learners.

## Schoolwide World Cup

Soccer is the internationally beloved game that brings the world together. Schools can embrace this global phenomenon by creating teams and assigning each group an actual World Cup participating country. Their uniforms can reflect the real flag and colors and the teams can learn some cheers in the matching native language, learn facts about their team country, and even read bios on the original players on **FIFA's home page**. Incorporating global lessons into P.E. class or recess is natural, fun, and quite simple when you look at global sports like soccer!

## International Game Day

Get kids moving and playing more than just tag on the playground. Kids universally have a wonderful ability to make up games with minimal equipment. Check out one of the following books to learn games that can easily be played at recess or on a dedicated game day: *Sidewalk Games Around the World* by Arlene Erlbach; *Kids Around the World Play! The Best Fun and Games From Many Lands* by Arlette N. Braman; *Growing Up Global* also contains a section detailing rules to playground games from around the world with a sampling found on the **Growing Up Global blog**. Also check out Creative Spirits to see **Traditional Aboriginal Games** from around the world.

Dedicate specific days in P.E. or recess to learn playground games from around the world. Globalize the lesson even more by locating the original countries on a map, determining what language the kids speak in that country, and calling each game by its native name.

## Student Performances

Talent shows with a cultural twist invite students to show off their capacities in front of the entire school. When sending out the call for students to perform at the school talent show, include suggestions for culture performances. Students can

- recite a poem in another language,
- sing a song in another language,
- perform an ethnic dance,
- showcase their martial arts routine,

- play an instrument from another country, and

- much more.

If the talent show has acts from multiple locations, the emcee can even include cultural information to enhance the experience, introducing the acts as if the audience were traveling around the world.

## Performances by Outside Groups

Like the student performances, inviting outside groups into the school offers an excellent way to make culture come alive for the students. Always leave a little time for students to ask questions—the interaction is an essential part of the experience. Another option is to hire a traveling performance group. For a fee, organizations like the **Bureau of Lectures and Concert Artists** provide programs to schools around the United States and Canada. Their repertoire includes a wide variety of cultural performances such as Chinese acrobats, Russian musicians, Argentine dancers, and Senegalese drummers that excite and entertain the kids while exposing them to cultural fine arts.

To get ideas of performances in your area, contact your local library, museum, ethnic church, or cultural center and inquire about popular groups they might know. Oftentimes traveling groups will offer a discount when already booked in the area. Schools can "piggyback" on programs already taking place at museums or other schools for a much lower price than the groups charge for stand-alone events.

## Friday Music From Around the World

Some schools play music over the loudspeakers on Fridays as a special treat to the students. Other schools begin their school news program with a different song each week. Schools can use every opportunity to globalize their environment, even by simply replacing these songs with multilingual music from around the world. Some of our favorite globally inspired music collections are found at **Putumayo Kids** and **Music for Little People**. In addition to these terrific record labels, **Dan Zanes and Friends** and **Red Grammer** are two American artists committed to a more peaceful world. Both do a great job juxtaposing American, folk-inspired music with sounds and artists from around the world to open up new and creative possibilities for their young listeners.

## Drumming Workshop

Many cities have African Drumming schools (or contact your local university's music department or African studies center), and workshops can be arranged so that children have the experience of rhythmic music making. Typically, this activity is West African inspired, but it also could include cultures from Latin America, the Middle East, and other parts of Africa, Asia, the Pacific, and Europe. Normally the drumming school brings in the drums and leads the lessons for small groups of children. Kids love to bang on the drums and are fascinated by the rhythms—usually accompanied by stories—from experienced teachers. Such drumming sessions work well in smaller groups, rather than trying to reach the entire school at once. Designate an isolated classroom to hold the workshops, and invite classes to each come in for a 20-minute demonstration. This time allotment can go up as children's ages and attention spans grow.

# Section 4: Global Fair/International Festival Activities

While schools are encouraged to incorporate global lessons throughout the curriculum and throughout the year, many schools also hold an annual, schoolwide international festival. In addition to the numerous activities listed above which can enliven the festival, here are some ideas that can transform your global fair or international night into an interactive experience that all children will enjoy. These festive events can be so much fun (and educational!) for families.

## Country Displays

Many schools choose to have booths or displays organized by countries, geographical regions, or even continents. In some cases, a class will do country projects, and each student or group of students will display their presentation on a table. At other schools, the parents' organization or international club will organize groups of parents to create displays to reflect their country of origin.

Pictures, maps, illustrations, articles, postcards, flags, or important information can be mounted on trifold cardboard presentation boards, including facts about the country such as capital, population, location, major cities, exports, landforms, and so on. To get beyond basic fact sharing, students can create presentations that emulate travel brochures, showcasing the top tourist destinations, culinary highlights, and major festivals, actually trying to lure visitors to their destination. When the information is clearly labeled and accurately researched, this type of exhibition not only informs the creators but also engages visitors to the International Fair in something far more interesting than a two-dimensional poster exhibit. On Kid World Citizen, you can see some **photos of Becky's displays during previous International Nights.** In the many International Fairs we've visited, the booths or tables that attract the most visitors include some type of hands-on interaction. Below are some of the more popular activities among elementary students:

- Black pipe cleaners and red, yellow, and green pony beads to make bracelets inspired by the flags of Ghana (or use other colors to make jewelry inspired by any country's flag)

- Making rubbings of any carved surface, whether it is wood, metal, resin, local coins, or an intricate carving reflective of a particular culture

- Simple games such as tangrams from China or mancala from Eastern Africa

- Trying on clothing used by the Bedouins in the Middle East to protect them from the sun and sandstorms

- Sitting on (and trying to balance on!) shepherd stools from Ethiopia

- Instruments for kids to touch or play with, such as a drum from South Korea or a tongue harp from Kenya

- Construction paper and straws to assemble "easier" flags

- Trying on bindis, bangles, and traditional jewelry or henna from India and Pakistan

- Tasting Mexican candy, Palestinian hummus, cookies from the Netherlands, goat's milk from Chad, or Argentine mate

- Playing with folk toys from China, such as a wooden top, bamboo dragonflies, or the jianzi (shuttlecock)

- Learning various yoga poses inspired by nature and animals

- Learning how to write one's name or a common word, like "hello" or "friend," in the script of another language

- Folding paper into origami cranes and other animals

## Cultural Fashion Show or Parade

A cultural fashion show is an entertaining and educational show in which students and faculty can participate—and show off their style inspired by diverse parts of the world. Teachers can ask interested children and adults to wear traditional apparel and accessories and walk the catwalk in front of their peers and parents.

With students, the principal, or a favorite animated adult from school as the emcee narrating the models' names, ethnic backgrounds, and details about the clothing, you can choose to play appropriate music from the cultures represented to accompany the show. In other cases, each participant speaks first about their choice of clothing, where it is from, when it would be used, and then exhibits the clothing. It is important to mention what the name of the clothing is (e.g., a sari, a bolero hat, a shamma), where it is used (e.g., in the highlands of Scotland, in the rural areas of Peru), by whom it is used (e.g., only women, only children), and if the clothing is only used for special occasions (e.g., a holiday, a certain time of year). Include jewelry, accessories, and even hairstyles!

If a parent or other community member has a particular talent, like operatic singing, in their language or they excelled at a sport in their country (especially if that sport is less well known in your locality, like cricket or handball), they might be invited to do a short demonstration as part of the Cultural Parade/Fashion Show. This also works in the Talent Show category.

## Passports/Stamps

Many schools reported that they created a "passport" for students to use during the International Event. When handed out to individual students, a blank passport can serve as a record of countries that students have "visited" during the International Event (or even as a record of countries studied throughout the year in class). Volunteers or teachers working the different country booths can dedicate a stamp for each country, and each student can be in charge of their own travel passport. If finding a stamp is too difficult, try using stickers to represent each country. In several schools, each booth had a few questions the students needed to answer (gleaning information from the display) in order to get their passport stamp.

Schools using passports reported that this tangible, concrete reminder of the event was enjoyed by all of the students, who were more motivated to make sure that they didn't miss a single table. Some teachers also noted that they collected the passports that following school day and gave a prize or held a raffle for those students who had collected stamps from all of the countries. You can use our downloadable passport template found in the Additional Resources at the back of this book.

## World Friend Bingo

A nice ice breaker for a school event like an International Festival or even for the first day of school to kick off a global themed week, month, or year is World Friend Bingo, a sort of human scavenger hunt. Following is an example of a Bingo Board you can use (this is particular to U.S. audiences; please adapt if you live outside the United States).

## (Find someone who . . . )

| W | O | R | L | D |
|---|---|---|---|---|
| Speaks more than one language | Knows where their grandmother was born | Knows where their dad was born | Has seen a movie from another country | Has seen a TV show from another country |
| Can say a sentence in Spanish | Can say a word in a language other than Spanish and English | Can name a currency (form of money) other than "dollar" | Can name a river outside the United States | Would like to live in another country |
| Owns a globe | Has traveled outside the country | **Free Space** | Can eat with chopsticks | Can find the country where their clothing was made |
| Owns a pet other than a dog or cat | Can name five continents | Knows the capital of Canada | Has a religious tradition that is different from yours | Knows the word for "soccer" used in most of the world |
| Was born outside the United States | Has a passport | Has eaten papaya | Knows what color saffron is | Can name a famous person born outside the United States |

Another version of our World Friend Bingo is ePals' **Cultural Bingo.** You may wish to mix and match categories and questions, depending on the background and interests of your own community. The key is to have fun getting to know each other!

## Movies for Classroom Discovery and Family Film Fun Events

When looking for media resources to be shown in class, films from various countries offer a fun and fascinating way to demonstrate various perspectives and can transport students to faraway places, without leaving the classroom. A 10-minute clip (or shorter) from a film like *The Story of the Weeping Camel* from Mongolia might suffice to create a powerful discussion prompt on different perspectives about material luxuries, survival, the importance of taking care of loved ones, being kind and considerate, different living environments, and communicating in various languages. It also can help build compassion and humanize an otherwise unknown culture.

Watching a film can go from a passive experience to an active, engaged, curious exploration and inquiry of big life themes and various academic disciplines. **Journeys in Film** offers thoughtful resources for actively learning and watching films. Its guides, available as free downloads on its website, have been created for Grades 6 and up, but for films on the list that are appropriate for younger audiences, such as *Like Stars on Earth* (India), *Please Vote for Me* (China), *Children of Heaven* (Iran), and *The Way Home* (South Korea), some of the activities can be adapted to slightly younger grades. See Chapter 3, Section 2 for an example of using a film to grow Language Arts skills.

Be aware of one additional challenge posed by these films: subtitles. Depending on the age and reading ability of your students, allow them to read the film, slowing down, repeating scenes frequently, or if you love the film, you can read it to your children/students. This may seem tedious, but it has benefits: Kids are reading alongside your pace, reinforcing their skills; you can skip an inappropriate word or idea (though we have tried to recommend films here which are safe to view in elementary school); and you can opt to spend more time on an idea you already are trying to teach in your class.

Reading subtitles builds important comprehension skills which countries around the world have gained as they have imported Hollywood films. Education-conscious nations like Finland almost exclusively air subtitled films and TV shows in order to cultivate a more literate national population. Finally, getting accustomed to reading subtitles can be like building a muscle—initially there is some discomfort, but as it grows, the initial pain or "stretch" from reading a film feels normal and it simply becomes an enjoyable experience.

Beyond classroom exploration, a foreign film event at school (like a School Film Festival or a fundraising family movie night) can serve as a terrific community event, shining a light on a new culture, introducing the audience to a new genre of art and expression, and engaging more parents. You might wish to offer snacks reflecting the culture in the film, have some opening dance or musical performances from that culture by local kids, teach a few words in the language spoken in the film, or have the ticket proceeds benefit a cause helping kids in that country.

## 25 Favorite Foreign Films for K-5!

Finding age-appropriate, high-quality movies from other countries, especially to watch with younger children, can be a big challenge. Action and story lines may differ drastically, and dubbing or subtitles offer a distinct viewing experience. Content is generally edgier than American audiences are used to and certainly that U.S. schools would be comfortable screening. An award-winning animated film from France or Japan may be considered PG-13 material, though many of the films don't receive the MPAA rating, making it even harder to choose a quality foreign film appropriate for all ages. With that in mind, here are a few of our favorite foreign films and our best judgment for audience ages:

- *Ponyo* (age 5 and up). A Japanese take on Hans Christian Anderson's "Little Mermaid" that's filled with wonder without the romantic obsession Disney's Ariel displays. This is an all-ages, girl- and boy-friendly absolute crowd pleaser.

- *The Red Balloon* (all ages). This film is almost completely silent, following a simple balloon through a day in Paris. Yet the simplicity masks the diversity of experiences which every viewer of any age may take away. It was acclaimed enough to win the 1956 Academy Award for Best Original Screenplay as well as the 1968 "Best Film of the Decade" Educational Film Award.

- *Linnea in Monet's Garden* (all ages). Swedish Linnea and her wise, elderly neighbor travel to Paris to see painter Claude Monet's

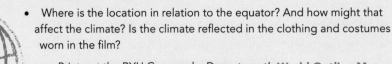

## Discussion-Thinking-Learning Exploration Guide for Watching International Films

This worksheet offers suggested points of exploration. In each category, you'll notice the points get slightly, progressively more complex, corresponding to a more mature learner. For example, the first bullet point can be discussed with viewers in first grade on, and the last might be just for Grade 5 and above. You can adapt these questions as a handout with space to fill in blanks while the film is watched or use it to guide discussion afterward.

### I. Geography and Location

- Where is the movie from? (If set in multiple nations, adapt answers to more than one location.)
- Find it on a world map or globe.
  - What language(s) are they speaking?
    - Where is the location in relation to the equator? And how might that affect the climate? Is the climate reflected in the clothing and costumes worn in the film?
      - Print out the BYU Geography Department's **World Outline Maps** for the region where the movie is located. Fill in the countries in the region, the capital cities, and for an extra challenge, find landforms and bodies of water.
    - Does the country seem as prosperous as your own? What hints from the movie indicate the level of wealth or poverty? Do you see signals of both wealth and poverty among different people from the same country?

### II. Identity and Characters

- Are the main characters children or adults?
- How many main/central characters does the film have?
- Do you remember their names?

garden for themselves. A gentle companion (no action or suspense here) to *The Red Balloon,* this art education film features the wonders of Paris and the Impressionists.

- *Frogs and Toads (Kikkerdril): Max's Magical Journey* (all ages). Journey through the vibrant Dutch countryside in this gentle tromp through nature with precocious 6-year-old Max and his buddy. It is a celebration of a child's imagination and discovery in the outdoors, dubbed into English.

- Have you heard these names before?

- What else do you know about them? For example, do they have many friends or few? Are they leaders or underdogs? Do they have a favorite food or snack? Do you know if they practice a faith? Do they have hobbies or favorite activities? What can you say about their home life?

- If your friends were going to act out a play similar to the movie, who would you cast as the various characters? Why?

### III. Setting

- Setting refers to places such as school, home, work, a desert, a farm, or an island. What is the film's setting?

- What is **similar** about the setting to places you are familiar with?

- What is **different** about the setting to places you are familiar with?

- Does anything surprise you about the setting?

- What adjustments to the life you are familiar with would you have to make to live there?

### IV. Challenges

- Can you name some of the challenges facing the main characters in the film?

- What did they do to overcome them?

- Could you imagine these challenges taking place where you live? Why or why not?

- Do you think they found a good solution? Why or why not?

- Are there some life lessons the movie conveys? What are they?

### V. Humor and Joy

- What makes the characters in the movie happy?

- Would this make you happy?

- What makes the characters laugh?

- Do you find the same things funny?

- *My Neighbor Totoro* (age 6 and up). American audiences unfamiliar with the fantasy creatures in Japanese animation may take some acclimating to *Totoro,* but we find our children are instantly transported by this film, which has become an all-ages classic. *Kiki's Delivery Service* is another age-6-and-up favorite from the same Japanese animation team. We've met so many kids who were inspired to study Japanese language as a result of their love for these movies and later by the anime genre in general.

- *Like Stars on Earth (Taare Zameen Par)* (age 7 and up). An 8-year-old boy in India, with discipline and learning challenges, is sent off to boarding school by his exasperated parents. An art teacher unlocks the boy's potential.

- *The Cave of the Yellow Dog* and *The Story of the Weeping Camel* (age 7 and up). These films show life in Mongolia that is innocent, real, and contemporary yet worlds away from what we know. Central characters are real families, not professional actors. Some aspects of nomadic life may be hard for children to watch (e.g., vultures feed on animal carcass, children are separated from their parents), but these are not in the context of any gratuitous violence or sinister character. Think of them more like a nature documentary. These would be good movies to watch actively: After a scene, pause and process together, then restart the movie and repeat.

- *The Secret of Roan Inish* (age 7 and up). In this contemplative folk-inspired film, the real Irish countryside is infused with elements of legend to captivating effect.

- *Winged Migration* (age 7 and up). In this nature documentary, follow familiar and rare bird species to and from all corners of the globe with keen cinematography that awakens the senses while it calms the soul.

- *Beauty and the Beast (La Belle et la Bête)* (age 8 and up). See the original French version, made in 1946, where Disney's inspiration came from. The cover art may seem scary to younger children, and the black-and-white effects feel far more sinister than Disney's animation, but with adult accompaniment, kids Grades 3 and up will enjoy this classic.

- *Azur and Asmar: The Prince's Quest* (age 8 and up). This French animation depicts the divides that come between two boys raised together yet from different races, classes, and religions. At a time when misunderstandings about Islam divide and mystify adults, this film can begin to show a way to a new generation.

- *Tales of the Night* (age 8 and up). From the makers of *Azur and Asmar,* this French animated film (completely dubbed in English) shares six short-story-format cultural fables from Tibet to the Caribbean Islands.

- *Alamar* (age 8 and up). Before returning to life with his mother in Italy, a young boy joins his father of Mayan heritage on an epic, bonding journey into the open Caribbean Sea off Mexico. This unscripted, semidocumentary film feels like a meditative plunge into nature's beauty.

- *Children of Heaven* (age 9 and up). A brother's love and care for his little sister as they seek her lost pair of shoes humanizes Iran's children in a universal story. The most challenging aspect is subtitled dialogue in Persian, so it's best enjoyed with stronger readers.

- *The Secret of Kells* (age 9 and up). This gripping, animated Irish film depicts classic Celtic folklore, art, and heroes. A feast for the eyes, ears, and imagination.

- *The Great Match* (age 9 and up). This may be fine for age 6 and up, except that in a few places there is a bit of cursing translated in the subtitles. For sports fans—especially soccer fans—this film conveys dedication to the sport even among the most isolated populations and the lengths that residents in the Amazon jungle, Mongolian plains, and Central African desert will go to watch the World Cup final. It's a nice depiction of how different, yet connected, we all are.

- Classics set in various locations around the world: *The Sound of Music* (age 6 and up), *My Fair Lady* (age 6 and up), *Anne of Green Gables* (age 6 and up), *The King and I* (age 8 and up), *South Pacific* (age 8 and up), *Oliver!* (age 8 and up), *Roman Holiday* (age 9 and up), *Fiddler on the Roof* (age 9 and up). When choosing one of these films to watch, note that times have really changed. You may want to take extra time to pause the film and discuss historical circumstances, social norms, and ethnic or gender stereotypes that were considered acceptable when the film was made. By taking the time to actively discuss and watch these films, you'll create an unforgettable learning experience.

## Show-and-Touch Tables

Country tables, also known as Show-and-Touch Tables, can serve as the backbone of an International Festival, offering information to the visitors about specific countries or regions. Elementary school–aged kids appreciate hands-on, tactile experiences that stimulate all of their senses. Here are some show-and-touch examples:

- Touching weavings, fabric, and textiles

- Running their fingers over wooden or metal carvings

- Trying on jewelry or clothing
- Seeing pictures (include modern cities and rural scenes, animals, people)
- Watching a colorful video montage with scenes from the country
- Listening to music either from a CD or by trying out instruments
- Smelling spices, coffee, tea, or flowers (place them in empty spice containers or small plates)
- Tasting a new flavor such as goat milk, seaweed snacks, or a new fruit like rambutans
- Using chopsticks to pick up dried beans

At Becky's school, she brought in a tiny shepherd stool/headrest from Ethiopia, and kids loved trying to balance on it. Another table had a water jug and she asked kids to try and balance it on their heads and walk around the gym. The Taiwan table was very popular, with a display of traditional toys such as Chinese yo-yos, wooden spinning tops, and shadow puppets for the kids to try out. The more hands-on the tables, offering tactile and multisensory experiences, the more successful they are at luring kids in. When children crowd around a certain table, wanting to have a turn at something, you know that you have piqued their interest!

## Guess the Flag Game

During special events, a table can be set up with a Guess the Flag game or other geography trivia. The games can be as simple as a read-aloud question and answer or as involved as a spinning wheel with different categories. The idea is to have fun and quiz kids about geography from around the world. One website, called **Printable Flash Cards**, has free, downloadable flashcards of the flags of the world. Another fun activity is a **flag puzzle**.

## Exploring a Country Through the Five Senses

Classes often invite guest speakers to come and talk about a specific country or culture in their class. Sometimes guest speakers are looking for an area to focus on and may not be used to speaking to young children. One suggestion is to have them introduce their culture using the five senses. Have them think of at least one object that the students might taste, see, hear, touch, or taste in the new country. This helps the speaker bring the lesson to the appropriate age group, while still introducing important aspects of the new culture. As an added bonus, kids who learn using their different senses are more likely to remember the lesson. **Kid World Citizen has an example of a lesson that uses the five senses to teach about Ethiopia.**

Teachers and after-school clubs also can use the Five Senses approach as a shorthand checklist for remembering to infuse global experiences throughout their classrooms. Can you think of ways to explore a country highlighted in literature, social studies, or science using each of the five senses?

## Passport Day

At Saint Mark's School in Marin County, California, Passport Day represents a culmination in global learning, giving, and citizenship for students, faculty, staff, and families and marks a highlight of the school year. In place since 2001, each year a new region, country, or culture is chosen at the K–8 school, and this is viewed as integral to the school's diversity and inclusion initiatives. As the school's website explains,

> The purpose of the day is to enjoy our differences and to celebrate values shared across cultures. On this day and throughout the year, Saint Mark's students are encouraged to ask themselves "How are we the same?" and "What can we learn from each other?," thereby seeking the deep similarities between ourselves and others that often lie beneath surface differences.

Jenny Getz, who started as a classroom teacher 20 years ago at the school and now serves as their director of Global and Special Programs, emphasized, "We really think a day like this is part of our continuous and ongoing focus on inclusion for every member of our community all year long. I would be sorry for Passport Day to be viewed as a one-off that occurs only once a year."

Homa visited Passport Day when the theme was India, and was impressed by the range of collaboration and community engagement that infused the program. Culture was presented as active, personal, and dynamic. In addition to long-term, schoolwide social studies and literature projects on display, special programs took place throughout the day.

For example, in yoga classes, concentration and breathing practices were taught to the children; in music, demonstrations by classical masters from the community were given; as various melodies and stories were shared, young ears became accustomed to beautiful new sounds; in art class, tiles were completed that would support an ongoing service program for a school in rural India; in P.E. class, children learned the rules of cricket and got to play the favorite Indian sport; a local Indian-born entrepreneur shared many innovative examples of how technology was being used in modern India to solve big, global challenges that could benefit millions; and of course, a feast of Indian cuisine was enjoyed for lunch (more elaborate for the teachers and other adults, simpler for the children). To learn more about Passport Day, you can visit the **Saint Mark's School website**.

## Section 5: Integrating Global Perspectives Into the School Environment Throughout the Year

While an International Night (or Week) highlights global studies over a short time period, there are many types of global projects that can allow students to connect with peers around the world throughout the year. Whether virtual or tactile, the following ongoing projects help keep global perspectives present in the school environment, while students make friends and build relationships with kids located anywhere.

### Video Chat With a Sister School

Set up regular video chats (via Skype or other platforms, like Google+, ePals, or Edmodo) with an elementary school in another part of the world. See the examples from Chapter 4 to learn more on how to connect with schools using technology, and see Chapter 4's section Tips for Setting Up a Successful School Partnership (or "Twinning Program") for guidelines on building a relationship with a partner school.

If you have not coordinated an official sister or partner school, programs like **Skype in the Classroom** will allow teachers to propose a lesson (or Skype topic) and let schools from around the world sign up to participate. For example, an elementary school in Houston, Texas, asked the question "What do you play at recess?" and was able to set up various sessions with schools from around the world during their International Week.

## Worldwide Cultural Swap Boxes

Through the **Worldwide Culture Swap**, schools can have their classes sign up to participate in a free cultural swap with other same-age classes either from different states in the United States or from different countries around the world.

Frances Diaz-Evans of South Carolina and the author of the multicultural parents' blog **Discovering the World Through My Son's Eyes**, shared her family's rich experience participating in Worldwide Culture Swaps and particularly the reaction of her son in preK. Her experience demonstrates that any age can gain a sense of wonder through this engaging global activity. As we learned about the many places from which they received packages, we could envision classrooms participating in the exchanges and the excitement of receiving a package from so many distinct places on Earth. Here's what Frances shared with us:

> *The best part* (of Worldwide Culture Swaps) *is that it has given our family the opportunity to receive tangible items from families in other countries which make it more "real" for us to learn about their culture. Some of these items my son has been able to take to school for "show and tell." He explains what the item is and where it comes from. For example, we received a rock in one of the packages, but it wasn't just any rock. It was a "Thunder-egg" (geode) rock from Oregon! It doesn't look like much on the outside, once cracked open you will see an exquisite beauty inside. From Norway we received pressed flowers and sand and sea shells that are from their local pebbly beach (we looked online for pictures so he can see where they came from); my son's favorite item in the package were the Norwegian chocolate bars. From South Africa we received a small rhinoceros toy, wildlife animal stickers, coins, and stamps. We also received beads with their significance, as well as brochures, homemade flag, and a lip balm. I printed out a map of South Africa so he can color, and stick the wildlife animal stickers he received in the package.*
>
> *From Florida we received the most fascinating item of all! Alligator teeth and "points" (a replica of a very rare and expensive arrowhead made by the native people in the region) where the family lives. We also received sand,*

*shells, sea sponge, marmalade, key chains, and postcards.*
*My son was really excited showing off the alligator teeth*
*to his classmates during show and tell. From England we*
*received Olympic memorabilia, perfect to teach him about*
*the Olympics (since we received it about the same time*
*the Olympics were on). From England we also received*
*flags, coins, custard, and a homemade DVD video of the*
*area where they live! From Hawaii we received a paper*
*lei and grow-in-water toy turtle (we were learning about*
*turtles), and how to make a luau shirt (folded paper*
*with instructions), and a fish made from palm leaves.*
*We also received stickers, a U.S. flag, macadamia nuts,*
*passion fruit jelly, calendar, and a newspaper, and lots of*
*information on Hawaii. Needless to say, this experience*
*has been educational and fun! In all of our packages we*
*received a personalized letter from each family, and some*
*even sent pictures.*

Once you are matched with a class, you decide together the extent of the swap: class letters, packages, postcards, or whatever the educators agree on. If more than one class from your school participates in sending and receiving, a display could be created with a world map marking the locations of the swaps, and even a touch table displaying the contents of the swap could be set up. The website has options for families who wish to participate, as well as for classes (schools), and there is also an option to only exchange letters through a pen pal program.

## Pen Pal Program

Since long before the Internet, pen pal correspondence has been considered one of the classic ways to make friends far away. Exchanging e-mails or pen pal letters with individuals or classes around the world improves reading and writing in an exciting way, while offering opportunities for making lifelong friends and dispelling myths about places and cultures we may never have had personal contact with. See Chapter 4's section Tips for Setting Up a Successful School Partnership (or "Twinning Program") to enhance the pen pal relationship. Use these sources for finding pen pals, so you can get started:

- *ePals* is a "leading provider of safe collaborative technology for schools to connect and learn in a protected, project-based learning network." ePals' free Global Community service features content from the National Geographic and Smithsonian Institute, offering connection to an extensive global network of vetted classrooms.

- *World Wise Schools*, a program of the U.S. Peace Corps, arranges for classes to be pen pals with Peace Corps Volunteers in monthly letter exchanges.

- *People to People International*, founded by President Dwight D. Eisenhower, includes a free School and Classroom Program that connects classes (ages 4–18) in different countries for e-mail and/or postal pen pal exchanges and projects that build cultural understanding. Registration for the academic year is held July through October.

- *School-to-School International* facilitates pen pal exchanges between classrooms in Guinea, West Africa, and North America.

- *Students of the World*, founded in France, has a free pen pal program matching classrooms around the world.

Finally, don't overlook your own network of friends and family with ties to schools around the world. Writing to a personal contact may be the simplest way to get started, but a drawback may be that you won't have the administrative support offered by some of the professional services.

*Safety caveat:* Particularly with online friends, adults need to be vigilant that they are dealing with a legitimate entity and supervise information that children are sharing. Personal information like home addresses should never be given out if corresponding as a class, and some sites recommend using nicknames or pseudonyms and never first and last names. If using snail mail, classes can send written letters in one bundle with the school's address as the return address. Or, to be extra safe, use the local post office for a return address.

# Section 6: Everyday Foreign Language Exposure

Language plays an integral role in understanding a new culture, yet many times is missing from our schools, especially at the elementary level. According to a 2010 poll commissioned by **NAFSA: Association of International Educators**, nearly two thirds (65%) of Americans surveyed believe that if our young people do not learn world languages, they will be at a competitive disadvantage in their careers. Yet only 25% of elementary schools in the United States offered any world languages in 2008, down from 31% in 1997, according to the Center for Applied Linguistics report *Foreign Language Teaching in U.S. Schools: Results of a National Survey.*

Including language lessons naturally internationalizes the curriculum and encourages children to learn a skill that comes easier the younger they are. Because budgets for language classes have been cut, fewer K–5 schools have a foreign language teacher on staff. Schools can incorporate foreign languages in lessons using the resources highlighted in Chapter 3, Section 8: World Languages. Below are a few informal ways for schools, classrooms, or clubs to strengthen language exposure and curiosity about diverse ways the world communicates.[1]

1. *Seeing leads to knowing.* Post foreign language words or phrases throughout the classroom or in a designated space. Exposure to words in various languages around key topics can be based on the various heritages of your students, composition of the community, places in the news, or any other geographic prompt. Special bulletin boards around words in many languages can serve as a point of pride and wonder.

2. *Sharing is caring.* Encourage students who study or speak another language to share a phrase or two per day or per week. This can build appreciation for bilingualism and classroom diversity; it might be the first exposure to a second language for many students and can embolden the second language speaker.

3. *Hear your community.* Invite parents, international students at local colleges, and other community members in to present about their language, preferably tied in to a learning unit already taking place, such as in science or math, or for your International Day/Week/Month events.

4. *Broadcast it.* Some schools have their morning announcements, or a phrase within them, repeated in a second language. This can help English language learners feel more welcome and also creates excitement in other students when they start to recognize familiar words they hear over and over. If the principal or another key leader repeats part of the announcements or a key phrase in a focus language, it will "stick" better, longer. Depending on the school population, announcements can be Spanish-English, or make a monthly or annual rotation of other languages present in the community.

5. *Talk to new friends far away.* Partner with classrooms where a different first language is spoken to create opportunities for the students to teach each other new words during video chats or while corresponding in other ways. This is one more benefit of supervised video chats and pen pals.

6. *Watch foreign films.* Age-appropriate, subtitled films offer an exciting lens into a new culture. Our 25 Favorite Foreign Films for K–5! list found earlier in this chapter can offer ideas. For more, see ***Growing Up Global***'s Chapter 8, "Watch the World—Read a Movie" with age-appropriate lists of films for Grades preK on up.

7. *Time for Kids: Around the World.* Think outside of the most popular languages. **Time for Kids** country profiles include "Native Lingo" sections for many countries, where kids can learn useful phrases and hear native speakers pronounce them in audio clips.

## "My Place in the World" Projects

Try a **geographical art project** with concentric circles cut out of colored paper that show "My House," "My City," "My State," "My Country," "My Continent," and "My Planet." An art project like this is a concrete representation of our geography and lets kids visualize how they and their community fit into the wider world.

## Map the Settings of Books Read

On a world map hanging in the classroom or library, teachers and students can mark the locations of the settings of books read. Students can watch the states/countries begin to fill as the year goes on, and teachers can use the visual reminder to see if any geographic regions are lacking in coverage. If you read several books from the same country, compare and contrast the details of the stories and settings. Also noteworthy are the similarities or differences between rural and urban settings. Students can add pins to the map when they read books independently as well, sharing what they learned about the setting with the class.

When Homa spoke to a parents group at the library in Eliot, Maine, the big map on the wall served as a great point of pride. They shared that not many people in their community get to travel overseas, but with the library's encouragement, kids participating in summer reading tried to "visit" as many countries as they could and were excited about noting this on the wall map.

## Daily Geography Trivia

Start the school day with world geography trivia publicized over the announcements, in the school news, or read by the teachers in individual classrooms. Choose geography questions which can cover topics like locations of places, specific physical and human characteristics, cultural questions, or the environment. Remember to record which questions were already covered so that the trivia touches diverse regions of the world without concentrating on only one area.

The **World Atlas** offers a giant list of facts about the Earth from which you can create trivia questions. The **CIA World Factbook** has country profiles and facts about the entire world that can also help to generate questions. The website and mobile app for the **National Geographic Bee** contains activities, quiz questions, and tips on studying for the Bee that anyone can use. You might even have a budding national champion on your hands!

Little Bennett Elementary School, a public school in Montgomery County, Maryland, has been hosting international activities since the school's opening in 2006. In addition to international nights, cultural calendars, and bulletin boards and displays, a year-long game was introduced by parent and PTA member Shiva Sobhani. Kindergarten through fifth graders were encouraged to work with their friends and families and follow a series of clues to find their principal as he traveled around the globe. In the game called "Where in the World Is Mr. Miller?" students received three clues each week and submitted responses to their teacher guessing Mr. Miller's secret location. The clues were revealed one at a time for 3 days, and a winner was randomly drawn from all the correct entries at the end of the week. Each Monday morning that person had the privilege of sharing on morning announcements where they located their principal. The game's bulletin board would then be updated to display a picture of the winner, along with the location, additional facts, and interesting notes about the place where Mr. Miller was found. Each quarter, a random winner from all the participants in the game would be awarded with an atlas. Children collaborated on finding the location, families worked with younger students in researching the clues, and entire classes could be seen with their teacher participating in the games.

## Exchange Student Panel

Many organizations bring exchange students to the United States to study while living with host families. These students often act as informal ambassadors for their home countries in their new host communities and may enjoy teaching people about their country, culture, customs, and family. Invite a panel of local high school exchange students to talk to your class or school or to answer questions from your students. Contact your local high school to see if it hosts any exchange students or contact the following organizations that place enthusiastic international students nationwide to find some nearby—or possibly start hosting yourselves.

- The *Council on Standards for International Educational Travel* serves as a not-for-profit clearinghouse of accredited exchange organizations serving youth at the high school level. Their Program Finder can start pointing you to programs operating in your state and offers guidance for starting new programs.

- *The Rotary Club* brings students from around the world to study and live with host families in the United States. Their students are required to give speeches to local Rotary Clubs and can be excellent candidates to come speak to elementary schools.

- *FLEX ("Future Leaders Exchange")* from American Councils sends students from Eastern European countries as exchange students who have been chosen because of their excellent leadership, communication, and academic skills. They are encouraged to volunteer and act civically responsible while in the United States and are truly ambassadors to their host communities.

- *The Kennedy-Lugar Youth Exchange and Study (YES) Program* provides scholarships to high school students from countries with significant Muslim populations. It is a highly competitive program, which brings excellent students to the United States and requires them to help educate Americans about their countries and cultures.

## Speakers From Around the World

To increase cultural awareness and widen the perspectives your students hear, invite speakers (individuals or even a panel of speakers) with a variety of cultural backgrounds and life stories to speak in your class or for schoolwide assemblies. While hearing speakers talk about their culture, home country, celebrations, or food offers an incredible experience, it is equally important for students to see professional speakers from a variety of cultures that are successful in their fields of expertise. In fact, these speakers do not necessarily need to speak about their culture; they can be coming to speak about their work as a scientist, pilot, doctor, or journalist. When students see that people from any background succeed in diverse fields of study or work, they can be motivated to strive higher.

Welcoming guest speakers into the class that hail from diverse backgrounds and have all made a positive contribution to important fields can also help dispel any preconceived notions that students might possess about the relative competence and value of people from different cultures. Meeting multicultural role models and hearing from them firsthand shows that people of all genders, ethnicities, and appearances have a positive influence on the world and deserve to be respected and emulated.

Once a speaker has accepted to come in, discuss clearly what topics they will cover, or have your students interview them with their prewritten questions. It is important to offer some initial guidance on topics to share or avoid so that information covered is age and subject appropriate for the children participating.

As you consider reaching out to your wider community, consider these sources for inviting in guest speakers.

- *Family members of students.* Many families have cultural connections: recent immigrants who grew up abroad or relatives who have lived, studied, worked, or volunteered in another country. Parents, and especially grandparents, can be offered the opportunity to share a completely different perspective than students usually hear.

- *Professional speakers.* Google your location and "speakers bureau" to find speakers near you on relevant topics. Universities, hospitals, professional business organizations, and clubs like Toastmasters, Rotary, or Kiwanis frequently have volunteers from within their staff, faculty, or membership that can come to your school to talk about a variety of topics.

- *Local foreign language periodicals.* Local newspapers or magazines are great sources for providing speakers, from scientists to athletes to activists. Check your nearest Spanish-speaking newspaper or Chinatown publication for leads on journalists or editors who might come to your school to talk about careers, writing, current events from a different culture's perspective, or other relevant topics. Ask parents who read in those languages if they might help to be on the lookout for speakers.

- *University student organizations.* Colleges have hundreds of student groups, many of whom encourage their members to volunteer in the community. For example, science, service, music, and international clubs may have outreach programs and can come out to schools to do demonstrations related to global environmental issues or other causes in which they are engaged. Check the websites of nearby universities and contact student organizations to see what they have to offer.

- *Individuals from area colleges.* Once you're investigating student groups at local colleges, also look for professors, international students, and administrators who make up a great, often under-tapped local resource that may be eager to share their research and life experiences.

## A Model of International University Scholars Impacting U.S. Schoolkids

**One To World**'s Global Classroom connects New York City youth with trained, international university scholars through in-person, interactive workshops that engage students in learning about world cultures and global issues. Interaction with Global Guides offers students a platform to break down stereotypes and expand their perspectives.

To illustrate, Themis, a Global Guide from Greece studying at Stevens Institute of Technology in Hoboken, New Jersey, offered a class of third graders an engaging and interactive two-part workshop on her country. In her visits, she engaged all of the students' senses—smell, taste, hearing, sight, and touch—so that they could imagine and explore the culture right from their very own classrooms. First, she shared the kinds of herbs her mother would grow in their garden, such as oregano, thyme, and basil. The students tasted olives, feta cheese, and fresh apples, and Themis shared where each of these foods come from around the country and how they are used in Greek cuisine. They also listened to traditional music, and Themis taught a little dance, traditionally practiced at family gathering and holidays! Themis showed the students beautiful images of the country, her neighborhood, and her house, as well as ancient Greek statues, which served as inspiration for the students' own art projects. Themis shared a Greek myth and had the students mold statues out of clay, based on their interpretations of the myth.

Face-to-face interactions like these form an unforgettable foundation for budding global citizens. We are impressed by this model of global education which harnesses existing resources to bridge local and global to build understanding and friendship. If you are located outside New York City, you can contact One To World for more advice and information on tapping into your nearby university's pool of international students.

- *Exchange students.* Numerous nonprofit organizations sponsor exchanges of teachers and students. As mentioned in the previous section, check with the **Council on Standards for International Educational Travel** to find specific organizations, or call your local high school. Many times the exchanges will last a semester or a year, and students may be encouraged to get involved in the community by volunteering. They can come to talk about life in their home country, differences and similarities between their country and their host country, their families, or what they do with their friends for fun, sports, birthday parties, favorite vacations—you name the topic, or have your students come up with a list of questions for the exchange student. Another option is to have a panel of students come in from different geographic regions so that your students can get a variety of perspectives. If you'd like to invite a university student, try their Office of International Students and Scholars for references.

- *Local talent.* Martial arts schools, dance troupes performing national and ethnic dances, and global musicians are all excellent choices for kids to expand their knowledge while having a fantastic experience and especially fun when our own students are members of the performing team. Before watching the show, it is helpful to give students the history and background of the art. After the performance, let the students ask questions and interact with the visitors to help the experience stick. Maybe it will pique their interest and they'll start a new hobby.

- *Peace Corps volunteers.* At the **Peace Corps World Wise Schools site**, you can request a returned Peace Corps volunteer from any region of the world as a speaker to your class to enhance your students' learning in almost any subject area. The site describes their purpose: "Their stories, projects, and experiences can provide U.S. students with unusually candid firsthand perspectives of cultures worldwide, views not usually accessible through textbooks, films, and other familiar media."

- *Skype an author* and *Skype in the classroom.* This brings speakers into your classroom for virtual visits from experts and student peers around the world (see Chapter 4 for more information on using Skype in the classroom).

## Multilingual Announcements

Several schools we spoke with asked students to volunteer to read the announcements in their native language, so the entire student body can listen to them in English and then a second language. At some schools, foreign language teachers or bilingual volunteers offer to teach a phrase a day in another language during the announcements. As touched on previously in this chapter, on the list of ideas for Everyday Foreign Language Exposure, spending a couple of minutes at the beginning of the day introducing Chinese, Spanish, Urdu, or Swahili may inspire students to begin studying a language they had not thought of previously.

## Incorporating Google Earth Into Lessons

We can't get enough of Google Earth. It is an astounding, eye-opening, free geographic resource that allows you and your students to fly anywhere on the planet and zoom from outer space down to street level to see cities, buildings, landmarks, ancient ruins, terrain, underwater ocean views—almost anything on Earth! Once you download the application onto your computer, you can begin to explore. It is helpful for teachers to preview and attempt to complete the activities before working with their students so that they can fully understand the program. Google Earth has **excellent tutorials and tips** and also contains classroom-ready lesson plans available for free.

Once you are comfortable with the Google Earth platform, try one of many ways to incorporate it into the curriculum:

- Look at real (current) views of cities. For instance, students studying Japan can take a virtual visit during the cherry blossom season.

- Take 360° visits to historical areas and ancient ruins, such as the Egyptian pyramids.

- Go on a scavenger hunt for landforms and physical features of Earth.

- Look at the street view of animal habitats. For example, if you're studying the rainforest, check out the street view of the Amazon River (where they mounted the camera onto a boat!).

- See evidence of, and the effects of, climate change.

You also can try applications to explore the ocean, Antarctica, or outer space. Learn more about incorporating Google Earth into the classroom and access **classroom-ready lesson plans**. This is armchair travel with 360° views so your students can "visit" places around the world without leaving their classroom.

## Take a Google Lit Trip

Another creative way to include Google Earth into the classroom is to journey with **Google Lit Trips**. Specially created for different age groups (including K–5), Google Lit Trips are downloadable files to be used with Google Earth that highlight the journeys of characters from famous children's literature. These free, interactive journeys place young readers inside the stories with relevant resources and media that delve deeper into the literature and provide thought-provoking discussions. To get a better sense of how these work and what they look like, preview the trips through tutorial videos available on the website. For example, Karen Arrington of Trinity Valley School in Fort Worth, Texas, developed this **example preview video of the Google Lit Trip for *A Walk in London* by Salvatore Rubbino**, adventuring all over central London.

## Geography Stars

Geography Stars was created by parent volunteer Sharon Deol in Austin, Texas, as a way to supplement geography education at her daughter's school. At this school, the program was run as an extracurricular activity with students doing weekly geography worksheets/research at home and submitting them in school to be graded by parent volunteers. For each worksheet submitted, students earned visa stamps that went into their Geography Stars passport. The program was so successful that Sharon is now designing Geography Stars packages for implementation by other schools.

Other schools have adapted Geography Stars to their own circumstances as a multi-week trivia program before or after school. In one variation, parent organizers choose two countries per week for students to study. These are announced in a flyer that goes home with students as well as during the weekly school announcements. Participating students are asked five questions about each country:

1. Locate the countries on a map.
2. Identify the continent.
3. Name the hemisphere (north or south).
4. Name one official language spoken.
5. Name the capital city.

Among schools that have tried morning Geography Stars, parents that could not normally volunteer during school hours appreciated the short and early time slot (7:30–8:00 a.m.), where they could come in to quiz participants. The students were extremely enthusiastic during the weekly morning meeting to show their skills, and several students at each grade level (including kindergarten) never missed a question. Each question was worth 1 point, so after answering the trivia about two countries each week, students could earn 10 points per week. At the end of the program at Becky's school, participants were awarded a laminated black-and-white world map that could serve as a placemat from which they could study more geography. Top performers earned a small inflatable globe from Oriental Trading Company.

Another variation on this geography-based activity is the **Passport Club**, started in 1994 in Olympia, Washington, and continuing today in hundreds more schools.

## Instill Meaning Through Service and Giving

We can't think of a better way to round out our list of ideas for integrating global perspectives throughout the year than to mention the significance of service and giving. Imagine if the excitement resulting from global learning at your school were coupled with making a difference, even if it's for lives far away. We've seen this played out repeatedly, whether learning about entrepreneurship by raising chickens and directing the funds from the sales of eggs to global projects via **Kiva** by the fifth and sixth graders at **Springside Chestnut Hill Academy** in Philadelphia, or by "walking for water," raising "Pennies for Peru," or donating outgrown bicycles, just to name a few of the examples we elaborate on in Chapter 5. When global learning combines with service to others, it's not just a memory for life, but it can instill purpose for a life well lived.

## Concluding Reflection

You can see the ideas shared in this chapter as a laundry list, a menu, or a buffet: You don't need to try everything to get a taste of the quality and value of global experiences, but taking part in whichever activities suit you or your school's inclinations can offer a satisfying experience. As we concluded in the previous chapter, remember to start with what you love. This helps the choice of which activity to try feel more authentic and enjoyable; it can help ensure that it sticks for a longer time and makes a more lasting impression on your students, while avoiding feeling overwhelmed by a new project.

As you try one or more of the items on the checklist at the start of this chapter, consider the following questions:

- Were your children/students as enthusiastic as you were when starting out?

- Did the enthusiasm continue throughout the experience?

- What might have made interest increase or wane?

- What were some of your realizations about organization, academic learning, and life lessons as you went along?

- Did other staff or volunteers share your interest in participating in the activity?

- What might attract more support next time?

- What adjustments need to be made next time to create a deeper, more authentic, less "touristy" global experience?

As you attempt and reflect on a new global activity from the checklist, we'd love to hear about your experience. Please contact us via www.globaledtoolkit.com!

## NOTE

1. List adapted from Tavangar, H. (2013). Growing up in a global classroom. In H. Hayes-Jacobs (Ed.), *Mastering global literacy* (pp. 67–84). Bloomington, IN: Solution Tree Press.

www.corwin.com/globaledtoolkit

# Infusing Global Learning Into Academic Subject Areas (With Special Consideration for Aligning Common Core Standards)

While many of the activities in Chapter 2 enhance students' overall social and academic experience at school or in clubs, the lessons and resources in this chapter are meant to be seamlessly incorporated into specific educational content areas. We realize it's unrealistic for most schools to undergo a transformation of their existing curricula, but we hope that simple considerations of global perspectives and the use of excellent, ready-to-use resources and lessons will make the transition to infusing global learning doable and painless. Expanding on what classroom teachers would already be covering, these lessons can reinforce concepts and at the same time showcase diverse cultures and perspectives from around the globe. In this area more than any other, teachers will play the lead role and serve as the primary facilitators of global learning in the classroom.

Examples have been deliberately chosen so that they are simple enough to not require significant new training of teachers and don't call for an overhaul of existing curriculum to be used. As simple tweaks or new ideas are infused into existing lessons, a global mindset—like a muscle that's always been there—will get stronger and be used more often. Students and teachers will create more and more extensions to the larger world and diverse cultures, more naturally, particularly as experience grows.

We have organized resources and activities corresponding to specific disciplines into the following sections:

- Section 1: "Global Competence" in the Context of the Common Core
- Section 2: Language Arts
- Section 3: Mathematics
- Section 4: Social Studies
- Section 5: Science
- Section 6: Music
- Section 7: Art
- Section 8: World Languages

## Section 1: "Global Competence" in the Context of the Common Core

In this chapter, we pay special attention to the Common Core State Standards. According to **the official website**, the Mission of the Standards is as follows:

> *The Common Core State Standards provide a consistent, clear understanding of what students are expected to learn, so teachers and parents know what they need to do to help them. The standards are designed to be robust and relevant to the real world, reflecting the knowledge and skills that our young people need for success in college and careers. With American students fully prepared for the future, our communities will be best positioned to compete successfully in the global economy.*

As of this writing, all 50 states, with the exception of 5—Texas, Virginia, Minnesota, Nebraska, and Alaska—have adopted the Common Core, so the standards are beginning to make up a vital part of instructional direction in the United States. Nonetheless, the final phrase of the Mission Statement, "to compete successfully in the global economy," remains elusive among many of the teachers with whom we have spoken, spurring many questions. For a K–5 classroom, what would it look like in practice to get students ready for a global economy? How is that implemented where resources are tight? What can teachers with minimal global exposure do to be true to that expectation? What resources are already out there to help realize this vision? In the following subsections, we offer sample ideas for including a global activity among Common Core Standards to try to answer those questions.

A further challenge of mandated standards is the fact that they define what students are expected to know and be able to do, not how teachers should teach. So the use of play with young children is not specified by the Standards, nor is the active use of resources from diverse cultures; yet these are widely accepted as offering rich learning opportunities in tune with 21st century learning and thus helping to meet the expectations of the Standards. Furthermore, while the Standards reference some particular content areas, like mythology and Shakespeare, they do not (and cannot) identify all the specific content that students should learn. We hope that the guide offered in our Toolkit helps point the way to content-rich curriculum that infuses a broader worldview.

Stepping back from the Common Core Standards' mission—which seeks to prepare American students for the future and success in the global economy—an awareness of "global competence" seems essential. According to the Council of Chief State School Officers **EdSteps project**, in partnership with the Asia Society Partnership for Global Learning:

> *Global Competence is the capacity and disposition to understand and act on issues of global significance. Examples of such issues are environmental sustainability, population growth, economic development, global conflict and cooperation, health and human development, and human rights.*

We particularly like that this definition encompasses knowledge alongside action and then offers examples of issue areas where global competence may be applied. While a variety of resources are available for middle and high schools, the development of global competence in academics for the lower grades is significantly weaker. Teachers often wonder how to engage the youngest learners with age-appropriate projects that will enhance global perspectives.

One place to start is by taking a fresh look at some of the most commonly taught lessons. The following table is meant to help teachers think beyond the typical lesson to bring up globally relevant issues in common units of study in many elementary schools.

# Examples of Global Lessons in Common Units of Study of Elementary School

| Farms | Read *Farms Around the World* by Catherine Veitch; look at **pictures of farms in many countries and states.** |
|---|---|
| Five senses | Learn more about a country by **using your five senses.** |
| Rainforest | Use Google Earth to **take a tour of deforestation in the Amazon rainforests.** Map the major rainforests of the world. Determine the languages spoken there. Consider the major environmental pressures on different forests. Put yourself in the shoes of local residents: How do you make choices in livelihood, preservation, and other issues across different priorities? |
| Pollution | Try the **Where Does Our Pollution Go?** lesson plan to discuss how the wind carries pollution around the world. |
| Conservation | Look at conservation efforts and nonprofit organizations across the globe. Why do some countries choose hydroelectric or wind power as a dominant power source? How are trash and recycling handled differently in different countries? |
| Water cycle | Follow the route of snow melting in the mountains to the tributaries of major rivers, such as **the Amazon**, Yangtze, and Nile, and back to the sea. |
| Families/ communities | What differences and similarities do you find in families and communities? Look at **schools**, **homes**, children (how many, how they are treated, how long they live at home, what jobs they are expected to do around the house), and sports around the world. |
| Careers/ famous people | Include examples of **inspiring leaders** from other countries. |
| Civil rights/ Martin Luther King | How far did Dr. King's message reach? Who inspired Dr. King and whom did he inspire? What groups of people are still fighting for their civil rights? Who are some of the national heroes in countries like South Africa, India, or anywhere else you may be studying. |
| Healthy eating | Learn about **where in the world our foods come from**; investigate healthy multicultural cuisine. Look up slide shows of school lunches or breakfast around the world. |
| Animals/ plants/insects | Discover native flora and fauna and habitats around the world; discuss hibernation (related to weather patterns) and migration routes with maps, such as **this lesson on monarch butterflies**. |

In each of these lessons, teachers can include the perspectives and experiences of groups of people beyond your local community with the complexity of issues increasing as students become more mature.

In the process of developing new curricula or revising existing lessons for global understanding, pose essential questions around learning goals. Teachers who want to deepen the international scope of their class can then apply the EdSteps Global Competence Matrix, which entails four key ideas that can be incorporated into any discipline and across disciplines. This Global Competence Matrix was developed by the Council of Chief State School Officers in partnership with the Asia Society Partnership for Global Learning, consisting of the following:

1. Investigate the World
2. Recognize Perspective
3. Communicate Ideas
4. Take Action

These four skills are essential for students' success in our interconnected world. To get a sense of how the **Global Competence Matrix** works in practice, this sequence may help:

- First, the students identify an issue of global significance, such as a specific environmental concern. Weighing a variety of sources and diverse media, students will research the local and global implications and combine the evidence to draw a conclusion.

- Next, they should examine their own perspectives on the issue, while recognizing the perspectives of others in the situation. It is especially important to take into account the cultural beliefs and influences of all parties.

- Using a variety of media and uses of technology, the students should then communicate their ideas; you can aim to reach a wider audience than the teacher, parents, or classmates by using technologies highlighted in Chapter 4.

- Finally, the class can make a positive contribution by taking action and putting what they learned into practice (see more in Chapter 5).

We recognize this represents a quite sophisticated skill set—high school students will stretch using this framework, too. But we have seen

## The Power of Pictures: Teaching Sustainability Through a Photo Exchange With India

One noteworthy example of an interdisciplinary project that encompasses the four points of the global competency matrix is a photo exchange developed by Pinki Shah, a fifth-grade teacher at the Manhattan Country School (MCS) in New York City. Ms. Shah's engaging study of sustainability combines math, social studies, art, and global learning while building a relationship with the HOPE Foundation School in Gujarat, India.

Over the course of 10 weeks, students from both schools exchanged pictures on how they used water, food, energy, and plastic in their communities. After exchanging the pictures, students were encouraged to ask questions, look for differences and similarities, and learn more about natural resources through the lens of human rights and international development. In the second year of the exchange, Ms. Shah's fifth graders had an opportunity to discuss selected photos with parents and visitors at an art gallery. Framed photos from the project were available in a silent auction to benefit the photography project and the work of the HOPE Foundation.

You can view the MCS students' sustainable photography that was exhibited at the Essie Green Galleries in Harlem, New York, and learn more **on their website**.

younger students learn under this rubric and as they use it, global competence develops more naturally and "sticks" for years to come.

## Section 2: Language Arts

Language arts classes lend themselves naturally to in-depth subject learning because teachers are able to cultivate necessary reading and writing skills in their students using materials from a variety of topics of their choosing. Teachers developing global awareness can make conscious reading choices that accurately portray cultures, books that represent a variety of global experiences, and stories that reflect different points of view and ways of doing things. While practicing Common Core skills such as reading for key details, describing overall structure of a story, or determining theme and setting, kids can simultaneously learn about the world and its many cultures.

The following table shows some examples of **Common Core Standards in reading and writing** that incorporate global learning.

| Common Core Standard and Grade | Example of Activity |
|---|---|
| *Speaking and Listening, Kindergarten–Grade 5 (SL.1–5):*<br><br>Participate in collaborative conversations with diverse partners about *grade-appropriate topics and texts* with peers and adults in small and larger groups.<br><br>Follow agreed-upon rules for discussions (e.g., listening to others and taking turns speaking about the topics and texts under discussion).<br><br>Continue a conversation through multiple exchanges. | Skype in the classroom: Teachers can either browse through ongoing projects that are looking for collaborators or develop their own project. For example, imagine interviewing a same-age class in Poland about what the kids like to do at recess outside or holding a Skype session with a classroom in New Zealand for a discussion around a book that both classes will have to read. These collaborative conversations with peers around the world deliver lessons in effective communication and active listening, as well as build relationships with diverse partners.<br><br>Use Twitter to enhance communication with classrooms around the world. Kindergarten classes following #kinderchat (or #1stchat, #2ndchat, and so on) not only share great global learning resources but also find other teachers who would like to pursue collaborative learning. When only 140 characters are allowed in a Tweet, this offers a succinct fulfillment of "agreed-upon rules for discussions" and can cover all kinds of texts and topics. For more information on Twitter, see Chapter 4, Section 1.<br><br>As an alternative to a digital conversation, teachers can look within their school for face-to-face discussions. As an ESL teacher, Becky has matched up groups of her ESL students with non-ESL students. She set up conversations across classes about a grade-appropriate topic or story, such as how they celebrate a certain holiday or things they did during the summer. This can show students in both groups the range of perspectives and experiences, right within the same school or community. After prewriting their questions, students really enjoyed finding similarities and differences between themselves and their peers. She frequently had the kids do Venn diagrams or journal entries about the conversations. One of her students exclaimed, "I always saw Nelly at lunch, but I never had met her before." It was a wonderful ice breaker and a great way for kids on both sides of the table to learn about their peers.<br><br>**The Global Read Aloud** is a like a worldwide book club, where hundreds of classes read a single, predetermined book during a set 4-week period, while making as many global connections as possible. Teachers decide how involved they'd like to be, and some classes use Twitter, Skype, Edmodo, **their wiki**, e-mail, regular mail, **Kidblog**, and other tools to connect with one, two, or more classrooms from around the world. There is one book for Grades 1–3 and one for the older elementary students. |

| | |
|---|---|
| *Writing, Kindergarten/ Grade 1/Grade 2, (W.K.1–2.6):*<br><br>With guidance and support from adults, explore a variety of digital tools to produce and publish writing, including in collaboration with peers. | One popular digital tool used to produce writing is a blog (see also Chapter 4, Section 2). With guidance from a dedicated teacher, classes can start their own class blog and have students take turns publishing their own writing. Chapter 4 includes lists of sample blogs, or see the Edublogger's **list of some wonderful classroom blogs** from around the world to help you get an idea of what a class blog can look like.<br><br>If you don't want to commit to a full blog yet, participate in some global collaboration projects already set up, such as "**Teddy Bears Around the World,**" where elementary students contribute to a blog and write about their "adventures" with their teddy bear, sharing cultural stories such as "Teddy eats Thanksgiving in the United States" and "Teddy celebrates his birthday in Costa Rica."<br><br>Another great example is the **100 Word Challenge**, which is a weekly creative writing challenge for children. The site gives kids a prompt and asks them to write about it, using 100 words, publish their writing on their blog, and then share comments with the many participants.<br><br>Technology and peer collaboration is not only for the older kids! Check out **this preschool class**, which asked students around the world to send them a picture of the view outside their classroom window and has shared the pictures they've received from Australia, Beirut, and Norway among others. Using digital photography, student artwork, and video, children are able to collaborate with peers on an age-appropriate project that is interesting and fun.<br><br>Use Twitter as a platform to share writing projects. There are **several kindergarten classes** who have worked together on **Twitter-based virtual exchange projects**. See Chapter 4, Section 1 for multiple uses of Twitter in the classroom. |
| *Reading Literature, Grade 2/Grade 3 (RL.2–3.2):*<br><br>Recount stories, including fables and folktales from diverse cultures, and determine their central message, lesson, or moral. | This standard involves fables and stories from diverse cultures. Teachers can use folktales that teach cultural values, such as *The Green Frog: A Korean Folktale Retold* by Yumi Heo, which discusses the importance of listening to parents and showing respect for elders. See our Additional Resources at the end of this book for an extensive list of multicultural literature. There are many lists online of such books, such as **this list of 50 multicultural books** from the University of Wisconsin-Madison or **this list of multicultural books** for upper-elementary students. |

*Reading Literature, Grade 2 (RL.2.9):*

Compare and contrast two or more versions of the same story (e.g., Cinderella stories) by different authors or from different cultures.

*Reading Literature, Grade 4 (RL.4.9):*

Compare and contrast the treatment of similar themes and topics (e.g., opposition of good and evil) and patterns of events (e.g., the quest) in stories, myths, and traditional literature from different cultures.

*Writing, Grade 3/Grade 4/Grade 5 (W.3–5.6):*

With guidance and support from adults, use technology to produce and publish writing (using keyboarding skills) as well as to interact and collaborate with others.

*Writing, Grades 1–5 (W.1–5.1)*

Write opinion pieces in which they introduce the topic or book they are writing about, state an opinion, and supply reasons that support the opinion. With each additional grade level, more sophisticated standards are added to this basic writing Standard.

**World of Tales** is a website with stories and folktales curated from around the world. Click on a continent or country name, learn some basic facts about the country, and read the story. Teachers will need to prescreen stories for subject matter and reading level difficulty. The site can be distracting in its use of advertising, sometimes placed at the start of a story, but overall it's a great one-stop resource for traditional tales.

---

Read and discuss the difference between **different Cinderella stories** or **"Gingerbread Stories" from around the world**, including such stories as "Runaway Rice Cakes," by Ying Chang Compestine, Eric Kimmel's "The Runaway Tortilla," and "The Runaway Latkes" by Leslie Kimmelman.

---

Once you have a selection of books for your students, have them work in groups to choose two stories from two different continents. Have each reader make a list of as many similarities and differences as they can between the books' settings, main characters, themes, and artistic or literary style. Based on these lists, they could write their own stories or use these similarities and differences as a basis for a class or small-group discussion. Extend the learning by referencing their locations on a map or including other culturally relevant lessons.

The class can set up a blog, such as **this project by Grade 3 students in Calgary** which is doing service and building their relationship with a community in Peru, learning about various cultures, compassion, and helping others. Their interactions with people commenting from around the world stands among their most valuable learning experiences (more on this example in Chapter 5).

---

Another project that encourages writing is ePals' **The Way We Are—A National Geographic Project**. In this project, students can collaborate globally via e-mail with a class in another region of the world. "Through e-mail exchanges, students will build friendships and learn about the daily lives and characteristics of the local environment of students" they've been matched with.

---

Use foreign films watched in the classroom as a springboard for writing opinion pieces. Prompts based on the film can include recounting the life lessons learned based on the plot, offering a movie review for a class newspaper or stand-alone assignment, or writing from the perspective of one of the characters in the film and how they overcame a challenge. This multimedia dimension can offer an exciting learning outlet, particularly for children who are less motivated by reading. See our recommended foreign films for K–5 list in Chapter 2 for movies to show the class.

Using the **UN Cyberschool lesson plans on the Convention on the Rights of a Child (CRC)**, have students write about their idea of the perfect summer day and then compare it with students in class. The lesson has students imagining an ideal world for children in the future, comparing their ideal day with the actual articles of the CRC, and discussing if every child in the world has childhood essentials. Finally, the class discusses their opinions on how their memories and experiences are related to the topic of human rights for children.

*Various Reading and Writing Standards for Grade 5:*

See **worksheet from iEARN** for details (can be adapted for younger grades, too).

In the **Kindred (Family History) Project**, students interview members of their immediate family, extended family, neighbors, or friends, asking them about experiences in their life that have been affected by the events of world or local history. Focusing on the impact on the family, events may include war, natural disasters, migration, important discoveries, monuments, famous places, and so on. See more on other phenomenal iEARN projects in Chapter 4, Section 4.

---

There are many other global lessons for elementary schools aligned with the Common Core on the iEARN-USA website, such as the following:

- **Cultural Recipe Book**
- **Global Art: Images of Caring**
- **The Teddy Bear Project**
- **Holiday Card Exchange**

## Out of Eden Walk: An Example of Using One Topic to Spur Deeper Learning Through Common Core Standards

With the kind permission from our friends at the **Pulitzer Center on Crisis Reporting's Education Division**, the table below demonstrates how one fascinating initiative, Pulitzer Prize–winning journalist and National Geographic Fellow Paul Salopek's **Out of Eden Walk**, can drive learning in many directions. The ambitious walk retraces on foot humanity's global migration in a 21,000-mile, 7-year odyssey that Mr. Salopek is taking. The journey begins in Ethiopia and ends in Tierra del Fuego, Chile. By the year 2020, the Out of Eden Walk will have accumulated an unprecedented chronicle of 2,500 generations of human life on Earth. Every 100 miles (160 km) Salopek is making a brief digital **Milestone** narrative for anyone to access. Each narrative consists of a visual panorama, photographs of the ground and sky, ambient sound at that location, and a short interview with the nearest person.

We think this initiative is bursting with global learning possibilities. The following table offers just a snapshot of many learning opportunities plugging in Common Core State Standards. The curriculum is used with permission from the Pulitzer Center and created for them by Dr. Heidi Hayes-Jacobs and the faculty at **Curriculum 21**. More material on this curriculum, from a unit titled **Who Am I?** can be found on the Pulitzer Center website.

## Common Core Lessons and Activities From the Out of Eden Walk

| Common Core Standard and Grade | Example of Activity |
|---|---|
| *Reading informational texts, Grade 4*<br><br>**CCSS.ELA-Literacy.RI.4.6**<br>Compare and contrast a firsthand and secondhand account of the same event or topic; describe the differences in focus and the information provided. | Identify through research two other explorers who followed a specific path and learned about original settlers. Is it a firsthand account of their journey? Find a secondhand account. Compare and contrast the accounts of the explorers you identified from research with Paul Salopek's firsthand accounts of his journey and goals. Then find a secondhand take on Paul's trip. How does the focus differ? |
| *Reading informational texts, Grade 4*<br><br>**CCSS.ELA-Literacy.RI.4.7**<br>Interpret information presented visually, orally, or quantitatively (e.g., in charts, graphs, diagrams, timelines, animations, or interactive elements on Web pages) and explain how the information contributes to an understanding of the text in which it appears. | Use a site such as Glogster to create multimedia posters online outlining the path Paul Salopek is walking, adding text, audio, and pictures to explain the problems or issues that he might encounter along the way. Students link individual glogs to others who share a connection or have a deeper explanation of a particular topic/issue.<br><br>Create a collaborative, annotated digital map at **Google Maps**. This could be created among students of your class or collaborating with another class following Paul Salopek's journey. Add different placemarks to locations of the walk. Students need to choose a title for each placemark and add a short summary of events taking place during Salopek's walk. |

*Writing, Grade 5*

**CCSS.ELA-Literacy.W.5.6** With some guidance and support from adults, use technology, including the Internet, to produce and publish writing as well as to interact and collaborate with others.

Students collaboratively work on **Wiki Spaces** as a central hub for storing their research connected to the Out of Eden Walk. The collaboration could be among classmates or by partnering with a class from another school and possibly from another country. Other media products created during the Out of Eden project will be embedded and shared on the wiki, linking it to students' research.

The class will use Skype to connect with other classrooms, experts, or people living in the countries Paul Salopek is traveling through. The teacher can use personal connections or sites like **Skype in the Classroom** or **Around the World With 80 Schools** to find Skype partners with whom they can connect their class. Students prepare a short presentation to explain their understanding of the Out of Eden project to the other classroom, expert, or people living in the countries on Salopek's route. In addition, the students will create open-ended questions to ask of connection partners. The questions should be created to learn different perspectives and opinions on Salopek's proposed journey. Students will then write a reflection piece that compares their understanding and learning from the Out of Eden project to those of their connection partners.

Students prepare a podcast news show to "inform the world" of the Out of Eden project. Starting by brainstorming their "news show" story, the class divides into groups and assigns roles to each group member (anchors/advertisers/music jingles creators, foreign correspondents, etc.) to write and storyboard the news show script.

*Reading Informational Text, Grade 6*

**CCSS.ELA-Literacy.RI.6.1–3** (1) Cite specific textual evidence to support analysis of primary and secondary sources. (2) Determine the central ideas or information of a primary or secondary source; provide an accurate summary of the source distinct from prior knowledge or opinions. (3) Identify key steps in a text's description of a process related to history/social studies (e.g., how a bill becomes law, how interest rates are raised or lowered).

Create a written, digital, or photographic policy brief in which the students discuss the ethics, problems, and solutions of human migration, which is housed on a class wiki and could be shared at a symposium on migration. This brief is based on both primary and secondary sources, recognizing the relative value and limitations of each. Demonstrate an understanding of a process that might lead to human migration.

| | |
|---|---|
| *Reading Informational Text, Grade 6*<br><br>**CCSS.ELA-Literacy.RI.6.6** Craft and Structure. Identify aspects of a text that reveal an author's point of view or purpose (e.g., loaded language, inclusion, or avoidance of particular facts). | Debate and evaluate arguments on both sides of the statement "Migration of humans from the beginning of their time on Earth to modern day has had a profound effect on the Earth, its resources, and people." Does Salopek ever use loaded language, inclusion, or avoidance of specific facts in his work? |
| *Integration of Knowledge and Ideas*<br><br>**CCSS.ELA-Literacy.RI.6.7–9** (7) Integrate visual information (e.g., in charts, graphs, photographs, videos, or maps) with other information in print and digital texts. (8) Distinguish among fact, opinion, and reasoned judgment in a text. (9) Analyze the relationship between a primary and secondary source on the same topic. | Use World Mapper or another such site to collect data on historical worldwide migration. Present the data using charts and graphs. Use this data for the written work listed later. |

## More Tools to Help Enhance Global Awareness Through K–5 Reading and Writing

For teachers and volunteers looking for high-quality, culturally accurate books featuring characters and settings based in diverse cultures and countries, one resource to help get started is **Worlds of Words (WOW)**. WOW contains a list of 25,000 authentic books from around the world held in the library at the University of Arizona College of Education. In addition to being able to search by title, region, or age level, WOW has downloadable resource kits with strategies, activities, and support on how to best use the multicultural literature listed.

See the Multicultural Book List in the Additional Resources at the end of this book for our own recommended reading list, organized by reading level, topic, and country or region of focus.

Teachers can use WOW to find appropriate titles (and summaries of the books) that are relevant to their class curriculum. For example, when talking about autumn and the different celebrations during this season, teachers can search "fall" or "autumn" and find numerous titles of books from around the world to read in their classes: from books about the Mid-Autumn Moon Festival in China, to birds flying south in the United Kingdom, to the migration of Monarch butterflies in Mexico. Make a list of the titles and request them from the local library. These picture books help children learn about the changes in nature and celebrations among people in diverse climates and cultures that take place during the season.

In addition to the quality fiction books found in the World of Words, teachers can purposefully choose nonfiction books that reflect a broad spectrum of cultures:

- Use autobiographies of people from around the world; for example, choose Nobel Peace Prize winners such as **Rigoberta Menchu**, **Nelson Mandela**, **Wangari Maathai**, or the **Dalai Lama**.

  Ask your students:

  ▸ Why is he or she admired around the world?

  ▸ What characteristics and values does this person have that makes him or her a good leader?

  ▸ Think about the challenges her or she overcame. What would be the hardest part about that time?

  ▸ If you could meet this person, what would you like to ask him or her?

- Read stories that show typical kids on an average day in other countries. For example, *Day of Ahmed's Secret* (Cairo, Egypt) by Florence H. Parry or *Ethiopian Voices: Tsion's Life* by Stacy Bellward. Also, check out the series **Child's Day**, which follows children in various countries throughout a typical day, from when they wake up until they go to sleep at night.

  After reading a couple of different stories, do the following:

  ▸ Make a Venn diagram or chart about the similarities and differences between the children in the books and their own lives or differences between lives in two books they have read.

  ▸ Talk about what kids eat, what they play with, where they live, who is in their family, how they get to school, how they learn—open your students' minds to distinct perspectives and ways of going through the day.

- What do all kids around the world have in common?

- What is something from the books that you would like to try?

- Select books that show children around the world celebrating their holidays, such as *The Best Eid Ever* by Asma Mobin-Uddin, *Day of the Dead* by Tony Johnston, *Lanterns and Firecrackers* (Chinese New Year) by Jonny Zucker and Jan Barger Cohen, or the compilation **Children Just Like Me: Celebrations** by Anabell and Barnabus Kindersley for UNICEF.

Include reference books that show the following:

- Where other kids live around the world like *Houses and Homes (Around the World Series)* by Ann Morris or *Wonderful Houses Around the World* by Yoshio Komatsu

- What kids around the world eat such as *What the World Eats* by Faith D'Aluisio or *Let's Eat: What Children Eat Around the World* by Beatrice Hollyer

- Where kids around the world go to school as in *A School Like Mine* by DK Publishing, *My School in the Rain Forest: How Children Attend School Around the World* by Margriet Ruurs, or *Kindergarten Day USA and China* by Trish Marx

- How people in diverse settings use and obtain basic natural resources, such as water, in books like **A Drop Around the World** by Barbara McKinney, **One Well: The Story of Water on Earth** by Rochelle Strauss, **A Cool Drink of Water** by Barbara Kerley, or **Our World of Water** by Beatrice Hollyer. (This list also crosses over for Science and Social Studies content.)

- Get to know the **UN Convention on the Rights of the Child**. Explore its content, discuss its relevance to each of your lives, and use it as a prompt for writing about what's really important from each child's perspective. The book **A Life Like Mine: How Children Live Around the World**, published by DK, offers a great start to learning about the important Convention on the Rights of the Child.

- For more resources, look at selections from independent publishers with excellent collections of books from global perspectives, like **Barefoot Books**, **Kids Can Press**, and **Charlesbridge**.

# Lessons on Africa, a Diverse Continent (Not a Country!)

Too often, units on Africa focus on the safari animals. This could turn into a valuable lesson on biodiversity and protecting their environment, but wildlife in Africa shouldn't be the sole focus of a study on the cultures or the continent. Other times, children hear about poverty or disease, like the AIDS crisis, which exists in some regions but does not define an immensely diverse continent. People refer to Africa as a country or single entity, but did you know Africa has well over 2,000 languages and many more ethnic groups in its 55 nation states? So when teaching about a region or a specific country, be careful not to generalize information and refer to "Africa" unless you are consciously referring to the continent.

Teachers can go a long way to dispel stereotypes by **teaching a variety of stories** from different countries in the continent. One book that counters stereotypes, *Africa Is Not a Country* by Margy Burns Knight and Anne Sibley O'Brien, gets to the heart of modern Africa: rural and urban families, living contemporary and traditional lives, and the children in their homes, enjoying their families, going to school, and playing with their friends. As an **introductory activity** (the book touches on 25 of the countries in Africa), kids can listen to the book and then can locate and color individual countries on a printable map of Africa as they hear them mentioned in the story; then when they really learn the geography, they can color blank maps. This link contains **a resource for labeled and blank maps of continents and regions**.

You can go further to teach children about this diverse continent. Here we look more closely at one country, South Africa:

1. *Choose a specific country.* The key is to not generalize about the entire continent. Remember, there are 55 countries and great variation. (Even the actual number of nations in Africa is disputed among experts.)

2. *Read a wide variety of stories.* Look for books that showcase rural and urban kids, fiction and nonfiction stories, folktales, biographies, and stories on innovation. See **this list** from KidWorldCitizen that helps children explore many aspects of South Africa through appropriate children's literature, and find more resources at the end of this book in the Multicultural Book List.

3. *Tie in lessons to your curriculum.* If you are studying biographies, read **Nelson Mandela's abridged biography for kids**. If you're studying civil rights, discuss apartheid. Science classes can look at poaching of the rhinos, desertification, water resources, or examine national parks in various countries.

4. *Go deeper with geography, beyond maps.* Talk about the southern hemisphere, climate in South Africa or Mozambique, and the reversal of seasons. Use Google Street View to take a "walking tour" of major cities, national parks, and landforms. Find some major festivals; talk about the values and traditions that are celebrated and, for higher grades, the role of religion.

5. *Make a connection with someone in a particular country of interest* (see Chapter 4 for global collaboration ideas). Choose age-appropriate conversations that give kids an insight into kids on the other side of the world.

# Section 3: Mathematics

Math may seem an unlikely area to help teach children about the world. Yet thanks to its lack of subjectivity, math may serve as an ideal lens through which to view the world, and even to grow in empathy.

Here are some examples of Common Core Standards in mathematics that can specifically relate to global learning:

## Global Lessons in Common Core Mathematics

| Common Core Standard and Grade | Example of Activity |
|---|---|
| *Mathematics, Kindergarten (K.G.1)*:<br><br>Describe objects in the environment using names of shapes, and describe the relative positions of these objects using terms such as *above, below, beside, in front of, behind,* and *next to.* | Use a book such as ***First Shapes in Buildings*** by Penny Ann Lane or ***Shapes Around Our World*** by Becky Ward to demonstrate shapes (pyramids, cube, circle, rectangle, etc.) in architecture around the world. |
| *Mathematics, Grade 1 (1.MD.3)*:<br><br>Tell and write time in hours and half-hours using analog and digital clocks. | Explain the reasons for time zones. One ELL (English language learner) teacher we spoke with displays extra (labeled) clocks in the classroom that are set to the time zones representing the homelands of the ELL students. This class then uses the comparisons as part of the telling time exercises they do during Calendar Math activities. If you have three clocks hanging on the wall, showing different time zones, ask, "What time is it in Beijing, China?" "What time is it in Lagos, Nigeria?" Not only are your students getting more practice in telling time, but they also begin to become aware that in other places of our planet, it is a different time of day or night.<br><br>While you read *World Team* by Tim Vyner about soccer around the world, students can practice writing and telling the time mentioned in the book. "One big round world, one small round ball. Right now, more children than you can possibly imagine are playing soccer." This book takes readers on a journey through time zones to witness kids everywhere playing soccer. |
| *Mathematics, Grade 2 (2.MD.3)*:<br><br>Estimate lengths using units of inches, feet, centimeters, and meters. | Talk about which countries use the metric system (almost all countries except the United States!). Estimate lengths and then find the actual measurements of students' heights, the lengths of their feet, the height of their desks, and the distance from their tables to the door in centimeters and meters as well as inches and feet. |

| | |
|---|---|
| *Mathematics, Grade 3 (3.MD.2):* Measure and estimate liquid volumes and masses of objects using standard units of grams (g), kilograms (kg), and liters (l). | Demystify metric measurement. To make an interdisciplinary lesson, the class could prepare an easy recipe from a particular country using metric units. |
| *Mathematics, Grade 4 (4.MD.2):* Use the four operations to solve word problems involving distances, intervals of time, liquid volumes, masses of objects, and money, including problems involving simple fractions or decimals and problems that require expressing measurements given in a larger unit in terms of a smaller unit. Represent measurement quantities using diagrams such as number line diagrams that feature a measurement scale. | Globalize word problems. Calculate distances between cities around the world in kilometers and meters. Investigate means of transportation between two cities (airplanes, trains, boats) and determine which would be the fastest and which your students would prefer. Use sports from around the world (such as World Cup soccer statistics or Olympic Gold Medals) in math word problems. Compare the heights of famous monuments such as the Eiffel Tower, the Egyptian pyramids, or the **world's largest skyscrapers**. |
| *Mathematics, Grade 5 (5.NBT.4):* Use place value understanding to round decimals to any place. | Examine currency and exchange rates around the world; convert home currency to other world currencies, rounding the conversions to the hundredths place. To practice currency conversion, ask members of the school community to bring in any foreign currency they may have to calculate the costs of simple items or solve more complex problems using money from one or more countries. If you don't have enough real foreign currency on hand, **print sample bills and coins** for dollars, Euros, Canadian dollars, and English and Australian pounds. Or print these **Money Worksheets From Around the World**. Try the World Food Program's worksheet **Playing With Decimals**. This offers students practice on addition and subtraction of decimals while considering the small domestic budgets of people in developing countries (less than $2 per day). To place this activity in context, you can see the short video **"A Dollar a Day—Kenya."** This video was shot in the slum where Molly Otieno, whom we discuss in Chapter 5, lives. |

# 30+ Geography-Enhanced Math Projects

Once you begin applying geographic knowledge and global awareness to math lessons, so many possibilities for exciting lessons emerge. The following are over 30 additional resources and activities to help boost mathematics engagement. Use maps to point out locations and talk about the original cultures, countries, and languages:

- Compare weather and seasons around the world. Start with the **Math Cats Weather Around the World** website.

  ▶ Find the differences between the temperature, wind speed, barometric pressure, and precipitation of different cities.

  ▶ Convert temperatures between Fahrenheit and Celsius. When looking at the Celsius numbers, try to guess what types of clothes a child would wear that day. Once converted, see if you were right!

  ▶ Compare temperatures on a continent or countries with the altitude of the places. How does the weather compare when traveling up or down the mountains?

  ▶ Find countries that have the most similar weather and determine their distances from the equator and from each other.

  ▶ Analyze average temperatures of different cities. Talk about how distinct geographical features determine climate.

  ▶ Categorize and graph cities according to temperatures. On a given day, look at all cities with highs of 10°–20°, 20°–30°, 30°–40°, 40°–50°, 50°–60°, and so on. Label them by colors on the graph, and then find and label them on the map. Notice their locations, and discuss similarities and differences.

  ▶ Create **weather glyphs** for different cities around the world. Compare and contrast the resulting pictures. For more advanced learners, talk about what advantages or disadvantages the areas have for growing crops or raising various kinds of livestock in the particular climate.

  ▶ Graph your local weather (**as seen on this lesson plan**) and pair up with another school in a different part of the world to compare weather.

- Investigate numbers in different scripts from other languages (such as Mandarin, Mayan, Arabic, or Roman numerals). Omniglot.com **has a chart of numerals in different writing systems** that would be helpful to use.

    ▸ Hang a poster in the room with the different numerals.

    ▸ Using flashcards of the different numbers, challenge students to try simple math problems, or try to put them in order.

- Display math tools and play logic games from around the world. In hands-on learning centers within classrooms, display math tools, aids, and games that originate from other countries, such as the abacus or games like **mancala**, chess, or **Nim**.

- Teach your students another method of solving math problems, for example, **this video showing the Ethiopian way to solve multiplication problems** or this **Vedic (Indian) method of multiplying**.

---

## Play the "What's Fair" Game (Grades 3 and Up)

Just about every child loves chocolate, but have you considered where it comes from and how it is made? Equal Exchange, the cooperative that sources fair trade chocolate, coffee, and other gourmet items and offers them for direct sale or school fundraisers, has created a simple, fun, educational game for children to consider what life for cocoa farmers is like, what the economic cycle of cocoa production and sales looks like, and, ultimately, "What's Fair." Here's an example of math and geography lessons building empathy. See the free downloadable PDF **curriculum guide**, pages 55–61, for instructions and game cards to play.

---

- Teach children the global origin of many math concepts and tools, both ancient and modern. Using this **Math Around the World Poster**, students can explore more than 50 accomplishments through rich illustrations and simple text, plus the location of each origin on the world map.

- Look at the different counting systems and their origins. Written for children, *The History of Counting*, by Denise Schmandt-Besserat, shows the relevance of numbers throughout human history and demonstrates the counting systems that different cultures have used throughout the world.

- Learn about latitude and longitude on Google Earth, a classroom map, or a globe. Have the students brainstorm places around the world that are meaningful to them, and then after locating them on the map, find their latitude and longitude.

  ▶ Make a list of 3 to 10 cities or countries that are the same latitude or the same longitude as your current location.

  ▶ Talk about differences and similarities in our weather patterns and seasons related to our locations on the globe.

  ▶ Decide which clothes would be appropriate to wear at different latitudes during different months of the year.

  ▶ Once students understand how to find latitude and longitude, give them a list of 10 major cities around the world and have them write down the coordinates.

  ▶ Give students 10 sets of latitude/longitude coordinates, and have students find which country they correspond to.

  ▶ Here is **an introductory lesson on latitude/longitude from National Geographic**.

- Locate your food origins. As a class, do the **Where in the World Is Your Food From?** project. For homework, have students visit their local supermarket and write down where different fruits and vegetables came from. Next, they can mark the origin of their produce on a world map. Using the map key and their rulers, have them figure out which foods have traveled the farthest (thereby using more energy) and which are grown nearby. Compare how many miles different foods travel (do it in kilometers as well!). If you do this project in different seasons, you can compare which foods are grown locally at which time of year. Discuss the implications of buying fruit and vegetables in season, and from local vendors, versus out of season (from the opposite hemisphere).

- Math can also be combined with art in awesome, interdisciplinary, global projects! Think about the following puzzles and patterns:

  ▶ **Islamic tessellations**

  ▶ **Chinese tangrams (another great source here)**

  ▶ **Indian Rangavalli patterns**

  ▶ Native American symmetrical patterns, such as **Navajo rug patterns**

- The iPhone/iPod/iPad app **iLiveMath: Animals of Africa and Asia** combines applied math skills and zoology, using multimedia (photos, videos, wikis, and audio) to challenge students at different levels of difficulty. Best for students in elementary school, the illustrated questions cover basic concepts such as calculating time, weight, and other measures.

- Participate in the global **Noon Day Project** by measuring your students' shadows and comparing results with their peers from around the world. Compiling the results online, children will collaborate with peers globally to measure the circumference of the Earth by using a method used by Eratosthenes 2,000+ years ago!

- Another global math project has students sharing local grocery prices. This **Global Grocery List Project** lets students around the world examine and compare the local prices of food such as oranges, eggs, milk, potatoes, coffee, and rice. The data can stimulate conversations about where the food is grown, how expensive or cheap it is to eat healthy in certain countries, and even how weather patterns would affect the crops and therefore the prices of what you might consider a common item but which might be a luxury elsewhere.

- The book *Math Games and Activities Around the World* by Claudia Zaslavsky includes so many games and art projects from literally every corner of the world. It is geared for Grades 5–8, but the majority of the activities can be adapted for children even as young as kindergarten. This book can serve as a nice companion for globalizing your math program.

- Teachers looking to learn more about math across cultures can check out the **Ethnomathematics Digital Library**, which has more than 700 articles, studies, and units in its online database, searchable by subject, geographical area, and cultural group. For further reading on cultural math resources, see the **International Study Group on Ethnomathematics (ISGEm)**.

---

## Math Class: A Portal for Project-Based Learning and Global Citizenship

Math teacher Kristen Goggin at San Francisco's Town School for Boys has unlocked fascinating global learning that goes way beyond the numbers. After taking a course on project-based learning through the **Buck Institute for Education**, she committed to trying the new methods with her fifth- and sixth-grade classes. She explains on her **blog**:

> The 5th grade boys work together to answer the driving question, "How do we as future working citizens/permanent residents, ensure that there is a livable wage in our country?" Through research and inquiry the boys worked to understand what minimum wage in the US is and considered cost of living in numerous geographic areas in an attempt to discover whether it is livable.

> The boys then set out to understand what local organizations in San Francisco were doing to alleviate poverty. The boys chose to create commercials for five local organizations before working through global poverty statistics.

> After looking at our local and national statistics on poverty, the boys were interested in looking at global statistics. Using these statistics we discussed graphs, scatter plots, stem and leaf plots, mean, median and mode.

> I emphasized the importance of looking out for our local, "glocal" community first, but introduced Heifer International through a reading of Beatrice's Goat with the 1st grade. The empathy they felt later led to a service learning action project, "Pi Day for Purpose" where the boys used rates, ratios, proportions and fractions to follow recipes for circular treats, create them, and sell them on March 14 (3/14, or Pi Day). They raised $906 and also collected over 100 cans. Using polling and voting techniques we divided up the money and cans between 6 organizations.

Through this description, we see the power of asking a driving question that motivates learners to offer real and creative answers, not simply offer a "right" answer students think their teachers want to hear. Then Kristen describes actual math lessons that otherwise might seem isolated from daily concerns or boring to students. Through this approach, basic math learning takes on urgency and relevance, and therefore, students connect personal commitment to the learning. They start with looking at needs in their local community, then branch out to national realities (understanding and calculating minimum wage all over United States), and from there naturally branched into global learning (introducing a cause like Heifer International and reading *Beatrice's Goat* about the impact livestock can make on a family living in poverty). Ultimately, the engagement becomes a lesson in empathy and global citizenship—going way beyond number crunching. Kristen's blog contains worksheets, videos made by her students, and more description on the project so you can try this with your own class.

For sixth graders, they engaged in a microfinance project, through Kiva (also see **Kiva in the Classroom**), where they not only learned math concepts required in the sixth-grade curriculum, but went further, to learn about profit, net and gross income, the business of banking and lending, taxes, and operating their own business, as well as collaboration, effective oral and written communication, leadership, initiative, and much more. As Kristen explained to us, involvement with Kiva and microfinance can be adapted for younger grades, and many of these benefits can be realized.

A great example of application to K–3 is through the **One Hen** book, website, and lessons available on the website. This also happens to be one of our favorite books; it is beautifully illustrated and teaches about the life circumstances, determination, and business acumen of a boy named Kojo who lives in Ghana and whose microenterprise grows into a successful business. Through Kojo's eyes, an understanding of otherwise complex issues of poverty, scarce resources, and investing becomes natural for younger children to grasp and empathize with. We have seen the impact of the story take on greater significance for children by the fact that Kojo's experience in the book is based on a real-life young man, now a successful entrepreneur.

## Section 4: Social Studies

Social studies class can incorporate history, religious studies, geography, anthropology, and civics—all natural entry points for learning about the wider world. This section includes a sampling of projects and resources that can be used to supplement K–5 social studies curriculum.

The Internet is packed with culture- and country-specific websites that help students go more in depth. At one elementary school in Naperville, Illinois, every grade is assigned a country and incorporates lessons throughout the year about their nation. For example, second graders study Japan and learn about celebrations, geography and climate, and some current events. They send home specific websites (such as **this wonderful and thorough resource for learning about Japan**) so their parents can encourage even more individualized study at home as kids explore global topics that they find most interesting.

For current events, **Youngzine** offers a "safe, well-lit website for children where they can learn about current events around the world without the bias, sensationalism and often inappropriate content in mainstream media." It also serves as community where children are encouraged to express their views; submit articles, book reviews, or travelogues; and all content is moderated by the editorial team.

Here are several examples of interactive, animated, culture-specific sites appropriate for elementary students:

- **Learn about Inuit culture.**

- **Play games that highlight Maori culture.**

- **Make your own virtual Ghanaian Kente Cloth.**

- Through interactive activities, **explore bits of African cultures.**

## Where to Find Global Lesson Plans With a Country or Culture Focus

Many organizations offer teachers global lesson plans that can be used for elementary school social studies classes. They might have detailed information about the countries in which they work, like a fun atlas alternative with real children's stories and pictures. Here are some examples of websites that offer online almanacs, filled with facts for kids about countries and cultures:

- **Cyber School Bus** from the United Nations has many online lesson plans and resources for teachers to use in their classes related to global issues such as poverty, discrimination, world hunger, indigenous people, and more. Not all of the lessons are for the elementary school level, but the information presented in the InfoNation and then Country at a Glance sections can be used as an online atlas to search for facts about countries around the world.

- **Time for Kids: Around the World** has articles about countries written for kids, including sightseeing guides, a history timeline, a "Day in the Life," and a follow-up quiz.

- **Global School Net's Online Expeditions** hosts virtual field trips using photos, videos, and text to take students to remote places.

- **The World Almanac for Kids** is an online, subscription-based almanac that includes information on the countries of the world.

- The **Study Corner** for National Geographic's GeoBee has preparation materials that teachers can use to teach kids about geography, maps, climate, and more. **National Geographic's Education** site also is packed with lesson ideas for various grade levels.

- **Facing the Future: Critical Thinking, Global Perspective, Informed Action** is an organization that provides curriculum resources to schools around the world. They have several lesson plans available for download that encourage critical thinking about global issues and teach about sustainability. Click on "Download Free Curriculum" on the top bar to search the different possibilities.

- **The Peace Corps World Wise Schools** section for educators has multiple lesson plans, including **this fabulous lesson**, "Building Bridges for Young Learners," that attempts to show the youngest children to compare and contrast one's own culture with those of other children around the world.

- **Stanford University Program on International and Cross-Cultural Education (SPICE)** offers multidisciplinary curriculum materials prepared by scholars at Stanford University on a variety of international themes for K–14 schools.

- **Project Explorer** offers a gorgeous, free, online global travel series especially for kids that includes an excellent collection of online videos made for kids along with photos, educational blogs, and lesson plans. They currently have material from about 13 countries around the globe and are continually expanding their reach.

## Online Games, Activities, and Apps

In addition to online information centers and atlases, a growing number of interactive games, apps, and activities allow students to read and weigh varying perspectives and then use critical thinking skills to solve whatever problems are presented. These games challenge students to gather information and synthesize it in order to understand or resolve global issues. Here are some wonderful examples of free online games:

- **Against All Odds** is an online game from the United Nations that lets kids experience what it is like to be a refugee. Because of the serious nature of the topic of refugees, teachers should play first and check out the resources beforehand to determine if their students are ready to tackle such a complicated concept.

- **Global Trek: Virtual Travel Around the World** is a web-based activity from Scholastic that allows students to choose a country to visit and then write a travel journey with guided questions. The site provides age-appropriate resources for each country ("Background Information," "Guided Tours," and "Meet the People") that help students learn in-depth information about each location.

- **In Search of the Ways of Knowing Trail** is a wonderful animated, interactive "choose-your-own-adventure" type of online game about the rainforest in central Africa, where students can learn how to make a better life for the animals and people that inhabit the rainforest.

- The **Peace Corps Challenge Online Game** is an interactive activity from the Peace Corps that places the user in the fictional African village of Wanzuzu. Students must solve issues touching on microfinance, water, sanitation, farming, education for girls, and using sustainable methods that are best for the village. Clicking through the cartoon story, students need to understand where the different people are coming from, gather facts, and then decide what the best course of action will be. This challenges their investigation and analyzing skills, plus exposes kids to the greater problems that many developing towns face.

- In **The Fin, Fur and Feather Bureau of Investigation**, the FBI and National Geographic present a series of geography-themed online missions based around the world. Students must engage their geography and problem-solving skills to use maps, texts, and images to solve the challenges.

- **Ayiti** is a sometimes tragic and always challenging simulation game, where students help Haitian parents and their children make decisions about work, education, community building, personal purchases, and health care that might brighten their future.

- Pinterest boards like **this one with Global Simulations and Games** include great finds. Keep checking Pinterest for new additions to various lists, including updates on Pinterest Boards for Becky (kidworldcitizen) and Homa (growingupglobal).

Many of the top educational organizations have apps for the iPod/iPad that help students learn more about other cultures and geography. The following apps (found at **iTunes** and other platforms) include both map resources and child-friendly atlases and are appropriate for the elementary school classroom:

- **History: Maps of the World**
- **Google Earth**
- **National Geographic** World Atlas, GeoBee Challenge, The World, and many other apps
- **CIA World Factbook**
- **Stack the Countries**
- **Jo in Paris**
- **Kids World Maps**
- **Geo Walk HD—3D World Fact Book**
- **Geo Challenge—Flags, Maps, and Geography Learning Game for Kids**
- **Barefoot World Atlas**
- **Tiny Countries**

## Section 5: Science

With a bit of creativity and initiative, science might be the most natural subject offering a global lens through which to view our world. Earth, water, air quality, climate, chemistry, physics, physiology, plant life, and animal habitats don't respect national boundaries, so they are inherently global in nature, inviting wider exploration and conversation. This fact in itself can serve as a launch for a global conversation. Vexing challenges stumping the best scientific minds are solved globally using collaborative teams located in different locales that experiment and study issues from diverse angles and approaches. In other words, introducing science in the 21st century is necessarily global.

Examples of resources from other sections, like climate and time zones (in the Math section) or resources from Oxfam and National Geographic (in the Social Studies section), can be readily applied to science curricula. Here are more resources for creating a global learning experience in science classes:

- **The Bucket Buddies Project** calls for students around the world to collect water samples from local ponds to answer the question, "Are the organisms found in pond water the same all over the world?" The lesson plans allow students to identify microinvertebrates in their water sample, share their findings on the website, and analyze the data.

- The **Global Learning and Observations to Benefit the Environment (GLOBE)** program is NASA's hands-on science program that allows classrooms to connect with scientists and science students from around the world. Schools can join their Student Climate Research Campaign and connect with classrooms around the world. While conducting science investigations and sharing their climate science studies, students will be inspired to look at climate-related environmental issues and Earth as a system.

- **ProjectExplorer.org** and STEM learning: Mentioned in the Social Studies section above, Project Explorer's library of 2- to 4-minute videos was created to introduce students to the features that make diverse cultures and countries so fascinating. Start at the homepage by choosing your learning level (e.g., Upper Elementary), pick a spot on the globe that has a project marker, and take off. For example, in the **Mauritius series**, learn how the island was formed, about the science and the ancient origins of the helicopter, how mineral deposits created gorgeous multicolored sand found only on that island, **how fish breathe**, and more.

    The **Project Explorer** series is continually growing (so keep checking in) and takes special care to address STEM (science, technology, engineering, and math) topics around the world, as well as subjects like local cuisine, traditions, history, industry, languages, and religions. If your class has a few minutes between activities, bookmark this website and use the time for a fun, smart exploration of a new location or topic.

- **Exploration Nation**, Digital Science Instruction is a subscription-based video lesson program for elementary and middle school students that was created in 2007 by Enzo Monfre at the age of 7 as part of a homeschool project. The program has since blossomed to include lesson plans for teachers, standards-aligned tools, and a team of kid explorers traveling the world doing real scientific research, which the lessons are based on. Content includes subjects like the Physics of Medieval Weapons, Biofuels, Walking With Mammoths, and Taking Flight With Newton's Laws. This is one of our few paid content recommendations, but given the youthful team and exciting science behind the lessons, we thought it well worth sharing.

- The **Daffodil and Tulip Project** was started by iEARN, which is one of our favorite organizations working to connect schools and teachers across the planet, and has a bank of great collaborative project ideas. The Daffodil and Tulip Project offers a science/math/writing/friendship experience that can be as simple or as complicated as a classroom is ready to take on. Classrooms around the world choose daffodil and/or tulip bulbs to plant during the same week in November. Students collect temperature data throughout the experiment, including when blooms appear, and report their results—both to their classmates and to their partner classes in other locales.

  We were fascinated to notice that on the project description page, we already saw participation from Jamaica, Israel, Iran, and the United States. iEARN reports that

  *participants enjoy interacting together while "waiting"*
  *for the blooms. Students have opportunities to use math*
  *skills, such as graphing, converting metric to English or the*
  *reverse, temperature conversions F to C and the reverse.*
  *In addition, they strengthen and practice science skills,*
  *i.e. hypothesizing what effects bloom date, collecting*
  *data, comparing and analyzing data. Also, students learn*
  *the importance of establishing and following a scientific*
  *protocol. The ultimate goal of the project is to promote*

*building connections between students and their teachers,
considering what affects plant growth, and peace!*

To learn more about iEARN collaborative projects, see Chapter 4, Section 4.

---

## The Tulip Project: A Global Science Collaboration

As the Global Initiatives Coordinator of Brookwood School in Manchester-by-the-Sea, Massachusetts, Martha Fox looks for interdisciplinary activities that allow students to experience global learning firsthand. The NAIS Challenge 20/20 program (see details on this in Chapter 4) is one such platform for making global learning connections, where Brookwood has access to Taking IT Global, an organization that facilitates collaborative learning to connect all types of schools around the world. Projects facilitated through these partnerships include their Kindergarteners' Monarch Butterfly Habitat Advocacy project with an elementary school in Edisto, South Carolina, and their fifth graders' coastal stewardship with a middle school in the Bahamas.

First-grade teacher Sarah Dawe works with her students on the Tulip Project. (Classes can join on the **Journey North** website.) Her students—and students from all over the world—plant Red Emperor tulip bulbs under the same conditions (i.e., at a designated depth, same distance apart). The classes log on to announce when they observe the first sprout and the first bloom. Over time, as schools report their first bloom and a red dot appears on the map, the students watch on the online map of the world to see when spring arrives in each region of the world. They discover that the arrival of spring is influenced by climate and geography and learn how these differences impact the seasons.

At the beginning of the project, students weigh, measure, and dissect the tulip bulbs. Then they work together to design and engineer systems for planting bulbs the required 7 inches apart using standard and nonstandard measuring materials such as unifix cubes, string, blocks, rulers, and a tape measure. Throughout the project, the children keep a scientific journal and sketch their garden during various stages. They get a chance to be citizen scientists as they record and share information with others, exchange ideas, problem solve, and deepen their appreciation for the outdoors. Finally, they create a pamphlet for their student booth at the school's Sustainability Fair to help educate others about the project. At the fair, they help visitors make recycled newspaper pots to plant their own Red Emperor tulips.

The Tulip Project serves as a wonderful example of how elementary learners can participate in a project that integrates science, math, art, writing, and sustainability lessons, while using technology to connect to others and share their findings—all leading to deeper global engagement.

## Create Your Own Collaborative Science Project and Your Own Wiki

If you haven't found a science collaborative project that is already set up, take inspiration from this group of students and create a wiki to teach kids across the country or around the world.

Students in Jeff Remington's class in Palmyra, Pennsylvania, near the home of Hersheys chocolates, benefitted immeasurably from a cultural, technology, and educational exchange with a school in Haiti, prompted by the creation of a wiki, a website developed collaboratively by a community of users, allowing any user to add and edit content. As the project report explains,

> To date, the Haitian students have benefitted from direct instruction that would not have been possible without the wiki. The most memorable educational experience for the Haitian students was a series of lessons on electrical circuits created and peer taught by the Palmyra students. The Palmyra students provided lab materials and video instruction that they posted on the wiki to teach the electrical circuit lessons. Since most Haitian students do not have access to computers or the Internet at home, the Palmyra students spent their time and effort creating the most meaningful educational Internet experience to maximize the Haitians' limited time on the Internet.

Depending on the unit of study appropriate for your grade, specific content of the wiki and the lessons can vary. This example highlights how exciting science class can be when kids teach kids, especially when they realize they are performing a service through their lesson, as these kids have. **Their project** went on to donate equipment to the school in Haiti and partner with Global Giving to sustain it. In this case, we see how globalizing a science lesson helps students learn the academic matter more deeply, as well as gain comfort using diverse communications technologies and develop skills of collaboration, communication, empathy, and generosity.

## Examples of Global Lessons in Common Science Topics of Elementary Schools

| Unit of Study | Lesson Ideas |
| --- | --- |
| Recycling and the Effects of Trash on Our Oceans | While studying local recycling, students can examine efforts around the world to recycle, look at the effect of littering, and what happens when recycling is not practiced in different regions of the world. The **PBS Independent Lens Film *Garbage Dreams*** has games and lesson plans for educators. |

| | |
|---|---|
| | Students can read articles such as **this one from Scholastic**, accompanied by a cause-and-effect worksheet, or **this one from the Ocean Conservancy** written with fourth graders. |
| | Watch **videos from the Ocean Conservancy** and learn about sustainable solutions in protecting our oceans. |
| | Use **lesson plans from the National Environment Education Week's extensive Ocean Curricula** for Grades K–4 and 5–8. These hands-on learning projects teach students about many of the current challenges the oceans are facing today. |
| | Learn about (and participate in!) the **International Coastal Cleanup**, a 25-year-old effort in 70 countries worldwide that brings adults and children together to "remove trash and debris from the world's beaches and waterways, identify the sources of that debris, and change the behaviors that allow it to reach the ocean in the first place." The lesson for the children is that we are all interconnected: Though they may live far from the ocean, many local water sources (streams, rivers, lakes) eventually connect up and lead to the ocean. Taking care of our local waterways and removing litter directly helps to keep our oceans cleaner. |
| Water Cycle and Conservation | Most elementary schools teach the water cycle and touch on water conservation. To internationalize the lesson, **Teach UNICEF** has developed lesson plans about the topic for Grades PreK–2 and 3–5. The unit introduces the importance of water on Earth, the water cycle, and then the causes and effects of water issues and why responsible water use and conservation of natural resources locally is healthy and safe on a larger scale. |
| | **Oxfam** has a wonderful collection of lessons for elementary schools as part of Oxfam Water Week, including videos, a slideshow, and activities for an all-school assembly. |
| | Watch the video clips (such as a little girl in drought-stricken Ethiopia) and read the articles (such as how Fatima from Angola collects water every day) that illustrate the concepts and encourage students to understand perspectives from children around the world. **Teach UNICEF** has other multimedia units such as Climate Change, Education, and Disability Awareness, too. |
| | There are age-appropriate, standards-aligned curriculum ready to use from **Water.org**. Lessons for elementary students about global water use fall under math, science, technology, and geography. |

| | |
|---|---|
| | The **Peace Corps Educational Portal** offers global stories and photos with accompanying text about access to water and water conservation to supplement water units. There is also a wonderful **interactive, online activity** (which is shared in the previous section on Social Studies) that allows the user to make decisions to determine who is polluting the water source. |
| Learning About Global Hunger | For upper elementary students, the World Food Program contains a variety of lesson plans on its **Teacher Pages**. One popular strand is **Teaching Hunger Across the Curriculum Through Molly's Eyes**. This is based around a popular **video series** by Molly Otieno, age 13 in Kenya, and is particularly significant around World Food Day, which takes place each year on October 16. |
| | Here are ways to adapt the lessons for older elementary students: |
| | Use the sheet **11 Myths About Global Hunger.** Ask your students: What is a myth? Then assign each particular myth to teams with the following activities: |
| | 1. Define at least three challenging vocabulary terms in each of the myths. |
| | 2. Restate the paragraph in your own words. If you were explaining this challenge to a friend or an adult, how would you explain it? What do most people think is the situation and what are the facts? |
| | 3. Go deeper: Look up a hyperlink that's embedded in the myth being researched, or look up a concept that is being explained. |
| | 4. What are some of the solutions that are being proposed to solve the crisis of world hunger? |
| | 5. How can you make a difference on this issue, or more specifically, on the myth you researched? |
| Animal Habitats and Climate Change | The study of animal habitats offers a natural link to geography as students examine the globe and determine the locations of different ecosystems. If you laminate your classroom world map, use dry erase markers to circle, label, and mark different regions. If your science and social studies classes study animal biomes and protecting endangered species, take the research one step further as you read climate case studies about human impact. On **Rainforest Heroes**, see how climate change is directly affecting people in Tanzania, Tuvalu, Ecuador, and other countries around the world in stories and pictures. |

## Section 6: Music

Music can touch a child and change their mood even if presented in a language the child does not understand. In **an article for PBS Kids**, Lili Levinowitz, cofounder of Music Together and professor of music education, recommends that children listen to a wide variety of genres, played with a variety of rhythms and in a variety of tones. An idea that we have long advocated, global music can naturally introduce students to the world through a rich universal language.

Your students will begin to experience not only the different melodies, beats, and instruments, but also the sounds of a distinct culture or language. Even when English speakers listen to a song that's sung in English but from Ireland, South Africa, or Jamaica, students may pull out new perspectives just from one song. Children's ears can become attuned to hearing English spoken (or sung) in various accents, a key skill of a globally competent learner. Then, they will start to imagine various scenarios painted by the song.

One nice song to begin with is "Beautiful Day" from **South Africa on Putumayo's Picnic Playground CD**, where listeners can imagine a whole scenario of sunshine, local candy and currency, scents like fish frying, and a joyful walk. Listen with your students to share what each person takes away from the song. We have found that exploring music from new places can serve as a wonderful launch to a country discussion and study, a calming activity for an ornery classroom, and of course, a way to build wider music appreciation and offer sheer enjoyment of diverse musical genres.

**LinkTV** streams diverse world music videos online for free. Preview and choose appropriate videos from various genres to share with your class. Not only will they benefit in hearing the music, but they will also be able to see the instruments and dances representative of other cultures.

Include instruments from around the world in your musical collection, and let kids experiment with the different ways to make music. **Sound World Instruments** sells a variety of quality, authentic world instruments. Also, check out the lovely book *African Musical Instruments* by Natalie Cooper. The detailed, colorful drawings are nicely paired with fascinating facts on over 20 unique instruments found throughout Africa. Kids love music, and learning about how distinct rhythms and sounds are made is one way to explore the arts and musical traditions of diverse cultures.

Section 3 in Chapter 2 contains additional ideas for incorporating music into global learning.

## Section 7: Art

Like music, elementary school art programs often provide the most natural entree to the wider world, and teachers of art and music may serve as the greatest advocates for incorporating cultural lessons into existing curricula. To support rich global learning that can happen through art class, tap into some of the following resources.

Use Google Art to **virtually visit museums around the world**, walking through the galleries and viewing art up close. As of this writing, the jaw-dropping undertaking holds 156 major collections from around the world, with close to 33,000 artworks on display. Free time in class can be spent browsing a gallery. Adults and children can go beyond simply observing the art by using the tools on the site to create slide shows of their own. Consider organizing shows around various themes: from colors, numbers, foods, alphabets of countries of origin, or objects, to more sophisticated topics around science, religion, images of home, school, or work.

Not to be confused with Google Art Project, collaborate with students worldwide in **the Global Art Project**, an International Art Exchange for Peace, which occurs biannually in April. Participants are invited to create a work of art in any medium that represents global peace and goodwill. The art is displayed in each participant's community and then virtually exchanged with their matched partners in one of countless countries around the world. It is displayed again in the new community.

The **Smithsonian's National Museum of African Art** offers many curriculum resources for educators related to Africa. In addition, the Guggenheim has **a clickable African map** showcasing pieces of art from the different regions in Africa. Other Smithsonian Museum collections, such as the **Freer and Sackler Galleries**, which focus on the rich cultural heritage across the continent of Asia, and the **National Museum of the American Indian**, carry not only extensive collections of multicultural art but also strong education programs as well.

The **Love Art: National Gallery London app** (for the iPhone/iPod/iPad, on iTunes) allows students to "touch" over 250 pieces of Western European art and read commentary by the artists and other experts.

**Art Miles Mural Project** is a worldwide, collaborative art project that has students creating murals of different themes, which will then be connected and displayed at exhibits around the world and online.

A variety of lesson plans online allow students to discover the use of masks in many cultures around the world (for example, see links on our companion site for **African masks** or for **masks worldwide**).

Because masks are so widespread, students might compare and contrast the materials, uses, colors, and designs of the masks of different origins.

# Section 8: World Languages

When people think of global education, foreign language learning may be the first thing that comes to mind. Justifiably so: Fluency in another language offers the clearest path to competency in a new culture and a portal to understanding the wider world. We hope that the many examples offered throughout this Toolkit demonstrate clearly that you don't need to be bilingual to take advantage of global learning. Nonetheless, language exposure can be a central part of global education—regardless of your fluency level in additional languages.

A great deal of scholarly research proves the benefits of language study. For example, "the bilingual brain develops more densely, giving it an advantage in various abilities and skills" (cited in **WebMD**, 2004). "Bilingual children have better working memory" (*Journal of Communication and Education: Language Magazine*, 2013). Other cognitive advantages include earlier, more complex vocabulary acquisition, stronger attention or focus, and encoding of sound (cited in **BBC News**, 2012).

Wealthy countries around the world have recognized the fact that this wiring of the brain through second language acquisition is most effective the earlier the learner starts, so these countries have committed to foreign language programs for young learners. According to **Julia Pimsleur Levine**, founder of **Little Pim** early language learning programs, "Of the 25 top industrialized nations, 21 of those introduce a second language to their citizens in kindergarten. The United States is not one of those."

In spite of the overwhelming case for teaching languages from an early age, U.S. schools seem to be going in the opposite direction. According to the Center for Applied Linguistics, "The percentage of elementary and middle schools offering foreign language instruction decreased significantly from 1997 to 2008: from 31% to 25% of all elementary schools and from 75% to 58% of all middle schools."[1]

The fact that U.S. schools have relatively few foreign language programs at the K–5 level makes any initiatives you can bring to your school more crucial than ever.

**ACTFL** (the American Council on the Teaching of Foreign Languages) has created a **21st Century Skills Map** that illustrates the integration of world languages with 21st century skills, such as the ability to communicate effectively with citizens around the world. Communicative competence is stressed, and language is taught as part of the curriculum during the regular school day. Content is not taught in isolation but rather relates to what students are already learning in math, science, social studies, art, music, and so on. Language classes reinforce concepts and give students another chance to practice critical thinking skills and develop cultural awareness.

In elementary schools that are fortunate to have a language component, students gain more competency when the language is used in authentic and practical settings, instead of limited language slots a couple of times per week. For example, Kolter Elementary is a K–5 foreign language magnet school in Houston, Texas, where students choose to study Chinese, French, or Spanish. The students acquire the language not only during their language classes but also during their art, physical education, and technology instruction. Instead of segregating the language, students use it in real-world, practical situations. This allows the students' fluency to flourish as they broaden their vocabulary and communicate with their teachers about diverse topics. In addition to developing their language skills, an effort is made to explore cultures as well through special events during the school day (such as folktale units, movies, student performances, and guest speakers) and during after-school programs and field trips (such as their own Tour de France or an international potluck).

There are several types of foreign language programs in elementary schools. The FLES (Foreign Language in the Elementary School) program is designed to be a sequential language program that aims to have students reach a certain level of proficiency in the target language. In FLES programs, the target language might be taught a couple of days a week.

Immersion programs (sometimes called bilingual programs) include instruction of content from the regular curriculum in the target language. Students are expected to acquire the target language by the end of the program, at least to some degree. FLEX (Foreign Language Experience) programs are designed to expose children to one or more different world languages, oftentimes to pique their interest and help them decide what language they might like to study in the future (for example, in middle school).

World languages are often taught differently in elementary schools and usually focus on the development of communication skills. Gradually, as oral comprehension increases, reading and writing skills are introduced. Students learning a new language develop proficiency but also an appreciation for the new cultures.

Common guidelines used in teaching foreign languages in elementary schools include the following:

- The teacher uses the target language for 90% to 100% of the class, helping students comprehend lessons using the target language instead of translating.

- Lessons are designed around themes with lots of opportunities for students to talk about topics that are meaningful to them. The Center for Applied Linguistics publication *Thematic, Communicative Language Teaching in the K–8 Classroom* can serve as a useful tool for designing thematic lessons.

- Teachers vary lessons to appeal to different learning types and interests and encourage active participation from students.

- Children sing songs, play games, listen to stories, and recite rhymes that are authentic and vocabulary rich.

- Learning about the target cultures is a natural part of classes, and cultural competence and awareness are explicit goals of the program; in many cases, this includes global collaboration and/or exchanges with other cultures and countries.

- In some cases, grade-level concepts are taught in the target language with the focus on developing communication skills while learning about the subject.

- Programs are staffed by certified teachers with a high level of language and cultural competence.

There is **a wonderful list of resources** specifically for elementary school foreign language programs also from the Center for Applied Linguistics. The list includes websites, books, journals, ERIC documents, and digests for schools who wish to start a language program, as well as resources for schools who already have a program in place.

Where elementary schools do not have a language teacher on staff and are not able to add one either because of inadequate funding, or lack of teachers with qualifications and skills, a plethora of basic foreign language exposure tools can still be used. For the younger elementary students, teachers can incorporate language lessons into the daily circle time or calendar time. Clear labeling of items in the class allow everyone (even the teachers!) to learn new vocabulary. After going over the numbers, days of the week, and months of the year in English, have students repeat them in the target language. Common classroom commands and phrases, such as "stand up," "put your books away," and "time for lunch," are fun to learn in another language because they are so often used and quickly learned. This can serve as an area for volunteers with foreign language knowledge to assist the class.

Teachers can search on YouTube or iTunes for children's songs in the target language. Incorporate songs into the daily routine, and after repetitive use, children will pick up on the verses and vocabulary used. For example, **Jose-Luis Orozco** has many CDs that introduce basic concepts and vocabulary in Spanish through song.

Teachers who are not native speakers may try the following resources to enhance their students' linguistic experience.

## Language-Learning Programs and Materials

- **Mango Languages** offers a program for children and adults to learn any of the 40 languages offered. Check to see if your local library or school district has purchased or would consider purchasing a subscription for the wider community's use.

- **Little Pim** is a DVD-based language program (now also available in digital download and apps in the iTunes store) using the Entertainment Immersion Method for children ages 0–6 in 10 languages plus English.

- **MUZZY**, the BBC language program, has two levels—preK to Grade 3 and Grades 4–8—that include DVDs, CDs, and interactive computer software for eight different languages.

- **E. L. Easton** has a large number of links related to language learning for multiple languages.

- **Rosetta Stone** is a subscription-based, online language study program, where students are advised to spend 30 minutes per day studying a language on the computer in engaging games and exercises in 20+ languages.

- FREE [insert desired language] Tutor Games are available for iPhone/iPod/iPad and are great for beginning language learners in Chinese, French, German, Italian, Japanese, Portuguese, and Spanish. Look for "FREE Chinese Tutor Games," and so on.

- **UCLA Language Materials Project** includes lessons for less commonly taught languages. Click on the "K–12 Gateway" link for age-appropriate lesson plans.

- Games, songs, and activities for multiple languages are available at **Hello-World**.

- **Ñandutí** is a comprehensive resource on foreign language teaching and learning in Grades preK–8.

We have found a seemingly endless supply of websites, apps, and programs for teachers to use with their students for language learning. Here are several resources for each of the popular languages taught in schools that teachers can use in their classroom to introduce world languages:

### Chinese:

Oxford University runs the **Centre for Teaching Chinese as a Foreign Language**, which provides resources that elementary schools can use.

The **ChinaSprout** catalogue carries a wide selection of language learning materials from various venders, including bilingual storybooks, textbooks, DVDs, and games.

### French:

The University of Alberta, in Canada, has **an excellent page of resources** to teach French as a second language, including curriculum guides for teachers who are not native speakers.

About.com also has **a list of many primary sites** in the French-speaking world and for the study of French.

### German:

The American Association of Teachers of German has compiled **a list of German resources** on its website.

### Hindi:

For teachers wishing to introduce their kids to Hindi as part of a lesson on India, **this short presentation on Hindi language and culture** was made by students in India with the Asia Society.

### Japanese:

The American Association of Teachers of Japanese has **a page of specially created multimedia resources and lesson plans** (free for downloading) that teach the language and culture of Japan for K–12. There are also a lot of **videos and lessons** that examine students' lives in Japanese elementary schools (with some language content as well).

### Spanish:

- **This is an excellent example** of how a teacher built up an elementary school Spanish curriculum put together by professors at the University of Minnesota. The site includes all of their lesson plans and a list of all of the materials used in their K–2 Spanish classes.

- **Mis Cositas** is a site dedicated to sharing materials for teaching Spanish and French. They have begun to add resources to Chinese, German, and Italian as well.

- **Cody's Cuentos** has classic children's fairytales in Spanish.

- **SEEDS** (Support for Elementary Educators through Distance education in Spanish) is a project designed to develop three distance education modules online for schools looking for classroom activities to teach Spanish language and culture in all curriculum areas.

---

## National Associations and Institutes for Language Teachers

These associations can offer professional development and human resources for enhancing school language programs.

*AATA.* The American Association of Teachers of Arabic and the **Arabic K–12** (the Arabic Teacher's Network) offer teaching materials and professional development.

*AATF.* The American Association of Teachers of French has an incredibly rich resource with web activities and classroom activities accessible to the public, tips for teaching with technology, and an advocacy wiki.

*AATSEEL.* The American Association of Teachers of Slavic and East European Languages shares a lot of appropriate resources for the classroom related to language as well as culture, film, and literature.

*AATSP.* The American Association of Teachers of Spanish and Portuguese offers workshops, publications, an Early Language Learning Forum (K–8), and classroom resources for their members.

*CLTA.* The Chinese Language Teachers Association promotes the study of Chinese language and culture, holds an annual conference, and publishes an online journal with resources for Chinese language teachers.

*NEALRC.* The National East Asian Languages Resource Center develops materials primarily for Chinese but also for Japanese and Korean.

*NMELRC.* The National Middle East Language Resource Center includes resources for language learners of Arabic, Hebrew, Persian, and Turkish with online links, programs, and professional development for teachers.

*NNELL.* The National Network for Early Language Learning has publications, workshops, and webinars for members interested in promoting language learning among young children.

## More Tools to Help Language Learners

- **Voxopop** is an audio tool that can be used to record online dictations or pronunciation drills (especially by native speakers). Students can then listen to the recordings and record either their responses or their practice.

- **Voki** allows students to make a speaking character with their own voices (speaking in the target language). In Voki Classroom, teachers can view and approve all of their students' Voki projects in one place.

- On the **Dvolver Moviemaker site**, students can make a simple animated movie, writing conversations that use current vocabulary and grammar in the target language.

---

## Best Practices for Building a Substantive Elementary School Language Program

When Winnetka (Illinois) Public Schools wanted to assess the effectiveness of their Spanish language program that had been running in their elementary schools since 1996, they took a systematic approach and uncovered important lessons we believe all schools could learn from. They shared their best practices at the annual meeting of the **American Council on the Teaching of Foreign Languages**, a vital association supporting foreign language teaching and learning.

Early on they saw the value of gaining credibility, perspective, and clarity from outside expertise, so the district called on the **Center for Applied Linguistics** (CAL) in Washington, DC. CAL has **extensive experience** in language education and assessment and a collaborative model of building foreign language programs in diverse schools. Together they determined three key evaluation questions:

- What are the strengths and potential areas for improvement in the design and implementation of the world language program?

- What resources or programmatic changes will promote alignment of the program with best practices in curriculum, instruction, and assessment?

- How can the district best move to a proficiency-focused model? How can curriculum design best support functional language proficiency? What professional development would best support the shift?

CAL and Winnetka worked collaboratively to develop a far-reaching evaluation process which consisted of analyzing current curricula; conducting surveys and well-organized focus groups with teachers, parents, and administrators, consisting of clear goals and methods; observing language classes; and conducting Student Oral Proficiency Assessment interviews in multiple grades to get an overview of speaking proficiency and listening comprehension at various grade levels. Finally, once all the collected data were analyzed, a comprehensive report was submitted to the district. This report helped to clarify the process leading to their assessment and recommendations and made the process entirely transparent—all of which furthers district support for the program.

The findings showed many strengths, particularly around infrastructure (human, community engagement, organizational, technical) in the district, yet student proficiency lagged. To achieve better results, they made the following recommendations:

- Set more challenging, yet realistic goals for increased language instructional time for each grade. Their new goal is 90 minutes per week per grade to make real language learning impact.

- Clarify all instructional goals (around language, culture, and content).

- Develop a common content-based thematic curriculum for the entire program, incorporating content objectives into every grade's language curriculum.

- Provide ongoing professional development for all world language teachers.

- Increase program visibility for language and cultures districtwide. (See text box on how this is being achieved.)

- Incorporate ongoing assessment into instruction.

- Establish monthly collaborative meetings for the world languages team.

- Provide dedicated leadership for the program transition.

*Raising Visibility for Languages and Cultures in the School District* A good way to start putting world languages on an equal footing with other core subjects is by incorporating them more widely and visibly into schoolwide activities. For example, students can read part of the morning announcements in Spanish; a "phrase of the day" can be offered for the students, teachers, and staff to learn in the new language; and areas of the school buildings can be labeled in the foreign language(s), for example, *Biblioteca* (Library), *Oficina de Enfermera* (Nurse's Office), *Oficina de Directora* (Principal's Office), *Baño de Niñas* (Girls' Bathroom), *Baño de Niños* (Boys' Bathroom), and so on. As CAL's experience has shown, students love being the "experts" in a language and can serve as language teachers for their regular classroom teacher; as they return to their classroom, they can share with their classroom teacher a specific phrase that they learned that day.

These goals came about gradually, not all at once, recognizing many demands on the school day and on student performance. Taking an iterative approach, administrators responsible for the foreign language program recognize some goals might be ready for implementation and others may be getting ahead of internal capacity, while ongoing learning encourages the revision of approaches. The model shows the power of collaboration (between parents, teachers, administrative staff, and with the outside expert organization), of honest evaluation, and clear goal setting.

# Concluding Reflection

The respected MetLife Survey of the American Teacher: Preparing Students for College and Careers, which surveyed teachers, students, parents, and Fortune 1000 executives, dedicates a significant amount of attention to the issue of global competency as it considers factors necessary for success in the new, global economy. The survey found "two-thirds of teachers (63%), parents (63%) and Fortune 1000 executives (65%) think that knowledge of other nations and cultures and international issues is very important or absolutely essential to be ready for college and a career."[3] Among public education thought leaders, the study cited quotes like "Teachers will have to broaden their own knowledge and be more aware of global issues students will face."

Despite the recognition of its significance, integration of global competency remains relatively rare in most schools. In our interactions with educators across the world, we have found that part of the reason for this gap between recognition and action lies in lack of training and tools (and therefore of confidence) to make the shift to global learning. Given the readiness of the youngest learners to embrace new cultures, languages, and ideas, we hope that resources like the many offered in this chapter can empower teachers to bring the world into their classrooms, to truly fulfill the needs of 21st century learners.

If the tools we offer seem simple, they are meant to be. We hope that the applications to diverse academic subject areas will allow small steps to begin right away and spur more ideas. For every upcoming unit you begin to plan teaching, please consider where a global dimension can be included. If you need to, write "GLOBAL" on a sticky note and place it prominently on your desk or on your computer as you are planning. Global considerations start to build like a muscle or habit—at first it might feel like a stretch, but with practice it's normalized—and you can get rid of the sticky note. For those educators with more experience in global learning, we have found that they can take the tools to go deeper, faster—for their students and in their own professional and intellectual development.

As practice is built around the integration of global themes in everyday learning, you will begin to find that you no longer have to make a difficult either/or decision between test results and global know-how, or between fulfilling mandated curricular requirements and bringing the world to your students. Successful implementation of global education can expand what you thought was possible and create a more fulfilling, productive, lifelong learning process for your students—and for you.

## NOTES

1. Rhodes, N. C., & Pufahl, I. (2010). *Foreign language teaching in U.S. schools: Results of a national survey.* Washington, DC: Center for Applied Linguistics.

2. American Council on the Teaching of Foreign Languages. (2012). *ACTFL performance descriptors for language learners* (p. 12). Alexandria, VA: Author. Retrieved from http://www.actfl.org/sites/default/files/pdfs/PerformanceDescriptorsLanguageLearners.pdf

3. MetLife. (2011). MetLife survey of the american teacher: Preparing students for college and careers. Retrieved from https://www.metlife.com/assets/cao/contributions/foundation/american-teacher/MetLife_Teacher_Survey_2010.pdf

www.corwin.com/globaledtoolkit

# Technology Tools to Connect With the World
## Unlocking Global Education 2.0

As we hope has become clear throughout this Toolkit, global education goes way beyond food, fun, and festivals, and it's also much more than going online to research standard information about a foreign country. Used properly, technology tools can build relationships near and far much more quickly, profoundly, and conveniently than ever before imagined. When they are creating opportunities for interaction, really getting to know people and situations regardless of their location, touching hearts, and teaching empathy, then the technology has done something amazing. *We think of this as Global Education 2.0, where it's ultimately about meaningful connections, not amassing apps and web links.*

The aim of this chapter is to help tap into and demystify education technology ("edtech") tools as a means of enhancing the experience of global learning and to build global competence.

This process also touches on the goals behind 21st century learning. Everyone has access to information—it's all a Google search away. But what your students will do with that information can be what distinguishes them. Research by the **Partnership for 21st Century Skills** has identified 4 Cs, which are the "learning and innovation skills" crucial to success in this century:

- Critical thinking and problem solving
- Communication

- Creativity and innovation

- Collaboration

These 4 Cs are part of a larger model that comprises "21st Century Student Outcomes," which include "Life and Career Skills" and "Information, Media, and Technology Skills," with "Core Subjects—3Rs and 21st Century Themes" at the base of the student outcomes. By 3Rs, they are talking about reading, writing, and arithmetic, plus other core subjects like world languages, science, geography, history, government and civics, and the arts. The 21st Century Themes identified in the model are global awareness; financial, economic, business, and entrepreneurial literacy; civic literacy; health literacy; and environmental literacy. Visually this has been represented by the figure below with "Student Outcomes" representing the top of the rainbow and "Support Systems" as the pools that lie at the base.

Our focus in this chapter aims to integrate various parts of the model, using Information, Media, and Technology Skills to advance global awareness, which will fuel stronger Learning and Innovation Skills (the

**Figure 4.1  21st Century Student Outcomes and Support Systems**

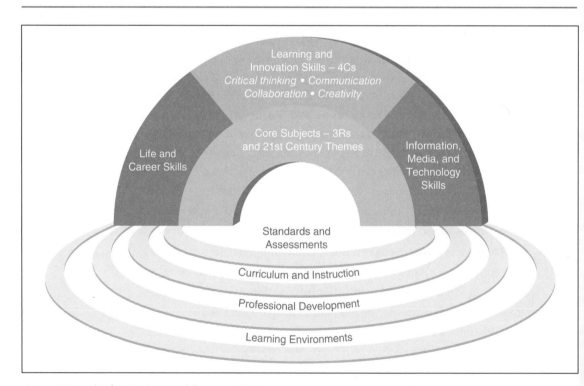

*Source:* Partnership for 21st Century Skills, www.p21.org.

4 Cs) and will be supported by the learning environments and curriculum/instruction you create or use. This also can serve as a basis for professional development material.

As we have seen, the sheer volume of tools and the rapid pace of change can leave teachers and parents virtually paralyzed, creating confusion about where to begin and causing them to seek comfort in turning off all technology and reverting to pencil and paper as their chief learning tools. This isn't bad in itself, but it doesn't need to feel this way, and "edtech" shouldn't be reserved for use by a few young "techies" in our schools. We hope that the tools and examples featured in each of the following sections will help clarify use, dissipate anxiety, and empower readers to connect with the wider world through the technology that is literally available at our fingertips.

We have organized this chapter into the following sections:

- Section 1: Social Media (Twitter, Facebook, Edmodo, and more)
- Section 2: Class Blogs and Wikis
- Section 3: Videoconferencing (Skype and Google+)
- Section 4: Online Clearinghouses for Lesson Plans
- Section 5: Digital Multimedia in the Classroom
- Section 6: Global Education Professional Development Opportunities

## Section 1: Social Media (Twitter, Facebook, Edmodo, and More)

Elementary school students shouldn't be using Facebook and Twitter on their own, but they are likely aware of these tools, and within 3 years of entering middle school, the majority will have a Facebook page, Instagram account, or whatever is the latest application for interactive sharing. Within a secured environment and a well-thought-out, guided project, classes can benefit from the positive uses of social media, setting the foundation for responsible "digital citizenship" and a lifetime of connectivity. Consider how you can use social media for social good.

An added benefit of exposing young classrooms to these tools comes from the example you set. Social media too often serves as a tool for exclusionary or bullying behavior—kids see what social events they've been left out of, or words fly that would never have been used face to face. But used in a guided learning environment, children will gain an understanding that social media tools can be used to connect with organizations and individuals making an impact on the world stage and that collaboration can be exciting, enriching, and take on various forms—even including the quieter voices in class. They can see that their Internet connection offers them power to do good, transcending cliques, material limitations, or geographic boundaries.

Adapting new technology offers an opportunity for the teacher to model positive digital interaction, while teaching that social media can be used for learning and expanding their mind, going way beyond entertainment.

## Twitter

Among too many adults and educators we have interacted with, **Twitter** has gotten a bad rap. "Why would I want to know when a celebrity goes to the bathroom?" and "My (teen or adult) kids have forbidden me from getting a Twitter account" and "You can't say anything of value in just 140 characters or less" are typical responses we hear. These views miss the power of Twitter and its growing influence as a compelling professional development tool (see Section 6 in this chapter for more on Twitter for professional development). Think of Twitter as a means to connect, communicate, and collaborate, and build friendships, compassion, and a genuine desire for deeper learning and engagement. We hope this section will show you how simple—and worthwhile—it is to get started. And if you are already using Twitter, share your experience with us: @growingupglobal and @kidworldcitizen!

## 12 Ways to Use Twitter in the Classroom

Twitter has so many uses in an elementary classroom. Try one or more of these 12 ways to Tweet your way around the world with your students.

1. *Engage parents.* Tweet relevant projects or news from your classroom and allow parents to follow back and instantly comment.

2. *Go to the primary source.* Follow relevant experts and hashtags such as **experts at NASA**, favorite authors, scientists, or historians. Try to engage them in short conversation by tagging them (*@theirname*) with a question— you never know who might respond!

3. *Start a movement.* Create your own hashtag. Let other schools know about it, and follow as it grows.

4. *Follow current events.* Many schools followed the #26Acts hashtag that urged citizens to do 26 random acts of kindness after the Newtown, Connecticut, school shooting that took 26 lives. Following a hashtag lets students in on the ground level of important movements.

5. *Gather real-world data.* Post a question ("What will you do for New Year's?" or "What is your weather today?") and follow the data on a map such as **http://twittermap.appspot.com**.

6. *Locate your followers.* If you ask your PLN (personal learning network) for their locations, check them on Google Earth and see who is the farthest and nearest classroom, what their terrain is, where the nearby cities are, and so on. **One fourth-grade class used this method called geoTweeting.**

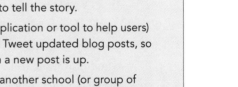

7. *Poll your followers.* Use **Twtpoll** to ask opinions on Twitter. Create a poll and graph responses as they come in from your followers.

8. *Recommend books.* Write short summaries (microblogs) of books read by students in class and keep them all in one place by Tweeting them from a single account. Some classes also live-Tweet a book as they read it together. When finished, compile the Tweets together to tell the story.

9. *Sync the class blog to Twitter.* Widgets (an application or tool to help users) on most blog platforms help to automatically Tweet updated blog posts, so parents and other followers are notified when a new post is up.

10. *Collaborate to tell a story.* Tweet a story with another school (or group of classes) and take turns adding to the plot. Use storify.com or twitterfall.com to put together the coherent story at the end, like the story of Goldilocks and the Three Bears, **tweeted by @grade1 and edited in Storify**.

11. *Update parents.* Live-Tweet field trips for parents or children who are home sick, including photos.

12. *¿Hablas español?* In a language classroom, follow Tweets in the target language. Create a community of language teachers who agree to Tweet once a week about recent projects or happenings in their class or town.

*Safety caveat.* When setting up a Twitter account for the classroom, many teachers decide to secure their Tweets from unwanted followers. Click on "settings," then at the bottom of the page select the box marked "protect my Tweets." This way no one will be able to see your Tweet except the limited followers that you approve. We recommend not using students' full names and asking parents to refrain from asking specific questions about their child on Twitter. Instead, they can send a direct message or e-mail to the teacher with any questions or concerns. Check with your school administration for additional social media guidelines, such as parental release forms for student participation.

## Facebook and Edmodo

Most schools block Facebook due to its social content. If your school allows it, you might consider using Facebook as a way to communicate with parents while teaching digital citizenship. **One first-grade class uses Facebook to talk about what they're learning, keep parents updated, and share student work and pictures.**

To demonstrate positive uses of social media, you could create a Facebook page of a historic figure, community hero, international icon, or made-up individual relevant to a lesson from your class (if your school firewalls allow). What might their interests be? What music, hobbies, books, places, and causes might they be interested in "liking"? The simple act of creating a Facebook page for Benjamin Franklin, Albert Einstein, or Sojourner Truth will test your students' knowledge of the history, circumstances, aspirations, and impact of that figure's life and times. Your Facebook page for the historic or fictional figure can demonstrate that social media can be used as a tool for raising awareness and doing good, well beyond the social pressure that young people sometimes find themselves in when engaged on Facebook.

**Edmodo** serves as a great alternative, surpassing Facebook's functionality, with powerful teacher-student-parent interface for productive communication and collaboration in a complete learning management system—which is free for users. It offers a secure social network where teachers can share documents, lessons, and ideas with students and other teachers; engage in discussions; and share content with classrooms around the world. This can be used as an iPad app or web-based interface. Some educators have described Edmodo as a "safer" Facebook: Teachers can share lessons with students (when they're absent, for extra credit, to collect and assign homework; and parents can check in on assignments), and students can share their work among classmates and with others around the world. For example, **a third-grade class from Pennsylvania set up virtual pen pals** with the purpose of respecting and appreciating different opinions, perspectives, and cultures of others.

## Other Education-Based Social Networks

*United Classroom.* A social network founded by enthusiastic, tech-savvy, young teachers, UClass is "where your class meets the world." Students are able to connect with other classes; share their thoughts and comments on videos, lessons, or questions; and collaborate on global projects. **For one project**, students were invited to share student-created content on "Where We're From." This particular project had students from the United States, Denmark, United Arab Emirates, and India sharing videos, pictures, and drawings about their neighborhoods.

*Diipo.* With a user interface similar to Twitter and Facebook, Diipo is another educational microblogging platform that encourages students to participate in discussions with their classmates or classrooms they have connected with online.

*Big Campus.* Big Campus represents an additional collaborative learning platform that helps classes collaborate with peers on projects, using forums, real-time chats, group discussions, and wall posts. In the resource section, teachers can access educationally relevant YouTube videos, websites, and more.

Share video/tutorials/songs via **SchoolTube**. Conduct **VoiceThread** projects, where students add their voice, narrating slide presentations; and create and share **Prezi** projects on the cloud, as an alternative to PowerPoint for presentations.

# Section 2: Class Blogs and Wikis
## Blogs

A blog is a website on which the users record opinions, information, or progress on a long-term project or share creative writing and multimedia production on a regular basis. Class blogs serve as a great tool of global collaboration and sharing, whether students are producing the blog posts or commenting on other students' writing, pictures, or videos. Blogs also offer an excellent example of Common Core Standards implementation as the kids do the reading and writing for wider audiences.

Here are some ways to get involved in blogging as a class:

- First, check out the **extensive list of class blogs at Edublogger**. The list includes blogs from around the world, organized by grade level (Grades K–8) and by subject. Read several different blogs to see some of the possibilities and ideas other teachers have tried. Notice that different blogs have different focus areas and share different types of posts. Decide what your class would like to share.

- As a class, read a couple of posts from class blogs that you preview first. To start, you can compose a comment together. This presents an excellent opportunity to teach your students about polite and respectful commenting and digital citizenship.

- The **Student Blogging Challenge** offers a free introduction to blogging that requires no experience. Twice a year (March and September), a challenge of 10 weekly tasks is announced. The tasks encourage students to improve their blogging and commenting skills while engaging with a global audience. Both class blogs and student blogs can register to participate.

- If you've decided to take the next step, set up your own class blog. **Kidblog** has a free platform set up by teachers that allows classes to blog in a secure, private space completely controlled by teachers. **One ESL teacher in Buenos Aires used Kidblog to discuss a book they were reading for the Global Read Aloud project.**

- Once you've set up your blog and have your students writing content, Tweet the posts using the hashtag **#comments4kids**. Educators check this hashtag and often give meaningful comments to kid bloggers. See more about using Twitter in Section 1 of this chapter.

- Get inspiration from some of the best class blogs on the web:

  ▸ **Mrs. Yollis' Classroom Blog**

  ▸ **Outside My Classroom Windows**

  ▸ **Mrs. Thiessen's Grade 4/5 Class Blog**

  ▸ **Global Grade 3**

  ▸ **The Denton Dynamos (fifth grade)**

  ▸ Ms. Smith's fifth-grade class blog **The Hive Society**

- **Global Teacher Connect**—featuring multiple classroom/teacher blogs

- Kathy Cassidy, author of *Connected From the Start*, where she shares her classroom blogging experience, has compiled a rich list of classroom blogs in **a Google Doc** geared to teachers of children ages 3–8 to give an idea of the variety of styles, voices, and methods that blogs can take. This serves as a great list for teachers who may be considering blogging but aren't sure how the blogs should look and get set up.

---

## Internet Safety Rules to Remember: Never Give Away Your YAPPY!

The seasoned bloggers in Linda Yollis's second-grade class share a simple Internet safety rule that guides their online activity in an **outstanding YouTube video** Mrs. Yollis made with her class. Among the nuggets of wisdom they share: "Never give away your YAPPY." A YAPPY is

- *y*our full name,
- your *a*ddress,
- your *p*hone number,
- your *p*asswords, and
- *y*our plans.

This motto could make for a good note to post in your classroom, on a Tweet, and for an early lesson in digital citizenship.

---

## Wikis

A wiki is like a blog but developed collaboratively by a number of users, allowing anyone in the invited community to add and edit content. The best-known wiki is probably Wikipedia, where users around the world can update encyclopedia entries. Wikis can be used to showcase projects that have been developed by students around the world with a common goal. They act like online databases that help to coordinate a group with multiple authors.

The **wiki called A Week in the Life** is part of the global collaborative Flat Classroom project, where students from schools around the world in Grades 3–5 connected for 10 weeks to work on a multimedia project together. The goal was to learn about each other's communities and the children that live in them and then present the information gathered with photos, videos, audio, or a slideshow. Each year a new batch of schools applies to participate in the project, which enjoys a strong global following.

Here are a few more terrific wikis to support your global learning:

- **The Global Classroom Project**
- **The Global Genius Hour**
- **Crazy Crazes**—sharing what's popular and trendy in a South African community, then going global
- **The Global Read-Aloud**
- **The Global Hello Project**
- The Centre for Learning and Performance Technologies has compiled a **list of 30+ wiki tools** for creating your own content.

## Section 3: Videoconferencing (Using Skype and Google+)

With the growth of the Internet around the world and developments in videoconferencing, it is now relatively simple for educators to connect in real time with other classes, with experts in various fields, or even to take virtual field trips through platforms like Skype and Google+. Sometimes, the most complicated part of arranging a call could be doing the math on the various time zones correctly and accounting for Daylight Savings Time. Free, simple time zone conversion sites like the **World Clock Meeting Planner** can help with that.

You can search a global directory of classes by student age range, language, and subject using **Skype in the Classroom**. With over 20,000 teachers registered on the site, ready to connect with other schools around the world, participating classrooms can "go" almost anywhere on the planet—and they do. The possibilities seem endless for teachers with a little creativity, enthusiasm for bringing technology into the classroom, and a passion for global education. **Skype is easy to use** once you have the equipment set up (webcam, microphone, and computer with a screen for kids to view—most of these are standard on laptop and desktop computers made in the past 5 years). Teachers can post projects that they are working on, ask for collaboration from other classes, or can browse through **exceptional examples of projects** that have already taken place. Teachers also can invite an expert to visit their classroom on Skype, virtually and literally making the world a smaller place.

**Google+ Hangouts** were created after Skype became established, but like other Google Apps for Education, Hangouts serve as a powerful learning tool, enjoying the backing of the creative Google team and their technology. Browsing on the **Google in Education** page, we found fun, easy-to-plug-into activities, like a **Google+ virtual classroom, powered by Hangout on Air and hosted by the Seattle Aquarium**. In this particular hangout, students (ideally in Grades 3–5) could "meet" the Seattle Aquarium's Giant Pacific Octopus up close and personal when they joined Aquarium biologists and educators on a dive into the Aquarium's octopus enclosure. Organizers encouraged prepared questions for divers and staff, and learning possibilities were vast. This is one of many examples showing engaged learning that doesn't depend on your location or material resources—as long as you have an Internet connection, monitor, and microphone—and a sense of exploration!

## Elementary Students "Study Abroad" (Virtually) and Plant Seeds for Actual Study Abroad

**Reach the World**, a nonprofit organization based in New York City, with ties to Teachers College, Columbia University, and named a Model Program in Geography Education by the National Geographic Society Education Foundation, takes classrooms and after-school clubs on virtual journeys by tapping into the energy of volunteer world travelers who serve as mentoring, global competence and live geographic literacy teaching resources.

For example, at PS (Public School) 36 in Harlem, New York, elementary-aged students connected with a traveler named Jheanelle in Barbados during their after-school program. These students followed her journey each week and videoconferenced with her several times a semester. Their teacher, Hannah C., noted that after each lesson, students became increasingly engaged and motivated to learn more about her and Barbados, fascinated that they could actually talk to someone in another part of the world. Whenever they chatted, they enjoyed asking Jheanelle about the Green Monkeys that are found locally as well as learning about local cuisine such as fried fish, coconuts, and potato wedges. During one videoconference, Jheanelle turned her video camera out the window to show her students the beautiful view of palm trees and beaches surrounding her homestay, and the students gasped in awe. The students also talked with Jheanelle about the challenges of studying for important college exams and strategies for making time to study.

Thanks to their interaction, the students did a better job retaining stories Jheanelle shared in her articles for their own classroom work and eagerly took these back home to tell their family members. The students frequently told Hannah C. how much they wanted to meet Jheanelle in person one day and travel abroad just like her, in most cases making them the first in their families to aspire to such a goal.

# Technology-Enhanced Communication and Collaboration

Communicating across cultures and working with others to resolve issues represent two important skills for the 21st century that require real-life practice. The majority of teachers we spoke with were excited about the possibility to introduce a global collaboration project into their classes. However, some believed that finding a partner class, setting up the sessions, and building the relationship seemed a daunting task. It doesn't have to be! Communicating with others outside of the classroom is made easier by the many services and programs now available online. The following offer a few good resources to start:

- **Connect All Schools.** In an historic speech in Cairo, Egypt, in June 2009, President Obama expressed his desire to "create a new online network, so a young person in Kansas can communicate instantly with a young person in Cairo." Since then, the secretary of state and secretary of education have both emphasized the importance of learning other languages, gaining global competency, and traveling to other countries. A number of organizations linking U.S. schools with others around the world are coming together in a new Connect All Schools consortium to meet a very specific goal: *to connect every school in the United States with the world by 2016.* Signing up and getting started follows **an easy three-step process.**

- **Global SchoolNet** aims to engage to students in 21st century learning and improve academic performance through content-driven collaboration. Matching teachers and classes to others around the world for global collaboration via e-learning projects worldwide, Global SchoolNet prepares students to become compassionate citizens with multicultural understanding. The database of teacher-led projects is searchable by date, age level, geographic location, collaboration type, technology tools, or keyword.

- **Epals** offers a platform to connect with schools around the world for the purpose of e-mail-based collaborative projects with digital content from National Geographic. There are active forums for students, teachers, and families to participate in discussions with peers worldwide in a safe online environment. It is currently one of the largest K–12 social learning networks on the web, and its members hail from 200 countries.

- The World Affairs Council in Seattle, Washington, has **compiled a document** that lists multiple organizations linking schools around the world in collaboration projects.

- **Around the World With 80 Schools** attempts to connect 80 schools from around the world through Skype in the classroom. Classes can sign up to participate and connect with other schools from around the world and blog about their progress.

- **Challenge 20/20** connects schools in the United States with schools in other countries. Together, students work to identify local solutions to a global problem. Through the globally based, experiential curriculum, the aim is for students to develop cross-cultural competency and communication skills. This online program is free of charge and open to all schools: K–12, public, private, and charter. It is administered by the National Association of Independent Schools (NAIS), and the online collaboration portal is run by TakingITGlobal, two outstanding leaders in global learning.

  ▶ Since its inception in 2005, Challenge 20/20 has connected thousands of schools, clubs, and after-school groups. Each year, more than 500 applications from nearly 60 countries are received, and NAIS pairs up best matches according to interest, seeking geographic and demographic diversity between partners.

- The **Flat Classroom Project** is a global collaborative project reaching students at all levels, K–12. The project was cofounded by Vicki Davis (United States) and Julie Lindsay (Australia) in 2006 when Julie (then in Bangladesh) and Vicki joined their classrooms together for the first time to study and emulate the emerging flattened learning environment. Since then, the concept of Flat Classrooms has grown significantly, and they share their learning and expertise in their fabulous book, *Flattening Classrooms, Engaging Minds: Move to Global Collaboration One Step at a Time* (Pearson, 2012). For elementary students, try the Flat Classroom projects "K–2 Building Bridges to Tomorrow" or "A Week in the Life" for Grades 3–5.

## Tips for Setting Up a Successful School Partnership (or "Twinning Program")

Beyond a fun, one-off video chat with a classroom far away, establishing a "twin" school or classroom can result in one of the richest learning experiences for everyone involved. It just takes some advance thinking and planning. Here are some tips to smooth the process.

*Before* you get started, consider these principles:[1]

- *Solidarity not charity.* First consider those in the partnership as your peers, with whom mutual learning will take place. A desire for charity may naturally emerge from interaction, but if you begin with the position that you will "help" the other children, your students will assume a superior, benefactor role, which is not conducive to the full twinning experience.

- *One-year (or more) commitment.* By making a longer-term commitment you will set out to get to know your partners and deepen the learning and relationship beyond a one-off fascination with those who seem so different.

- *Set goals and integrate them.* Identify a few outcomes (academic as well as social) you hope to realize from the commitment and where you can integrate the classroom twinning with the general curriculum.

- *Classroom to classroom, not pupil to pupil.* Make this a united effort. You'll begin to see variations across people in their classroom, better sustain the partnership, and be able to encourage individual efforts from among your students.

- *Consider common learning and action themes.* For example, you could have a joint project related to peace, the environment, or creating more inclusive classrooms, concerns that children on both sides of the twinning program will share. This can serve as a proactive platform for working together and helps students get to know each other on a deeper level.

- *Partnership shouldn't depend on the technology.* In fact, success might be measured by how well the class does when handling glitches. Be ready to plan around asynchronous time zones, lack of adequate bandwidth and Internet connection, sound and video limitations, long delays in receiving replies to letters or e-mails, and miscommunication. Discuss these possibilities; look for back-up solutions.

*During—conversation prompts.* Below we have listed just a few starters for conversations, e-mails, or letters to your school partners. Generally, remember to begin with similarities and build from there, especially if a significant income or cultural gap exists between your twinned schools. If engaging in live video chat, it might be best for students to write down questions before their first few conversations so they don't freeze on camera and lose out on interesting content. Teachers also should make sure to monitor their students' communication carefully, to avoid inappropriate language and topics, or watch for stress triggers.

- Say "hi!" Teach each other various ways you say "hello" and greet friends—especially fun during video chat.

- What time do you wake up in the morning, and what do you have for breakfast, lunch, or dinner? (This can be one or three different conversations.)

- Describe your family for each other.

- Discuss local climate/temperature/environment. The classes can teach each other about specific local weather phenomenon (such as a tsunami, snow storm, earthquake, or tornado).

- Describe the subjects you are studying at school. Comparing social studies or history content can be a good start.

- Describe how you play during the school day, what your favorite sports are, and possibly teach each other playground or other favorite local games.

- Discuss upcoming holidays and how these are celebrated. Try to put less emphasis on the material aspect of the holiday (e.g., opening lots of presents).

- For video chat, share your national anthems for each other. You can also see if they know some of the same (traditional, folk, or pop) songs and sing all together.

- Showcase and then observe a skill or talent such as a regional dance, sport, song, instrument, or other fine art.

- Compare and contrast summer breaks: the length, the month they begin, typical weather, favorite activities.

- If you will engage in a joint service activity, like cleaning up trash around the school, making gifts for local senior citizens, or getting inspiration from an idea highlighted in Chapter 5 of this Toolkit, start discussing that. Share perspectives and challenges, and brainstorm how you can help.

*After.* Take time to reflect on the twinning process and activities soon after each encounter with your students and on your own as a facilitator. What did the students learn? What surprised them? What would they like to talk about next time? Some reflection can be done as a class discussion and some as individual journaling. For teachers, if you have a professional learning network (or any "posse" of colleagues), share the experience and invite feedback.

## Lessons in Global Partnership: One School's Story

The Packer Collegiate Institute in Brooklyn, New York, has learned many valuable lessons through its partnership with the Ndonyo-Wasin Primary School in the Samburu region of Kenya, a part of the world that is about as different from Brooklyn as can be imagined. They work with a small nonprofit, the **Thorn Tree Project**, that supports three schools in the remote region of East Africa. Due to limitations on technology availability in Ndonyo-Wasin, communication between schools is done by mail and in person.

Teachers and administrators agreed that instead of a small, superficial project, the goals would be to teach the children about the school, the Samburu, and Kenya while building students' capacity to understand and see the different perspectives over a longer period of time. Their shared philosophy was that building a relationship and learning about Kenya should not just be a 1-day or 1-week project, but part of a systematic integration, built into the scope and sequence of the existing curriculum.

Packer undertook a redesign of the curriculum, beginning with involvement from the teachers. For example, the kindergarteners learn about family structures in this community: that they are nomadic and that their parents are herders and so the children board at school. The third graders study the native tribes of the local New York City area and make comparisons between the Lenape American Indians and the Samburu tribe, their reliance on the land and livestock, and why one culture virtually disappears and one doesn't.

Because there is no Internet and limited access to electricity, there has been no real-time communication between the students. Instead, they write letters, paint portraits made from photographs, and make videos at both schools to exchange with each other. Students learn a few words of Samburu, the local language; Swahili, one of the national languages; and about the geography of the Samburu region of Kenya. They learned what children "need" and discovered, for example, that toys were not on the list.

The students in Kenya took pictures, wrote the text, and made beautiful books via online publishers like **Blurb** and **MyPublisher** about life in their school and their community, so the Packer students could use the books as a learning tool.

While school assemblies were exciting and enjoyed by students, the teachers at Packer were careful not to exoticize this society where warrior-age men still dress in traditional clothing with beads and bright colors and maintain rituals and cultural customs that are essential in their culture. By keeping the learning grounded in empathy, humility, and appreciation, the children could understand more profoundly the challenges and joys of a starkly contrasting way of life.

## Maximize Inclusion During Video Chats—Skype Jobs Chart

When circumstances do allow for real-time communication with a partner school, a few thoughtful steps can be taken to ensure wider inclusion. Videoconferencing in the classroom shouldn't be exciting just for the most outgoing, conversational children. Silvia Tolisano, the quintessential 21st century educator whose work is found at **Langwitches**, came up with a "Skype jobs" list (see the following chart) to show how to include more children with wider interests and strengths to each contribute to the success of video chatting in the classroom.

Jobs can be assigned by the classroom teacher and rotated on a regular basis, or just a couple times per year if kids seem content and settled in to their assignments.

## Widen Your Horizons: Try a "Mystery Location Call"!

One fun variation on the video call is the "mystery call" (often called "Mystery Skype") where teachers set up a call with a class or person in another city, state, or country and a series of questions, with geography, climate, and culture clues, are asked between the two groups to guess where they are located. Physical maps, Google Earth, atlases, and whiteboards for group work are among the tools used for this simple, fun, interactive inquiry-based learning activity. Pernille Ripp is a fifth-grade teacher in Wisconsin who shared her classroom's experience and how-tos for Mystery Skyping in **an article in Learning & Leading With Technology**. Pernille shared this reflection with us: "I have always searched for a way to bring geography alive; doing Mystery Skype allows students to take control of their learning and apply it to real-world problems. With an emphasis on critical problem solving and adaptability as questions are posed, students relish the opportunity to solve the challenge presented." What a great experience!

# Skype Jobs Chart

| | |
|---|---|
| Calendar | Responsible for adding scheduled Skype calls to embedded calendar on classroom blog. |
| Greet | Greets the partner school. Makes initial introduction. Talks about geographic location. |
| Share | Shares something special about school, city, state, or country. Could be song, dance, souvenir, project, sports team, etc. |
| Q & A | Asks specific questions for data collection. Responsible for keeping conversation fluid. |
| Photographer | Responsible for documenting connection via still images. |
| Videographer | Responsible for documenting connection via movie clips. |
| Backchannel Writers | Documenting conversation, questions, answers, and classroom happenings during the connection with backchannel chat. |
| Backchannel Cleanup | Responsible to save backchannel chat as Word document and cleaning up duplicate comments and mark questionable statements to be verified. |
| Blogger-Skype | Blogs Skype connection live on classroom blog. |
| Blogger-Word Problem | Creates a math word problem from data, questions, and answers from the Skype connection. |
| Google Earth | Finds location of Skype partner and measures distance in miles and kilometers. |
| Google Maps | Responsible for adding placemark of Skype partner's location to embedded map on classroom blog. |
| Infor Station | Responsible to search for any data questions on the spot. Verifies questionable information as well. |
| Data Entry | Responsible for entering data collected into embedded form on classroom blog (e.g., distance in miles/km, temperature in F/C). |
| Elapsed Time | Responsible for noting time Skype call started and ended as well as calculating elapsed time. |

Source: Used with permission from Silvia Rosenthal Tolisano, www.langwitches.org. This table also appears in *Mastering Global Literacy*, edited by Heidi Hayes-Jacobs, Solution Tree, 2013.

## Getting the Most From
## Your Skype/Google+ Calls

Kathy Cassidy is a seasoned primary teacher and technology user. She shares her considerable experience in her excellent e-book, *Connected From the Start: Global Learning in the Primary Grades*, with practical tips for technology use. Here are her tips for making the most of a video call in a classroom:

- Have a clear goal in mind. Will you be introducing all the children? Asking them if they have any patterns (one of our topics of study) in their classroom? Finding out what their weather is like? Practicing counting together? Extra questions that come up during your call are great, but start with a plan and then you can be flexible if need be.

- Talk to your students ahead of time about behavior. They will probably get excited and forget, but I still try anyway. I let all of the students have a chance to see what they look like on the camera before our first call each year so that they can concentrate on the purpose for the call and not on the chance to see themselves on camera.

- If possible, hook your computer up to a projector so that all the children can easily see what is on the monitor, even if they can't see the computer itself.

- Give as many of the children as would like to a chance to talk, even briefly.

- Keep the call short. It is better to have another one later and to end the call on a high note.

- Talk about the call after it is finished. What did we learn? Did we use our best manners? What goals should we set for our next Skype conversation? Are there other things you would like to know about that class? (pp. 24–25).[2]

# Section 4: Online Clearinghouses for Lesson Plans

Search the Internet, and it might seem like there are millions of websites offering teachers lesson plans of varying quality and depth. Throughout this Toolkit we have mentioned hundreds of specific examples of lessons that can be used in the elementary classroom to increase global awareness. In this section, we will note some of the exceptional clearinghouses online for lessons that will increase global awareness.

## Eighteen Clearinghouses for Global Lesson Plans

1. **PBS Learning Media** has lesson plans searchable by grade level and subject matter. Choose social studies, and then filter by topic (such as anthropology or African cultural studies) for a rich variety of cultural activities that encompass several disciplines. When you join their mailing list, you'll also receive updates on lessons around current events and popular PBS programming.

2. **Curriculum 21**, with electronic resources, searchable lesson plans, and professional development services, originally was developed around the work of Dr. Heidi Hayes-Jacobs, offering practical models to update schools' curricula. Curriculum 21 is the work of educators around the world who are attempting to transform school curriculum to reach the needs of 21st century learners.

3. The **Global Education website** gives teachers resources about current global issues, such as case studies, country profiles, lesson plans, as well as collections of photos, videos, and related links. These are geared toward upper-elementary students.

4. Primary Source, dedicated to "educating for global understanding," has a website rich in teaching resources, including **Teacher-Created Curriculum** and an extensive list of **Resource Guides and Bibliographies**.

5. The **Critical Multicultural Pavilion** from EdChange is a clearinghouse of links and lesson plans that increase cultural awareness in children.

6. **TeachUNICEF** boasts a portfolio of free, global, interdisciplinary educational resources for Grades preK–12. Its mission is to foster global citizens who "understand interconnectedness, respect and value diversity, have the ability to challenge injustice and inequalities and take action in

personally meaningful ways." The lesson plans, stories, and multimedia are searchable by topic (such as climate change or education), grade level (such as Grades 3–5), or media type (video, text, or audio clip).

7. The Peace Corps runs the **Coverdell World Wise Schools site**, which contains lesson plans informed by volunteers' experiences from around the world, arranged by geographical region, subject area, and grade level.

8. **TeachGlobalEd.net** contains high-quality, online modules and class activities; includes primary sources; and has many web connections categorized in five world regions: Africa, East Asia, Latin America, Middle East, Slavic and Eastern Europe. On its website, if you click on each region, several have a tab specifically for "Elementary Resources."

9. **Oxfam** has worked with teachers in the United Kingdom to develop and provide hundreds of free online resources, lesson plans, and classroom ideas to promote the goal of empowering young people to be "active Global Citizens." The organization is promoting education that helps students understand the global issues that affect their lives and take action toward a more peaceful and sustainable world.

10. At **Core Knowledge** you can use the search function to look for lesson plans related to different cultures such as "Mexico," "Taking Care of the Earth," or "Deserts."

11. **The History Channel** uses video clips, photographs, and articles to inform students about history. See useful links under "Ancient History," "Holidays," and "Places" that can be appropriate for elementary students. For example, compare a beautiful photo gallery of Egyptian pyramids to galleries of Latin American pyramids.

12. Resources from the Asia Society's Partnership for Global Learning are numerous and of excellent quality. Here are a few good K–5 resources:

> ▸ **Elementary Lesson Plans**, which increase global awareness, are specifically designed for elementary-aged students, using global music, art, literature, and celebrations. They also have a **downloadable toolkit** for setting up an after-school program for global learning.

- ▸ The "**exchange matrix**" describes the general process of assessing and guiding partnership relationships, from warm-up and establishment to implementation and reach.

13. The **Global Virtual Classroom** project is a collection of free, online educational activities that help students around the world work together to research, communicate, and create via the Internet.

14. The **European University Institute** in Florence, Italy, runs this site, which contains links of history and culture for most countries in the world.

15. **Tech for a Global Early Childhood Education** lists available resources for educators working with young children (ages 2–8) and interested in using technology to create global learning experiences in their classrooms. The activities are easily adapted for elementary schools.

16. **Global Wisconsin** makes the case that international education is both essential to students and demonstrates how to integrate this into current teaching practices. Wisconsin's additional International Education resources can be found on the **Wisconsin Department of Public Instruction website**.

17. **My Wonderful World** is a National Geographic–led campaign with resources to help schools expand geographic learning. Their downloadable toolkit contains hands-on tools to help kids increase geoliteracy as they learn about the world.

18. **KivaU**, an education initiative of Kiva, which has brought the power of microfinance to diverse people as lenders and borrowers worldwide, offers resources for educators and students to take a hands-on approach to complex topics such as entrepreneurship, international development, and financial inclusion. Starting with students in Grades K–2, teachers can cover themes like "needs versus wants," "sharing and why it's important," "what is money (currency)," and "giving back." Lessons are aligned with Common Core Standards and offer examples for extensions to various academic areas.

# iEARN: The World's Largest Nonprofit Global Classroom Network

**iEARN (International Education and Resource Network)** claims to be the world's largest nonprofit global network for teacher collaboration. In a safe and structured environment, members can select an online project and determine how they can integrate it into their classroom. Teachers and students then enter the online forum to meet one another and collaborate with their peers on the shared projects, which can truly foster global understanding. Over the years, we have met the hard-working and dedicated people behind the global network and remain impressed by their dedication to quality global education and connections.

In the following phenomenal examples, iEARN has provided detailed instructions for the lessons, student and teacher goals, a timetable, and resources (e.g., books, website) and has aligned the lesson with several Common Core Standards, all through top-notch global collaboration projects that can be viewed online:

- *The Machinto Peace Project.* This is an authentic project that gets kids thinking about kids that live in parts of the world that are experiencing conflict. Classes read *Machinto*, a Japanese picture book, and share their responses with another school around the world via videos, videoconferencing, or another method of global collaboration. Finally, the children research and locate areas of conflict in the world and create their own picture books that will be delivered to the children in a conflict zone. Here is one school's reflections on participating in the **Machinto Peace Project**.

- *Cultural Recipe Book.* In this project, students research the recipes of typical dishes from their heritage, as well as the origin of the ingredients and recipes, and the legends and stories behind them.

- *Global Art: Images of Caring.* After studying works by Mary Cassatt, students make observations of her style of expression on the subject. Then, students create a piece of artwork that illustrates their idea of "caring." Drawings are scanned and uploaded to an online gallery where students can view the artwork created by students from other countries and discuss them.

- The *Teddy Bear Project.* Matched with a class in another country, students send a visiting stuffed animal to their partner class and then communicate via e-mail about their adventures with the Teddy Bear.

- *Holiday Card Exchange.* After connecting with partner schools, students research their matched country's past year in terms of significant events (political, economic, disasters, triumphs, news) and develop a project to convey their findings to their partner classes. The classes compare and contrast between events, relationships to other world events, and the global impact. Finally, they make New Year's cards to exchange with each other via post mail, along with photos.

# Section 5: Digital Multimedia in the Classroom

To reach different types of learners, to model diverse modes of communications as a 21st century skill, and to cultivate a dynamic learning environment, tap into the rich variety of audiovisual aids available for little or no cost to teachers and students. Multimedia includes text, photographs, videos, animation, sound clips, and other graphics. Teachers can use these global images and sounds as a writing prompt, to inspire conversations, to literally illustrate places the students are studying, or to showcase current affairs. Going beyond simple text allows educators to reach all learning levels of students, and their images can spur more immediate reactions. Engage your students with the following collections of multimedia from around the world.

## Global Photography

Well known as the world leader in stunning photography from around the world, keep *National Geographic* in mind as an excellent resource to supplement classroom lessons.

LEARN NC, the K–12 teaching and learning resource from the University of North Carolina School of Education, features **Around the World in Multimedia**, which offers a collection of more than 2,000 high-resolution photographs and audio recordings from Asia and Latin America, with historical and cultural context and related lesson plans.

The *New York Times* Learning Blog has a weekly feature called **What's Going On in This Picture?** done in collaboration with Visual Thinking Strategies in which they publish a *Times* image without a caption or any other clues about its origins, then invite students to write in to discuss what they see in it. Full information about the image is posted 24 hours later. This activity is intended to boost skills according to Common Core competencies, and while most are oriented to older learners, teachers may get inspiration from these for younger learners, too.

**TrekEarth**'s mission is "to foster a global community interested in photography from around the world." Its members upload engaging photographs organized by themes (such as "Overcrowded Vehicles" or "Diwali") or categories that cross borders (such as "Daily Life" or "Festivals"). Users can also explore destinations, which is especially useful if the class is studying a particular region of the world.

## Global Videos and Audio Clips

48 hours of videos are uploaded to **YouTube** every minute. Instead of wading through videos aimlessly, subscribe to YouTube accounts of organizations like the Jane Goodall Institute, Free the Children, or other causes your class may wish to follow in order to get latest updates on their work (ideas of organizations and causes may be found in Chapter 5). Here are seven YouTube channels for education worth following:

1. National Geographic
2. Discovery Channel
3. Smithsonian Videos
4. American Museum of National History
5. Khan Academy
6. MIT
7. REEL Nasa

Also notable is **SchoolTube**, which contains educational videos uploaded by students and teachers from around the world.

The goal of **ProjectExplorer.org** is to encourage awareness of the world in students through its free, online multimedia educational materials. Using videos, photographs, educational blogs, and lessons plans, ProjectExplorer.org has a global travel series based on age (there is one for upper elementary) to foster cross-cultural understanding. This is an incredible way for students to "travel" and learn about other cultures without leaving the classroom!

The History Channel has **several categories relevant to global studies** (especially "Holidays," "Places," and "Ancient History") and appropriate for older elementary students. In each category, there are related videos and articles.

The Smithsonian's Museums of Asian Art have **great podcasts** of concerts, stories, from around Asia.

The **Global Oneness Project** education program offers curriculum, discussion guides, and "conversation cards" to become more deeply engaged with the issues and ideas raised in their film and media content. It all arrives in an attractive package with booklets, DVDs, and cards. Though ideally suited for high school students, some of the films in the set can be suitable for elementary ages. The materials provide ways for educators to introduce global themes, environmental issues, and multicultural awareness in class. The Global Oneness materials also can offer excellent faculty and staff development: Watch the short films and use the study/discussion guides as prompts for your own learning.

## Build Empathy: Enhance Your Google Search to Include Perspectives From Diverse Nationalities

Students can try to see the world from different perspectives simply by altering their usual search configuration on Google (or any favorite search engine). As **Alan November** pointed out to an Asia Society Partnership for Global Learning conference, this is a way to use technology to build empathy—put yourselves in the shoes of a person in the country you are researching about. What would their search look like? You can do this by using the **Root Zone Database**, which lists Internet country codes. For example, if you want to search for news about kangaroos in Australia, type "site:au kangaroos." A search for earthquake news in Japan would be "site:jp earthquake." Experiment by comparing the results you'd get conducting a search as you normally would and then as you would with the Root Zone Database.

## Tapping Into News Outlets From Around the World

You can use national or local periodicals to bring world affairs into your lessons or class discussions. However, to really understand global issues from different perspectives, accustom yourself and your class to read and hear the compelling arguments from the actual communities where they are taking place. By reading articles and examining polls, analyzing infographics, or watching the news and slide shows sourced from another country, students start to build the "muscle" of weighing diverse perspectives.

When conscientiously practiced, this helps build empathy, too, as students can look at an issue from the perspective of one whose circumstances are very different than their own. For example, seeing a slideshow or news analysis from a Japanese news source following the devastating 2011 Japanese tsunami illuminates the human toll as well as heroic recovery efforts that might have been overlooked from a North American news source. This also can be practiced for learning about how national holidays might be celebrated elsewhere, if you prefer to start looking for stories with a more positive angle.

One simple recommendation that has carried a great deal of traction with teachers and parents since the release of *Growing Up Global* is to simply "change your homepage" on your personal computer. Whether you switch your homepage to the BBC or Canada's CBC, or stretch a bit further to Al Jazeera or **Japan's Nippon News** in English, you can start to get a taste for issues on the radar of people living in other parts of the world to truly widen your own perspective with minimal effort.

To better understand how to integrate news and media literacy into your elementary classroom, see this article from the **National Association for Media Literacy Education**, which contains additional scholarly references, case studies, and integrates a commitment to these key themes:

> *(1) the use of inquiry to guide lesson development,*
> *(2) the role of ambiguity and uncertainty in otherwise*
> *structured learning environments, (3) the use of*
> *scaffolding and planning to limit and shape students'*
> *experiences with a variety of unpredictable media texts*
> *in the classroom, and (4) written reflection on how*
> *individual teacher values and motivations contribute to*
> *the unique classroom culture.*[3]

In addition to culling stories from trusted individual foreign news sources, you can use the following resources to locate articles about the same topic but told from a range of perspectives.

1. *Newspaper Map*, the source of over 10,000 newspapers, is searchable by clicking on a pinned location on the world map or filtered by language.
2. *Online newspapers* are available from around the world, listed by country or region.
3. *Primary Source: Educating for Global Understanding* promotes history and humanities education by providing educators with learning opportunities and curriculum resources for K–12 educators. The teacher-created database of primary sources includes films, audio clips, artifacts, newspaper articles, books, and activities to teach about global issues, especially from underrepresented groups and their histories.

# Section 6: Global Education Professional Development Opportunities

While great resources for global lessons seem abundant, teachers also need support and continuing education to best use the resources and meet other colleagues with similar interests—particularly if you wish to sustain the effort and continually improve the quality.

We find ourselves in a new era of professional development (PD), not limited to local classes or a narrow set of experiences. Personal learning networks (PLNs), a key component of 21st century education that supports collaboration and sharing, may comprise peers in any country around the world from whom we can learn best practices from any school and educational system. As you get more comfortable collaborating in PLNs (through Twitter, blogs, Nings, in-person conferences, webinars, Facebook and other social media groups, professional associations), you will find (or create) more specialized groups suited to your particular interests. Try some of these sources for building your global education teaching expertise and practice.

## Join a Ning

A Ning is as an online platform where users can create their own social networks, sharing information about their work and interests within their personal pages on the platform. We have seen Nings used effectively as a professional development, sharing, and discussion tool.

**The Educator's PLN**, the personal learning network for educators, is a popular Ning or dynamic learning community which anyone can join to share resources, ask vexing questions, and learn from other practitioners. Additional excellent, specialized Nings we have consulted in the global education space include **Curriculum 21** and the **Global Education Conference**. The **Flat Classroom Ning** describes itself here:

> *This educational network supports the workflow and collaboration of the award winning* **Flat Classroom Project** *and* **NetGenEd Project**. *Students, teachers, expert advisors, judges and people interested in learning more about our projects and being part of them are invited to browse discussion groups and multimedia.*

Members can connect and share their multimedia projects on the site and participate in chats, leave comments, view the calendar of events, and collaborate through live classroom connections.

## The Global Education Conference–Free, Online, Flexible

An excellent resource for facilitating global professional learning is the totally virtual **Global Education Conference**. Every year during the International Education Week in November, the multiday, around-the-clock event connects educators and organizations worldwide, offering a platform for diverse voices to share their experiences and learn from each other. "It is designed to significantly increase opportunities for building education-related connections around the globe while supporting cultural awareness and recognition of diversity." Educators who wish to learn more can search the hundreds of archives from past conferences for relevant topics and listen to the sessions from their computers. We have participated online as presenters as well as participants, in our pajamas, in the midst of making dinner, and with a group of colleagues around a conference table. Flexibility is part of the beauty of it.

The organizers, Lucy Gray and Steve Hargadon, have grown a global network, curating the latest innovations in global learning and inviting participation from anyone interested in sharing or learning the multitude of ways to connect students to the world. They've expanded the Global Education Conference offerings beyond the week in November to include Google Hangouts in collaboration with **TakingITGlobal**, another leader in global education. Participation is free, online, and open to anyone who may be interested.

## To Start Collaboration, Join a Learning Circle

Teachers who engage in collaborative classroom projects with colleagues around the world convey a palpable sense of excitement and profound commitment to global learning. It's not unusual to hear that such collaboration has transformed their teaching and sense of their work. One way to begin and find support among like-minded colleagues is to participate in a **Learning Circle**, which, according to iEARN, *"is made up of a team of 6–8 teachers and their classes joined in the virtual space of an electronic classroom. The groups remain together over a 3–4 month period working on projects drawn from the curriculum of each of the classrooms and organized around a selected theme. At the end of the period the group collects and publishes its work."*

iEARN's network facilitates these circles, with a **free online guide** to better understand the mechanisms and benefits of this approach. Read the guide then join a circle!

### Get Inspired by a Short Talk via TED; or a Lesson via TED-Ed

Learn from the world's best experts (in virtually every field) at your own convenience by using TED (Technology, Entertainment, Design) talks as a professional development resource. Constantly updated, TED started as a global conference of forward thinkers, which shares its powerful talks free for viewing online at ted.com. TED has grown to include TEDx conferences, which are independently organized events in the spirit of the original TED conferences but located around the world, sometimes with a particular theme, such as EDU, exploring innovative ideas and practice in education. Talks can serve as a great team-building tool for staff meetings to prompt a Tweet to other educators for feedback or for your personal inspiration. Here are just a few talks to consider watching to get started:

- *Sir Ken Robinson, "Changing Education Paradigms."* Probably the most popular TED talk ever that's about education. Description: "Creativity expert Sir Ken Robinson challenges the way we're educating our children. He champions a radical rethink of our school systems, to cultivate creativity and acknowledge multiple types of intelligence."

- *John Hunter, "Teaching With the World Peace Game."* Description: "John Hunter puts all the problems of the world on a 4′ × 5′ plywood board—and lets his 4th-graders solve them.

At TED2011, he explains how his World Peace Game engages schoolkids, and why the complex lessons it teaches—spontaneous, and always surprising—go further than classroom lectures can." See more on John Hunter's methodology (with a link to the TED video) in Homa's piece for Edutopia, "**How Fourth Graders Are Achieving World Peace.**"

- *Chimamanda Adichie, "The Danger of a Single Story."* Description: "Our lives, our cultures, are composed of many overlapping stories. Novelist Chimamanda Adichie tells the story of how she found her authentic cultural voice—and warns that if we hear only a single story about another person or country, we risk a critical misunderstanding."

- *Eli Pariser, "Beware Online 'filter bubbles.'"* Description: "As web companies strive to tailor their services (including news and search results) to our personal tastes, there's a dangerous unintended consequence: We get trapped in a 'filter bubble' and don't get exposed to information that could challenge or broaden our worldview. Eli Pariser argues powerfully that this will ultimately prove to be bad for us and bad for democracy."

- *William Kamkwamba, "How I Harnessed the Wind."* Description: "At age 14, in poverty and famine, a Malawian boy built a windmill to power his family's home. Now at 22, William Kamkwamba, who speaks at TED, here, for the second time, shares in his own words the moving tale of invention that changed his life."

- *Elizabeth Gilbert,"Your Elusive Creative Genius."* Description: "Elizabeth Gilbert muses on the impossible things we expect from artists and geniuses—and shares the radical idea that, instead of the rare person 'being' a genius, all of us 'have' a genius. It's a funny, personal and surprisingly moving talk."

- *Sugata Mitra, "Build a School in the Cloud."* Description: "Educational researcher Sugata Mitra is the winner of the 2013 TED Prize. His wish: Build a School in the Cloud, where children can explore and learn from one another. Onstage at TED2013, Sugata Mitra makes his bold TED Prize wish: Help me design the School in the Cloud, a learning lab in India, where children can explore and learn from each other—using resources and mentoring from the cloud."

- *Angela Maiers, "You Matter."* Description: "Angela Maiers is an education and technology consultant from Des Moines, Iowa, who shares with us how two words can change a life."

- *Patricia Ryan, "Don't Insist on English!"* Description: "Long-time English teacher Patricia Ryan asks a provocative question: Is the world's focus on English preventing the spread of great ideas in other languages? (For instance: What if Einstein had to pass the TOEFL?) It's a passionate defense of translating and sharing ideas."

- *ShaoLan Hsueh, "Learn to Read Chinese With Ease."* Description: "In just 6 minutes, ShaoLan walks through a simple lesson in recognizing the ideas behind the characters and their meaning—building from a few simple forms to more complex concepts. Call it Chineasy. Watch this over and over with your students to learn dozens of Chinese characters, and get excited about tackling a new intellectual challenge."

- *Anything from TEDxNYED archive.* These talks all explore and share innovations and great ideas in education. Simply type "TEDXNYED" into the YouTube search bar to discover diverse voices on education, sharing powerful ideas in this annual event.

- *TED-Ed*. This more recent initiative of TED is designed to expose "the voices of the world's greatest educators." Pairing exemplary educators with extraordinary animators, TED-Ed curates an ever-expanding library of educational videos. For example, have a look at a lesson from Jackie Jenkins (junior school principal at the United Nations International School) on **Greetings of Peace Around the World**. As you will notice, in the TED-Ed format you are encouraged to "Think," "Dig Deeper," and "Discuss." In the case of this lesson, "Think" includes five multiple-choice and three open-ended questions based on the content presented in the 3-minute video. "Dig Deeper" offers additional resources to explore. For this lesson, it's a link to Jenkins's school and more about the United Nations.

After you've enjoyed lessons from a few TED-Ed videos, you are encouraged to make your own "flipped" classroom lesson. In fact, educators can use any educational video that is on YouTube and create their own lessons, adding context, questions, and suggestions for follow-up. A **video tutorial** on our Companion Site shows how to create your own lesson from a favorite video.

## Use Twitter to Grow in Your Teaching Practice

Lydia Spinelli, the director of the Brick Church School in Manhattan, and an educator for over 30 years, summed up her experience using Twitter for us:

*I was surprised to learn from a colleague that Twitter*
*is an extremely powerful professional development*
*tool. Once I tried it, I realized by following the people I*
*respect in the educational world, I can keep up to date*
*with the latest research and debates.*

To tap into the power of Twitter for professional development, use the tutorial information located earlier in this chapter, and go further to enhance your learning and grow your professional network. When you include the targeted hashtag (indicated by use of the #, pound symbol) in your Tweet, you are sending your note to the community that follows this discussion. We have found those people and accounts that follow these hashtags to generally be a thoughtful, encouraging, continuously learning group of tech-savvy teachers and thought leaders. Table 4.2 has a list of useful educational hashtags to follow. Join the conversation to connect with other teachers.

## Table 4.2  #Hashtags for Education

| Grade Specific | Educational Chats From Other Countries |
|---|---|
| #kinderchat | #auedchat—Australia education |
| #1stchat | #cdned—Canada education |
| #2ndchat | #ClavEd—educational French speakers |
| #3rdchat | #EdChatIE—Edchat Ireland |
| #4thchat | #edsg—Singapore educators |
| #5thchat | #finnedchat—Finnish educators |
| #6thchat | #skolechat—Danish educators |
| | #ukedchat—UK education |
| **Subject Specific** | **General Chats** |
| #mathchat—Math | #edchat |
| #scichat—Science | #edtech |
| #engchat—English | #education |
| #artsed—Art | #globaled |
| #musedchat—Music | #langchat |
| #SSchat—Social Studies | #k12 |
| #esl—English as a second language | #ESDGC—education for sustainability and global citizenship |
| #flteach—Foreign language teachers | #flatclassroom |
| | #homeschool |
| | #socialjusticeED |

## Global Education Professional Development and Training Resources

When you are ready to go deeper, try one or more of these providers of high-quality educational materials, workshops, seminars, webinars, conferences, or experiential learning facilitators:

- **Primary Source** offers a rich variety of professional development programs for K–12 educators. With the aim of connecting teachers to people and cultures around the world, they provide learning opportunities in the content areas of Africa, Asia, Latin America, the Middle East, and the United States. Their core offerings include school-year seminars and intensive summer institutes. For interested and qualified teachers, they lead study tours to different regions of the world, including China, Japan, and Ghana.

- **Asia Society Partnership for Global Learning (PGL)**, in addition to the premier (yet more intimate) annual conference focusing on global education, also hosts the National Chinese Language Conference, webinars throughout the year, on-site trainings for schools and districts, and more.

- **World Savvy** "prepares the next generation of leaders to learn, work and thrive as responsible global citizens in the 21st century." In this context, World Savvy offers a menu of workshops (2-hour) and institutes (half-day, full-day, and 2-day) focusing on a range of global issues and methods for integrating world affairs into classroom instruction, as well as customized professional development.

- **AFS-USA**, known as a leader in high school education exchange programs, has developed an excellent **Educator's Portal** with resources for building global competency and bringing the world to your classroom.

- **IREX Teachers for a Global Classroom** is an excellent program offering professional development and scholarships for travel to far-flung countries is for middle and high school teachers, but we like it so much we wanted to list the program. Encourage your colleagues in upper grades to apply and have them come back to share their experience with you, your students, and colleagues.

- **World Leadership School** helps K–12 schools "make the shift towards 21st century approaches to teaching and learning" through services such as consulting, professional development, teacher coaching, curriculum design, and support for schools that want to build sister school relationships in Asia, the Middle East, Africa, and Latin America.

- **The International Society for Technology in Education (ISTE)** might be considered the 10,000-pound gorilla of education technology. Attend its annual conference with thousands of other educators and technology professionals and see the latest products and applications in connectivity, learn from best practices in tech integration, and attend presentations by leaders in the field. Tap into special interest groups such as the **Global Education Conference ISTE Summit** during ISTE to build your professional learning network.

- The **Building Learning Communities Summer Conference** is a professional development institute by November Learning, which brings together K–12 education thought leaders and always includes a global education component.

- **Curriculum 21** offers a suite of professional development services, from on-site PD to webinars and strategic planning services, as well as its annual training conference. Its work aims to transform curriculum and school designs to match the needs of 21st century learners, particularly focused around curriculum mapping for 21st century skills.

- **Powerful Learning Practice** conducts "professional learning for connected educators" through regular online courses, webinars, publishing original material, active social media engagement, and more resources.

- The **Global Education Benchmark Group (GEBG)** annual conference comprised primarily members of the GEBG from independent schools, but the conference and the group's learning can serve as valuable professional development for anyone interested in this field of work.

- **ASCD** is a leading "membership organization that develops programs, products, and services essential to the way educators learn, teach, and lead." Its professional development around 21st century skills include a large collection of resources on the website, conferences, and in-person trainings led by top practitioners in the field.

- **NAFSA: Association of International Educators** represents a vast network, particularly at the higher education level. Its work includes studies and initiatives on **internationalizing**

**curriculum**, supporting international students and scholars, policy advocacy for global education at many levels, and large annual national and regional conferences.

- The **Comparative and International Education Society (CIES)**. is a scholarly association dedicated to increasing the understanding of educational issues, trends, and policies through comparative, cross-cultural, and international perspectives. CIES organizes major national and regional conferences and events showcasing research in the field.

- **International Council on Education for Teaching (ICET)** hosts a World Assembly of educators from all over the world, as well as other trainings and an online community for educators.

- **International Society for Teacher Education**, like ICET above, serves members from around the world, holds an annual seminar, and focuses on scholarly research, as well as networking among members.

- **Teaching Tolerance**, a project of the Southern Poverty Law Center, offers online professional development tools with such topics as Reflective Teaching, Classroom Strategies, School Climate, and Teaching Diverse Students.

- **Facing the Future** offers a variety of professional development options for individuals, districts, and state departments of education, all of which include standards-based global issues and sustainability curriculum resources.

- The **Tanenbaum Center for Interreligious Understanding** offers a 6-day intensive course on Cultivating Global Citizenship, as well as shorter workshops around building inclusivity in various settings and circumstances.

## University-Affiliated Professional Development Focused on Global Ed

Students enrolling in schools of education, particularly at the graduate level, can take advantage of a growing quantity and quality of university programs with concentration in global competency and bringing the world to the classroom. For those not enrolled in a degree program, consider the following university programs that offer professional development with a shorter-term, lower-cost commitment.

To find a nearby university-affiliated PD program for global education, start with the network of **National Resource Centers**. A large number of centers (125) have been established at colleges and universities throughout the United States with funding from the U.S. Department of Education under Title VI, "to establish, strengthen, and operate language and area or international studies centers that will be national resources for teaching any modern foreign language." This program was established in 1965, thanks in part to the launch of Sputnik in 1957, when the federal government acknowledged the need to build capacity in critical languages and knowledge of countries and cultures and has been run continuously ever since. Each program will have its own flavor and focus, according to the strengths and interests of the university and departments in which it is housed. According to its website, the National Resource Centers support

- teaching of any modern foreign language;
- instruction in fields needed to provide full understanding of areas, regions, or countries;
- research and training in international studies;
- work in the language aspects of professional and other fields of study; and
- instruction and research on issues in world affairs.[4]

One excellent online resource developed under the Title VI program is **Outreach World**, containing contact information for the entire national network as well as educational materials relevant to all global regions, grade levels, themes, and disciplines.

- The **University of Oregon, Global & Online Education, through the Office of the Associate Dean for Global and Online Education**, with leadership from Professor Yong Zhao, has taken its commitment to the development of educators for the 21st century to a whole new level. They've launched their Oba learning platform for ongoing distance learning, cloud-based collaboration, and a wide suite of services "built by global educators, for global learners."

- **Harvard University's Think Tank on Global Education** runs a 2-day, annual event assembling a range of global education leaders, researchers, and practitioners.

- The Institute of Design at Stanford University, known as the d.school, carries a suite of programs **to teach educators design thinking**. At the root of this thinking is the cultivation of empathy, a critical virtue of global citizenship. A **multimodule, free virtual design thinking for educators course** is available through Edutopia, in collaboration with Stanford's d.school and IDEO, as well as the **Design Thinking for Educators Toolkit** and the possibility of taking in-person courses in design for educators on Stanford's campus.

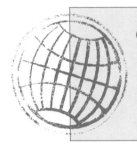

## Grants for Educators

Looking to infuse some fresh cash into your programs, professional development, or to fund travel learning? Consult **GrantWrangler**, where grants for teachers can be found organized by grade level, subject area, or deadline.

- The **University of Chicago's Center for International Studies** hosts an annual global education conference, has tailored training, and shares more in its **Educator Resources**.

- The **University of Minnesota's Institute for Global Studies** offers Summer Institutes for educators on a variety of global issues.

- The University of Denver's Center for Teaching International Relations' **International Studies Schools Association** holds an annual conference and offers teachers "professional development opportunities in content areas and methodological approaches related to contemporary themes in international studies" in its national K–12 network.

- The **University of North Carolina at Chapel Hill World View** program offers a wide range of seasonal professional development and resources to keep educators focused on 21st century global education.

- The **Global Competency Program**, a thoughtful, comprehensive, personalized course of study designed for inservice teachers to complete over a period of 18 months, has been created by global education leaders World Savvy; Teachers College, Columbia University; and Asia Society. It was announced in June 2013 for a first enrolling class in Fall 2014.

- Check in with the offerings at **Coursera**, an example of a source for MOOCs, or massive open online courses, which curates courses from over 80 top universities around the world, including teacher PD with a global dimension.

## For More, Follow Global Teacher Education

Global education programs and resources represent a fast-growing, fluid, and dynamic initiative of universities and professional development organizations across the United States and worldwide. Follow information on the website **Global Teacher Education**, curated by a team of professionals committed to global education, for updates on programs and research.

## Travel Opportunities for Educators at Reduced or Zero Cost

Recognizing how important it is for teachers to actually travel abroad to teach about the world, a number of organizations offer full or partial scholarships for educators' travel. Here are some of these organizations, which you can access on the Companion Site:

- Various programs through the **U.S. Department of State Bureau of Educational and Cultural Affairs**
- **The Fund for Teachers**
- **The Earthwatch Institute Educator Opportunities**
- **American Councils for International Education**
- **Study Abroad, Volunteer, Intern, Teach, and Jobs Abroad**
- **Toyota International Teacher Program**
- **Turkish Cultural Foundation**
- **Transatlantic Outreach Program to Germany**
- **Korea Society**
- **Qatar Foundation International**
- **East-West Center**
- **U.S. Center for Citizen Diplomacy**
- **Fulbright Exchange Program**

- **IREX Education Projects**

- **National Endowment for the Humanities Summer Programs**

- **Omprakash Volunteer Abroad Grants**

- **Global Exploration for Educators Organization**

- **EF Educational Tours**

Note that these programs may change from year to year, often carry strict deadlines for applications, and may require a full year of advance planning to line up participants, funding, and professional development around the trips. Check back frequently with the programs.

## Additional Reading for Global Education Professional Development

- Binaya Subedi, B. (Ed.). (2009). *Critical global perspectives: Rethinking knowledge about global societies.* Charlotte, NC: Information Age.

- Cassidy, K. (2013). *Connected from the start: Global learning in the primary grades* [E-book]. Virginia Beach, VA: Powerful Learning Press.

- *Educating for Global Competence: Preparing Our Youth to Engage the World* (PDF) is a text based on interdisciplinary instruction research from Harvard University's **Project Zero** and pedagogical work by global education institutions such as the **International Baccalaureate**, the **Asia Society**, **Oxfam**, and **Facing History and Ourselves** (Boix Mansilla and Jackson, Asia Society, 2011).

- Hayes-Jacobs, H. (2010). *Curriculum 21: Essential education for a changing world.* Alexandria, VA: ASCD.

- Hayes-Jacobs, H. (Ed.). (2013). *Mastering global literacy.* Bloomington, IN: Solution Tree Press.

- Hunter, J. (2013). *World peace and other 4th grade achievements.* New York, NY: Houghton Mifflin Harcourt.

- Lindsay, J., & Davis, V. (2013). *Flattening classrooms, engaging minds: Move to global collaboration one step at a time.* Upper Saddle River, NJ: Pearson.

- Kist, W. (2012). *The global school: Connecting classrooms and students around the world.* Bloomington, IN: Solution Tree Press.

- Peters, L. (2009). *Global education: Using technology to bring the world to your students.* Washington, DC: ISTE.

- ***Ready for the World: Preparing Elementary Students for the Global Age***, a publication of the Asia Society (2010) "is a guidebook that offers strategies and resources for elementary schools on how to integrate international knowledge, skills, and experiences into their programs, and help our next generation become globally competent."

Photographic Books to Begin Opening Up the World:

- Kindersley, A., Kindersley, B., & UNICEF (1995). *Children just like me: A unique celebration of children around the world.* New York, NY: DK Children.

- Menzel, P., Mann, C. C., & Kennedy, P. (1995). *Material world: A global family portrait.* San Francisco, CA: Sierra Club Books.

- Menzel, P., & D'Aluisio, F. (2007). *Hungry planet: What the world eats.* New York, NY: Material World.

The list below includes titles offering important intellectual underpinnings for global education, or the bigger-picture view:

- Darling-Hammond, L. (2010). *The flat world and education: How America's commitment to equity will determine our future.* New York, NY: Teachers College Press.

- Friedman, T. (2005). *The world is flat.* New York, NY: Farrar, Straus and Giroux.

- Stewart, V. (2012). *A world-class education: Learning from international models of excellence and innovation.* Alexandria, VA: ASCD.

- Tavangar, H. S. (2009). *Growing up global: Raising children to be at home in the world.* New York, NY: Ballantine Books/Random House.

- Wagner, T. (2008). *The global achievement gap: Why even our best schools don't teach the new survival skills our children need—and what we can do about it.* New York, NY: Basic Books.

- Wagner, T. (2012). *Creating innovators: The making of young people who will change the world.* New York, NY: Scribner.

- Zhao, Y. (2009). *Catching up or leading the way: American education in the age of globalization.* Alexandria, VA: ASCD.

- Zhao, Y. (2012). *World class learners: Educating creative and entrepreneurial students.* Thousand Oaks, CA: Corwin.

# Concluding Reflection

This chapter centered on the use of technology, but we started it by talking about relationships, touching hearts, and teaching empathy—components of what we consider Global Education 2.0, where the hardware needs to be made servant to the "heart-ware," and not vice versa. This implies a process that is interactive (learning is collaborative and relationship driven), iterative (not a one-time do-and-through, open to change, and next generation technologies), dynamic ("failures" signal a lesson, not an end, and problems can be solved through multiple approaches), and human centered (children's learning and well-being are at the beginning, middle, and end of any consideration about technology). Ultimately, keeping this balance in mind can pave the way for meaningful connections forged by lifelong learners, and such a lofty goal can seem more attainable.

The young learners you'll be influencing with the tools in this book stand firmly in the "digital native" category. For them, going back to unplugged, screen-free learning does not appear to be a feasible option (though knowing *how* to do that also serves as a great asset), nor does learning that focuses only on the country in which they reside—in a sense making them "global natives," too. Whether you find these realities scary or exciting, such a cultural shift will inevitably impact the learning process, particularly for K–6 learners, who still have much formal education to go.

Upon reflection on so many tools for connecting classrooms with the wider world and making new friends in faraway places, what is one thing you hope to try out right away? Can you collaborate with a nearby colleague to support each other in the effort? What about building a borderless PLN to deepen your own learning? As you keep in mind tech tools to try, consider how qualities like empathy, flexibility, compassion, respect, patience, and gratitude (virtues of global citizens) can be integrated into the conversation—among educators and for your students—as well as how both the hard tools (tech) and soft ones (human virtues) can work together to enhance test scores and academic performance, alongside social cohesion and a sense of purpose.

## NOTES

1  "Before" guidelines adapted from our own experience and a presentation by W. J. Egnatoff, PhD, Faculty of Education, Queen's University at Kingston (2010). *Bi-national learning and the Internet: Grassroots experiments in global education.* Presented at Canadian Institute for Distance Education Research.

2  Cassidy, K. (2013). *Connected from the start: Global learning in the primary grades* (pp. 24–25). [E-book]. Virginia Beach, VA: Powerful Learning Practice.

3  Moore, D. C. (2013, March 13). *Bringing the world to school: Integrating news and media literacy in elementary classrooms (JMLE 5:1).* Philadelphia, PA: Temple University, Center for Media and Information Literacy. Retrieved from http://namle.net/2013/03/06/bringing-the-world-to-school-integrating-news-and-media-literacy-in-elementary-classrooms

4  From http://www.nrcweb.org/about.aspx. Language also found at http://www2.ed.gov/programs/iegpsnrc/index.html

# Charitable Giving and Service

## Ready, Set, Make a Difference!

Over 100 million children worldwide who should be in school do not attend primary school, with more girls than boys missing out. Of the kids who are in school, 66 million primary school-age children attend classes hungry across the developing world, with 23 million in Africa alone. Overall, 870 million people in the world do not have enough to eat. This number has fallen by 130 million since 1990, but progress slowed after 2008. Even in the United States, the number of households living on less than $2 per person per day, considered "extreme poverty" for even the poorest countries, more than doubled between 1996 and 2011, from 636,000 to 1.46 million. The number of children in extremely poor U.S. households also doubled, from 1.4 million to 2.8 million. Worldwide, over a billion people live on less than $2 per day.

As our students learn more about kids around the world, these sorts of statistics can get personal: With greater familiarity about diverse settings, stories, and ways of life—especially if they start communicating with real people in new places—their sense of fairness emerges. With encouragement and guidance, greater awareness and connection prompts kids to want to do something about immediate crises, like natural disasters and the lack of books, or more systemic challenges, like access to education, water, and nutrition. You don't have to tell your students the statistics we share above, but as facts about life on Earth come to light, kids will gain a sense of stark needs, particularly of other children living in different circumstances.

Our intention in this chapter is to provide many tools to help you take service-oriented action. This doesn't stem from a need to be busier; rather, it's an outgrowth of a natural inclination for empathy and compassion that global learning instills. To reach this point of effective service and action, we've broken down this chapter into the following sections:

- Section 1: Thinking About Service-Learning

- Section 2: Engaging in Service: Who, What, Where, Why, and How

- Section 3: Fundraising With a Purpose: Resource Building That's a Win-Win-Win

- Section 4: Amazing! Examples Highlighting What It Looks Like When Kids Make a Difference Globally

- Section 5: 12 Take-Aways From Awesome Kids Changing the World for the Better

# Section 1: Thinking About Service-Learning

One middle-school teacher in Canada described his students' reactions the first day at school after the tsunami in 2004. They had formed a relationship on Skype with a school in Indonesia, which fortunately was not affected by the disaster. But when they realized their friends on the other side of the world had relatives and friends in affected areas, their first question was "What are we going to do to help them?" This empathetic reaction comes naturally when people in affected places far away become real—become friends—to our kids.

By getting involved in a specific cause, children take away profound lessons as they become more aware of the global community. Kids may assume that everyone has access to the same resources and activities that we do. The first time we talked with our kids about the scarcity of water in some places on Earth and the need to carry back heavy containers of fresh water from a well, our young children innocently asked why the women didn't just fill it up from their faucet. When a child in an ESL (English as a second language) class explained that he went to school only on Tuesdays, the other children were incredulous: "But why only 1 day per week?" He explained that the teacher only came to his village on Tuesdays because she had to visit other classrooms the other days. An understanding as basic as the suburban child's grasping that not everyone has a driveway or a garage connected to their home can launch into a larger conversation around different ways that families—near or far—may conduct their daily lives. Expanding perspectives can take so many forms.

When teachers and parents model an awareness of social injustice around the world, along with a giving spirit, students will follow their lead. They will get the satisfaction that they have made a difference in the world for others and start to learn to delay their own needs in favor of someone else's. Awareness and action become cultivated like an innate muscle—it's there, but it takes exercise and practice to realize it and strengthen it.

The examples and action steps offered throughout this chapter are informed by some of the basic principles guiding service-learning. (To learn more about the characteristics of service-learning, see the resources found at the **National Service-Learning Clearinghouse website**.)

The National Service-Learning Clearinghouse defines service-learning as

> *a teaching and learning strategy that integrates meaningful community service with instruction and reflection to enrich the learning experience, teach civic responsibility, and strengthen communities. Through service-learning, young people—from kindergarteners to college students—use what they learn in the classroom to solve real-life problems. They not only learn the practical applications of their studies, they become actively contributing citizens and community members through the service they perform.*

We believe this definition offers an ideal start for implementing meaningful service activities in schools that are going global.

# Section 2: Engaging in Service: Who, What, Where, Why, and How

The following points can help you answer the basic questions around service and giving opportunities that will impact the lives of children in your community and across the planet.

1. Decide what type of charitable project best fits your objectives, values, preferences, and resource capacity:

   ▸ Will you be raising funds or collecting items to donate?

   ▸ Will the entire school participate or only certain grades, classes, or clubs?

   ▸ Would you like the organization you support to focus on a particular need? For example, collecting eyeglasses or sports equipment, building a well and learning about clean water initiatives, or raising money to fight hunger or to aid victims of a natural disaster.

   ▸ Is it important that causes or geography tie in to existing curricular priorities (e.g., if a grade is studying Mexico, do you want the service activity to take place there?), or will these choices be kept separate?

   ▸ If you are collecting items, will someone coordinate drop-off, storage, shipment, and payment for shipment to the intended recipients? This step often makes the collection of goods prohibitively more difficult than raising funds.

   ▸ How many adult volunteers are committed to the project, and how much time can they invest per week or per month? Make sure that expectations are aligned with human and financial resource capacity. If projects are overly ambitious, this could result in burnout or disappointment and not be repeated in future years. Starting small is often preferred, so schools can continue the project and go from strength to strength.

2. Use a variety of tools to help research which organizations fit your goals:

   ▸ At **Global Giving** you can learn about a variety of projects around the world. The website serves as a clearinghouse for numerous preapproved organizations, both in the United States and around the world. Users can search the database by topic, by region, or by current situations in the news.

   ▸ Inventory your own community. When Michelle Saylor, an assistant superintendent in the Bellefonte Area School District in rural central Pennsylvania, wanted to set up connections with schools and programs around the world in her previous districts, she wasn't sure where to begin, so she wrote to her school's staff to see if they might have some personal connections with anywhere in the world. The response was so positive that outreach started with those contacts and has been maintained over several years. Certain staff, such as the music teachers, gave her the most enthusiastic response, and she ran with their suggestions.

▸ Get inspired. The Internet is full of stories about kids making a difference all over the world. The websites **Kids Are Heroes** and **Global Youth Service Day**, which is a project of **Youth Service America**, offer hundreds of examples of real kids making a real difference in so many ways, as well as practical guidelines. **DoSomething.org** is geared for teens but also offers adults working with kids many "how-tos," "action tips," and strategies for making a difference near or far. We hope the examples included in the section below might also offer inspiration for your own activities!

▸ Evaluate the charities. **Guide Star** offers users financial information and reviews from people familiar with the agency; **Charity Navigator** offers impartial evaluations on thousands of charitable organizations. What are their annual goals and results? How efficiently do they use their funds? What is the impact the organization has had?

▸ Be wary of organizations that do not disclose financial information or do not answer your questions. Even if they have nothing to hide, they might simply be overstretched. Transparency is a powerful tool.

▸ Follow Facebook and Twitter accounts of charities and organizations you admire to stay on top of their regular developments and assess if that's who you'd like to align your school's service with.

▸ For more ideas on charitable organizations, see the many recommendations in *Growing Up Global*'s Chapter 9 on Service and Giving as well as its Appendix on Action Steps.

3. Integrate learning into the service.

▸ When you have chosen your charity, work with the teaching staff to integrate lessons into the curriculum or in school activities. We have often seen a fundraising pamphlet get sent home, the parents might write a check and return it, and the children are not involved in any of the steps. Thus, kids will completely miss out on the learning or impactful lessons that are inherently part of the initiative.

▶ When the school incorporates presentations and hands-on learning and involves the students in raising the money, the kids begin to grasp the meaning of the project. For example, Becky's kindergarteners were raising money for a women's and children's shelter. The teacher asked the kids to each write down three chores they would do at home to earn money for the fundraiser. The parents needed to "sponsor" the chores in the name of the charity, and the kids had to "work" for their donation. This simple but meaningful way of involving the kids meant that the money passed through their hands, and as philanthropists, they became a part of the giving.

▶ Check with the organization for lesson plans it may have developed to accompany the project. In addition, some organizations provide speakers or at least materials to support a proper presentation. Involve the children in learning about the location, the issues, and the background information so they will be more intrinsically motivated to participate. Students who broaden their cultural horizons and understand that they are part of the solution will grow into more compassionate adults. By encouraging our students to work as a team, we help them begin to see how they fit into the larger global picture and learn many life skills along the way. This encompasses many key attributes of 21st century learning.

▶ For a comprehensive guide to planning and thinking about service-learning, see *The Complete Guide to Service Learning* by Catherine Berger Kaye, a trusted international authority on this topic.

4. Build in reflection and celebration.

▶ According to the *K–12 Service-Learning Project Planning Toolkit*, the final components of a typical service-learning project include Reflection and Demonstration/ Celebration. These steps may be overlooked or avoided due to time constraints or unfamiliarity with the process, but they can mean the difference between making lifelong impact or getting forgotten by busy children and families.

Reflection involves "activities that help students understand the service-learning experience and to think about its meaning and connection to them, their society, and what they have learned in school." Demonstration/Celebration entails "students, community participants and others publicly shar[ing] what they have learned, celebrat[ing] the results of the service project, and look[ing] ahead to the future."[1]

# Section 3: Fundraising With a Purpose: Resource Building That's a Win-Win-Win

When planning for the year, rethink your traditional approach to fundraising. Most schools must try multiple sources of fundraising, from box tops and store receipt programs to wrapping paper, pizza dough, and school events to cover expenses and activities. Use school fundraising as a win-win-win when your school or classroom tries going global: Turn an annual necessity into an unforgettable connection with bigger impact. If done in the context of larger learning goals, then the benefit multiplies. Here are a few outlets worth investigating. They sell high-quality items which can benefit your school while educating on an important cause *and* giving back to the countries of origin. These can offer tangible ways to begin creating real connections:

- *Greenraising.* Started by elementary school parents who wanted to make a difference through their fundraisers, this extensive fundraising catalog is eco-friendly and globally conscious, with items like recycled wrapping paper, reusable lunch containers, and more. It's a joy to browse through.

- *Global Goods Partners.* Buy handmade, fair-trade jewelry, accessories, and other gifts; support women's enterprises around the world; and earn a percentage back for your own cause. What's not to love?

- *Equal Exchange.* A pioneer in fair-trade gourmet foods, this worker-owned cooperative organization trades directly with small farmer cooperatives worldwide. Nonfood items partner with Ten Thousand Villages, and the entire organizing, shopping, and browsing experience offers a fascinating lesson in itself.

- *Grounds for Change.* This organization offers fair-trade coffee and a coffee-of-the-month club for fundraising.

- *Heifer International.* This organization offers a suite of simple, thoughtful service-learning and fundraising programs through their website.

- *Hand in Hand, Sustainable Suds.* For every bar of soap purchased, this start-up will donate a bar to save a child's life. Its motto is "Buy a bar, give a bar." It saves 50 square feet of rainforest for every bar purchased—this is a powerful lesson in science, math, sustainability, and social studies in and of itself. Additionally, to help alleviate poverty in the United States and the developing world, the organization makes a donation to fund microcredit loans. This reflects a growing trend in socially responsible business, starting small, but with a goal to make a difference. We like efforts like this not only for the example of giving back and making impact but also for the entrepreneurial lessons children can take away by getting involved in selling or purchasing high-quality items like these.

## Section 4: Amazing! Examples Highlighting What It Looks Like When Kids Make a Difference Globally

*"Unless someone like you cares a whole awful lot, nothing is going to get better. It's not."*

—From *The Lorax,* by Dr. Seuss

Use the links in previous sections for researching the names of many good organizations you can support. In this section, we offer 20+ examples of more organizations, but this time they are mentioned in connection with kids making a difference and show what their involvement has looked like. These mini "case studies" can highlight some of the key elements in starting or sustaining globally engaging service and philanthropy, and we hope they spur your imagination to do your own outreach, from your classroom, club, home, or as an entire school.

# Global Grade 3 and Pennies for Peru

*This Global Project, which began as a deeper inquiry into our Social Studies curriculum, has become one of the most POWERFUL and engaging learning experiences I have been lucky enough to be a part of in 25 years of teaching. Flattening the walls of the classroom and sharing our journey with the world has touched each one of us in ways never imagined. I have been forever changed by this magical learning journey. (Laurie Renton, third-grade teacher)*

In 2010, a videoconference call with a teacher on leave and travelling through Peru with his family sparked a groundbreaking initiative for Calgary, Canada, third graders. Based on what they learned from the call, they wanted to make a difference in the lives of children in the village of Q'enqo, Peru. Initially they intended to raise money for sports equipment for the Q'enqo school but soon discovered far greater needs. The people of Q'enqo and the organizations that supported them requested the support be channeled toward a school library. Realizing they shouldn't try this on their own, the **Global Grade 3** partnered with the charitable organization **Mosqoy** and the nongovernmental **Q'ente Textile Revitalization Society**. In the project's second year, they began blogging their observations and experiences, significantly ratcheting up their learning experience and personal involvement.

In the 2 years since the start of the project, a **very old and dilapidated building was completely transformed and repaired** to become the community library, outfitted with furniture and books, with close to $5,000 raised. Evidence of the kids' dedication came in the form of personal initiatives, like kids donating their allowance money, running lemonade stands on weekends, and even requesting that donations to Q'enqo be made rather than bringing gifts for a few birthdays. The third graders got the entire school of 700 students involved by initiating spirit days, sharing progress on morning announcements, and hosting a four kilometer Pennies for Peru fundraising walk.

As much as the experience demonstrated how students can make a difference around the world, they also grew academically. For example, customs and cultures introduced through textbooks came alive. They got lessons in economics, like how much further the money goes in Peru than in Canada and how resourceful people can be when lacking conveniences we take for granted in North America, from brooms to paint brushes. In math, they learned how to count donations well beyond their grade level, converted currencies, tracked hits on their blog's revolver map each day, and calculated mentally how many web hits occurred (e.g., "If we had 3,948 on the revolver map yesterday, and we are at 4,274 today . . . how many hits were there?").

Writing for a global audience on the blog and replying to comments made students more aware of the need for crafting better sentences, using effective vocabulary, collaborating more successfully, and conveying interesting content to "reel in" readers. Meaningful lessons about digital citizenship and online safety taught within the security of a classroom took place when confronting the challenges of an active website (like rude or "spam" commenters).

We are impressed that the blog isn't just about victories but also chronicles the surprises, setbacks, and challenges along the way, particularly regarding sustainability for "recipients" whose culture and living conditions differ drastically from that of the donors. The challenges create a more realistic—and meaningful—experience for the children. By the end of the school year, children express how much they have been affected by the entire experience, from walking in the heat for four kilometers like the children in the village (except that they have comfortable shoes and aren't on harsh, mountainous terrain, which they acknowledge and now can empathize with), to trying to raise funds, to having a clearer picture about life in the Andes, communicating with people around the world through their blog, and feeling like their lives have been changed forever by this year-long experience.

It's crucial to mention that this would not be possible without a dedicated teacher, Laurie Renton (and many supportive staff, parents, and friends—she is quick to point out), who was moved to make a difference and bring her students along on a journey of global citizenship and change making. Her example also shows that small steps, taken on a regular basis, conscientiously, as opposed to a herculean, uphill burden, sustains the effort. It also takes great commitment, extra research for lessons, willingness to learn new technologies, and a very open mind.

# Project-Based Learning and Driving Questions

When setting out to make a difference through involvement in a global project, your class may be engaged in deeper learning, focused action, and authentic inquiry. If the project drives the core of learning as evidenced by several examples in this section, such as Pennies for Peru and Ms. Goggin's Fifth-Grade Minimum Wage Project (highlighted in the Math section of Chapter 3), this is considered project based learning (PBL).

To better understand PBL, we looked to the Buck Institute for Education, which has created a suite of products and services for advancing 21st century teaching and learning, with PBL at the core. Its publication *Project Based Learning in the Elementary Grades* explains the Institute's approach:

> In Project Based Learning, students are pulled through the curriculum by a meaningful question to explore, an engaging real-world problem to solve, or a challenge to design or create something. Before they can accomplish this, students need to inquire into the topic by asking questions and developing their own answers. To demonstrate what they learn, students create high-quality products and present their work to other people. Students often do project work collaboratively in small teams, guided by the teacher.

This approach is distinct from learning a concept then adding on a project to demonstrate the learning, which the Buck Institute describes as the "**dessert**," not the core PBL.

To help focus the project work, ask "driving questions." These are usually open-ended questions that illuminate the purpose of the project in a succinct question, invite multiple answers, and help guide roles of both teachers and students. To keep the driving questions in mind, you can post them in a prominent location in the classroom, on a class blog, or at the top of relevant worksheets. See this checklist of **PBL Essential Elements**.

## Water.org and a Pinterest Board

There are so many ways that kids can make a difference to help get clean water to other children around the world. Water.org shared with us their terrific **Students in Action Pinterest board**. We learned about bake sales that earned double their goal since customers paid extra when they learned that sales were intended to help others in need; art by kids posted on Etsy that would benefit water causes; and a little girl named Izzy, who hopes to change the world with her video and blog series by telling others about the water crisis. When you complete a project, take a photo, and share it with the world! You can also find out about some of the fundraisers started by kids through **Give .Water.org**, and learn and share information from the organization's **free curriculum**.

## Put Some Meaning Into an Empty Water Bottle

According to a United Nations Children's Fund (UNICEF)/World Health Organization (WHO) **report**, every 21 seconds a child dies from a water-related disease, but these diseases, like diarrhea, are so easily preventable. To make a difference on this issue, have the children collect change in empty water bottles to symbolize where their money will go.

## Healthy Kids for a Healthy World: Rachel's Walk for Water

We learned about Rachel from our friends at **Citizen Effect**.[2] Rachel had seen the impact one person can make when her brother initiated a Badminton Challenge while he was in fourth grade and she was in first. Their school principal and P.E. teacher gave permission for kids to pay $1 to play badminton before school once a week, where all proceeds went to a local homeless shelter. So in second grade when Rachel learned the profound impact the lack of access to clean water had on people's lives in Sanganguna village in India, she knew she had to do something. Her family got right behind her, hoping to start something that would involve everyone at her public school for more than a day as well as offer a healthy activity for the kids.

After several meetings with her principal, they came up with a Walk for Water (W4W). They partnered with Citizen Effect, which connected with Sports Authority stores to donate 500 pedometers. Then Rachel's mom, representatives from Citizen Effect, and Rachel herself gave presentations at school during lunchtime to explain (1) the need for clean water for kids in India; (2) the importance of keeping fit in their own lives, and how the pedometers could help; and (3) how they could get sponsored by family and friends—one penny per step they took on W4W Day to help build wells in India. The kids at school got excited!

A W4W Day was held on a Saturday at the school fields, with the PTA, principal, and many teachers supporting the effort, along with many children and parents and lots of simultaneous activities. For example, one mom brought gallons of water for the kids to carry across the field to recreate the experience of so many of the world's children walking from a faraway well to assist their families, and games were set up around the grass.

Those pennies-per-step added up to so much more than anyone had expected. In one year, Rachel's Walk for Water project raised $2,700 to build a well in India. She went over her goal, so she contributed $1,000 to help fund a foster home in South Africa. As of this writing, she's 10 years old and working on a new project, which she calls Baskets for Beds, to help provide beds for homeless shelters in Detroit. In this project, kids will play basketball on their grade's team and get sponsors for their games played.

All these projects take considerable effort and have benefited tremendously from supportive P.E. teachers, the principal, and parents, as well as partnership with an organization that can help provide know-how, facts about needs, and ideas for generating funds and community support. They also show how combining awareness with activities they love, like various sports and games, can make giving more fun and more effective—building that compassion muscle!

## A Class Wiki Expands Learning and Brings Technology to School Children in Haiti

Earlier in this book, under the Science lessons section of Chapter 3, we shared the example of Jeff Remington's students near Hershey, Pennsylvania, teaching students in Haiti about electrical circuits through a wiki. We mention the project again here, since we see it as much about giving as it is about learning. This is not a wealthy, well-traveled community, yet through fundraising at school where kids found creative ways to raise funds, including one fourth-grade boy's birthday party gifts reaching $200 that would be donated to Haiti, partnership with a local foundation, and expansion to the **GlobalGiving platform**, Mr. Remington's class initiative has collected over $25,000 (with a total goal of $75,000). Funds have gone toward purchasing Classmate PC laptops, ancillary computer support items, and ongoing training for the Haitian students. These investments "provide Haitian students with immersion in technology, academic enrichment, and the development of collaborative problem solving skills crucial to the future success of post earthquake Haiti."

Mr. Remington summed up their experience:

> *We have been able to touch lives in ways we had not thought possible. The Palmyra students have developed technological and project management skills on a level that could not be attained in a traditional classroom. In addition, the Palmyra students have participated in numerous humanitarian outreach projects that directly benefitted their peers in Haiti with an unparalleled personal connection. The Palmyra students learned about Haitian culture and languages through Skype videoconferencing and video wiki created pages highlighting Haitian traditions such as Carnival.*

## Molly Otieno and a Flipcam

The World Food Program gave a compact video camera to a fifth-grade girl from Kibera, the largest slum in Nairobi, Kenya, to document her daily life and conditions, her friends, and family. Watch the **videos of Molly's life** and have a discussion with your kids on a range of topics, such as the following:

- Find Kenya on a map or globe. Then find Nairobi, Molly's home city.

- What did you notice about life and conditions in the area where Molly lives?

- How would you describe Molly's school?

- In spite of few possessions, how was her attitude?

- How do you think hunger impacts learning?

- What do you think is possible and worthwhile to do for Molly or other kids facing a shortage of good nutrition?

On World Food Day in October 2012, the depiction of Molly's life through her camera's lens resulted in over 50,000 donations in honor of Molly and her community. Interact on Twitter by using the hashtag #mollysworld or have your students send video messages about their own lives on behalf of food for all, whether it's sent to Molly and the

World Food Program or to your own community. Compare similarities and differences with the lives of children around the world and record the ways you, your class, or organization will make your mark. (Or make a video of your group dancing to a favorite Michael Jackson song. As you'll see in videos of kids in Kibera and in Italy, everyone seems to like Michael Jackson, and that shared interest can serve as a starting point for connecting with kids in very different places.)

When Homa shared Molly's World with a group of eager fourth graders, they seemed mesmerized by the entire process—seeing Molly's life, seeing the reaction of children in Italy, seeing how food donations can profoundly impact the educational prospects of the children in Kibera and similar communities, and even learning about life in a modern slum, in a community so different from their own. They were eager to raise their own funds for the World Food Program and make their own video to send to Molly and other children involved in this project. Share a few of the videos with your class or a group of your children's friends, let it sink in, ask some driving questions, and see what their reactions and ideas for action may be.

See the **World Food Program site** for lesson plans and various activities compiled around raising awareness of hunger challenges globally.

## An Elementary School's Race Against Hunger

With support from international hunger relief organization **Action Against Hunger**, students, faculty, and administration from Chicago's Belmont-Cragin Elementary School learned about hunger around the world then partnered with their local high school and middle school for a Race Against Hunger—but it was the younger kids who initiated the project and took the lead.

Students sought pledges for the laps they ran around the high school track and proudly shouted out the amounts they had raised—$3, $4—as they completed each lap. As the **Service-Learning Blog covering Chicago Public Schools** noted, "It was clear that the amounts were not important; the fact that students brought so much enthusiasm and energy to address the problem of world-wide hunger was important."

The Action Against Hunger model offers direct support to schools and organizations taking on the challenge of global hunger and encourages anyone to make a difference.

In one year, over 17,000 students at 70 schools across the country tried fun runs, bake sales, dance competitions, talent shows, and penny drives in the **Race Against Hunger** campaign. They learned how every amount makes a difference:

- $5 purchases a lemon, banana, mango, or orange tree for a farming family; this helps them eat fresh fruit daily, prevents soil erosion and desertification, and provides much-needed shade.

- $25 helps a farmer buy enough maize, groundnut, or millet seeds for one agricultural season and provides training on how to maintain crops for a healthy harvest.

- $35 provides a 30-day crucial treatment for a severely malnourished child in the Democratic Republic of Congo.

- $50 aids a family in times of emergency with necessities like blankets, cooking pots, and soap.

## KidKnits

**KidKnits** began when 9-year-old Ellie knit a hat out of yarn made by women in Rwanda and realized "you're never too young to change a life on the other side of the world." Working with her parents, a message of global citizenship and activism has already reached thousands of children who want to make a difference through the tangible act of knitting a hat.

You can purchase a kit with yarn that is hand-spun by women in Rwanda or Chile, helping to lift their families out of poverty. Along with the yarn purchase, students can benefit from the KidKnits curriculum prepared by Ellie's parents, which integrates reflection and action into 10 flexible lesson plans on creative problem solving, mathematics, world cultures, narrative play acting, and reflective journal writing. Students across the country that have participated in knitting with KidKnits have gone on to give their knit hats as gifts to loved ones, to local shelters, and to hospital patients, so the gift gives back on both sides of the process—at the stage of purchasing the yarn as well as after making the caps.

Homa tested out KidKnits with her fourth-grade daughter and nine of her friends. The kits were even better than expected. They came with two round looms in a colorful handmade (reusable) bag made by women in Liberia, natural wool yarn made in Rwanda, simple instructions, and keepsake tags from recycled aluminum collected in Nairobi's Kibera slum (the home of Molly in the previous example from the World Food Program, which the fourth graders also had learned about), with a book-mark-sized card on one side that read "One ball of yarn. One woman. One day's salary. One way to change the world." Then below that is a photo and name and age of the woman who spun the yarn and a bit of her life story. On the reverse side of the card, our children wrote their information and story to share with the hat's recipient. The knitting was simple to learn and baby hats (donated to a local clinic) were relatively quick to make. We enjoyed the simplicity and tangible benefit of this project, which helped us feel a real connection with the women who worked hard to provide various parts of the kits and with Ellie and her family that took the initiative to build an organization that made giving and making easier for us.

## Flag Pins to Help Victims of Natural Disasters

After a lesson on Dr. Martin Luther King Jr.'s dream for a better world, the fourth graders in Amber McCabe's class at Brecknock Elementary School outside Lancaster, Pennsylvania, decided they needed to do something beyond their rural community. They had heard about the ravaging earthquake in Haiti and tsunamis in Japan and wanted to help children in those two countries. Following research in class, they decided to create and sell flag pins made of a safety pin with colored beads depicting the Japanese and Haitian flags.

According to their principal, Lyn Hilt:

> The class discussed a goal for fundraising and decided $50 or so would be a reasonable goal to set, and, well . . . $700+ later, students' pin sales resulted in a sizable donation for the relief efforts. This was totally a student-run project. They designed everything, created the pins, advertised, sold them, and managed the project. It was so wonderful to see! Their teacher supported them every step of the way, and they were so proud to contribute to the cause.

They chose to channel their funds to **Save the Children**, which provides development aid and disaster assistance to children around the world, supplying food, medical care, education, and help to rebuild communities.

## Girl Scouts World Thinking Day Participants Launch a Bigger Project

When Girl Scout Troop #4015 in Pacific Palisades, California, represented India at **World Thinking Day**, an annual event held by Scout councils all over the world meant to help girls realize they are a part of a global sisterhood, their connection to India became much bigger than a day's worth of activities. Once they started brainstorming about ways to give back, using the **GlobalGiving** website to learn about needs and projects, they decided to aim for **donating bikes to girls in India**. Every girl in the troop got engaged and excited about this. For their annual Girl Scout Cookie sales, the Troop of 10 fourth graders decided to give back 50% of their cookie profits in order to buy bikes for girls in India. This resulted in 10 bikes for 10 girls from 10 girls. As their troop leader reported, "It's been wonderful to watch the girls really go for this project. We are really proud of them and they are proud of themselves!"

## Deliver a Message to a World Leader

When Heidi Hattenbach first heard that 30,000 children die every day from hunger, she recounted, "It hit me so deeply. I cried. It just didn't make sense, so I decided to do something about it."

This was about 30 years ago, and Heidi joined an organization called Youth Ending Hunger (YEH), mobilizing other young people to speak out against hunger and find creative ways to help stop it. At the time, there was a terrible war and famine in Ethiopia. The governments of the United States and the Soviet Union (which was an amalgam of states stretching from Central Europe to Central Asia, with its capital in Moscow) were sending weapons to the war zone. The people at YEH were encouraging citizens all over the world to write letters to the presidents of different countries demanding the leaders of the world take responsibility for the children who were dying. Because of Heidi and many other young activists, the organization collected 65,000 letters from people in Europe, Africa, the United States, and Canada. Some of the messages in the letters were conveyed in pictures by children too young to even write. YEH organized a delegation to deliver all the letters to Soviet President Mikhail Gorbachev in Moscow. One person from each country in which letters were written was chosen to go. Heidi was among them. Her friends and family raised the money to pay her way to go.

Mikhail Gorbachev was out of the country the day Heidi and her friends from 12 countries walked into the Kremlin carrying several heavy bags of letters, but Mrs. Gorbachev greeted them with huge hugs and told them of her own hope of ending hunger. She promised to pass on their message and letters to her husband. The delegation was invited to speak about their mission on Russian television, where their words reached over five million people!

Today, letters are written less and less, but they speak powerfully. Write to a world leader, to a member of Congress, or to the head of a corporation to demand justice or change where you believe it is needed. Use statistics and facts to make your case. Such an exercise can show students how loudly numbers speak and how they can drive decision making and emotions. Letters via "snail mail" can make real impact—just imagine young Heidi and peers from around the world with 65,000 letters. Today, electronic letters and petitions also create great impact.

For example, 10-year-old Mia from California petitioned her favorite smoothie chain to stop using nonbiodegradable Styrofoam cups which harm the Earth, animals, and use 57 chemical by-products in their creation. She wrote a **petition on Change.org** and gathered over 130,000 signatures. The company is now committed to phasing out Styrofoam, and she has since joined their youth advisory board.

Likewise, the fourth graders in **Mr. Wells's class in Brookline, Massachusetts**, used Change.org to petition Universal Pictures when the film *The Lorax* was being released. They noted that while the spirit of the book revolved around environmental stewardship, the film's marketing materials did not. Their appeal included concrete suggestions for the website, for activism, and for learning, and after 57,000 signatures were collected, it seemed the big movie studio agreed to the whole campaign! This has been an exciting victory for the students, who didn't just write a petition but "made posters, **wrote a script in the style of Seuss**, then **shot a video**! They've also been reaching out to everyone they know, lighting a fire under this cause, then graphing your signature count to track the progress of their project."

---

## A Writing Prompt: How Will You Change the World?

After reading some of the examples in this chapter, try this writing prompt: "If you were going to make a difference in the world, what would you do and why?" This can help get creative ideas flowing and make initiatives personally significant to students. You can go an extra step to ask, "What steps do you think you'd need to make to have a successful effort?"

Finally, you could consider letting your whole community know what you care about by writing a letter to the editor. Equal Exchange's **curriculum guide** has instructions for writing one effectively on page 23.

## Sleeping in a Box to Raise Awareness on Homelessness

Peter Larson was "sleeping out" in a refrigerator box outside his home from first grade until he graduated from high school, every year, on November 12 to December 31 as a part of the Interfaith Outreach & Community Partners annual housing campaign in Minnesota, where temperatures dropped as low as 10 degrees below zero during his Sleep Out.

On his **charity website**, you'll learn about the critical need for housing among families in his community who are turned away from shelters. Peter says, "It's hard to think about how the kids in those families are getting by and that some of them go to school with me." With determination and a long-range commitment, he's raised over $400,000, providing housing for more than 450 local families.

We were impressed by the fact that Peter stayed committed to this cause for so many years and took such a tangible action. Many parents of elementary school-aged kids wouldn't be comfortable allowing their child to sleep outside in frigid conditions against the elements, but clearly he stayed safe with parents and community members watching over him. By engaging in a consistent, meaningful, difficult activity year after year, a strong sense of social commitment has been instilled in Peter, which will stay with him well beyond his teen years, and he's surely inspired many more around him.

## Tangible Gifts Leave a Lasting Impression

Like young Peter who slept in a cardboard box to raise awareness on homelessness, elementary school–aged children respond sincerely to tangible needs. You can encourage children to feel more connected to their local and global community through tangible gifts and projects. Just like having a home, kids understand the need to go to school and to play. Collect items that enable other kids to enjoy these basic rights. Help children in your local community or in war-stricken countries by having your students donate school kits, sports equipment, backpacks, and shoes through a trusted organization. This concrete and tangible project will make your own kids' school and play experience that much more meaningful.

## Free Rice

When students play the online game **Free Rice**, 10 grains of rice are donated through the World Food Program for every correctly answered trivia question. Students can choose to answer questions in English, Science, Languages, or Geography. Many classrooms, like Becky's, played this game whenever there were a couple of minutes transitioning to a new activity or waiting to get called to a school assembly. You can take it a step further and set up a Free Rice Challenge like schools throughout Canada have done. Vie with classrooms in the same school, across your school district, or on a global scale. Students in Canada **played this challenge for just 7 days and ended up donating enough rice, grain by grain, to feed 200 school children in Cambodia.**

## Go Meatless on Mondays!

Kids in Baltimore, Maryland, practice "**meatless Mondays**," a health, nutrition, and environmental initiative that the entire public school district has embraced. They learned that "if every American goes meatless on one day a week for a year, that would be the equivalent of removing 8 million cars from the road." They're healthier for it, do something tangible for the environment, and have enjoyed new foods, too. Participation from schools around the country is growing. It's a simple, tangible way to make a difference and feel better too.

## Andrew in Ghana Helps Kids in Somalia

When energetic **Andrew Adensi-Donnah** from Ghana—a country where the average person lives off of $7 a day (or $2,555 per year)—was 11 years old, he wanted to do something about the severe hunger crisis in the Horn of Africa. So he designed his own bright orange "Save Somalia" shirt and dedicated his summer to going door-to-door fundraising for the famine. After just a few months, in spite of the fact that many of us in North America would consider Andrew and his neighbors to be "poor" financially, he raised $500 and plans to do much more. As a result of his effort, Andrew was profiled on the BBC and in the United Nation's World Food Program blog.

## A 5-Year-Old Girl and the Power of Nets

In 2006, when she was 5 years old, Katherine Commale learned about the devastating impact of malaria after her mother, Lynda, saw a

PBS documentary one night and couldn't sleep. The next morning Katherine asked her mother what was the matter, and Lynda told her how upset she was to find out that a child dies of malaria every 30 seconds. Katherine immediately began to count to 30 and realized they had to do something.

With her 3-year-old brother, Katherine built a diorama to represent an African family in a hut. Using a piece of tulle and a toy bug, she created a short skit showing how nets protect sleeping children when the nets are tucked in their beds. It's a simple concept the young children immediately understood. Katherine and her mom soon made a presentation at their church and raised $2,000, then began visiting more churches. During the holiday season, children from Katherine's church and local community, as well as her neighborhood friends, hand decorated more than 600 gift certificates, allowing gift givers to purchase bed nets (which cost just $10 each to save a life) in honor of a friend, teacher, or family member. The certificates were a huge success, as has been their entire campaign, which has taken off nationally and internationally. They have met with world leaders and were profiled on CNN and in the *New York Times*, among others.

Since the original diorama was made, the Commales have become spokespeople for the UN Foundation's program **Nothing But Nets** and have raised more than $180,000. Nothing But Nets is a terrific program engaging families, classrooms, and sports teams at every level on preventing malaria and saving millions of lives. Katherine's project didn't begin on a huge scale, but with a simple story depicted in a shoe box. Start with one step and see where it takes you.

## Little Red Wagon—The Movie and the Cause

In 2004, at age 7, Zach Bonner was determined to help the victims of Hurricane Charley near his home outside Tampa Bay, Florida. He pulled his red wagon around his neighborhood, asking for donations of supplies, water, food, clothing, tarps—anything that might bring comfort to those who had lost their homes from the storm. His effort, with the support of friends and family, resulted in 27 truckloads of relief supplies and a nonprofit organization, the **Little Red Wagon Foundation**. As he learned more about social needs, he grew most concerned about the plight of homeless children and started on long walks—first across his state. Then by age 12, in 2010, he walked across the United States, almost 2,500 miles from Tampa to Los Angeles to raise awareness on homelessness. This made him the youngest person to accomplish such a feat. You can see Zach's story come to life in a Hollywood-made feature film about his quest, *Little Red Wagon*.

## Video Games to Play Virtually, Make a Difference Actually

Club Penguin, a division of Disney Online, is the "number one virtual world for children." Through its Global Citizenship initiative, Coins For Change, children who play on its site are encouraged to "help change the world by donating virtual coins they earn playing games online to real world causes that matter to them." Kids can direct donations to provide actual medical help, build safe places, or protect the Earth. Since 2007, more than $6.5 million has been given to projects that helped hundreds of thousands of kids and families around the globe.

A network of gaming for meaning, learning, and impact is growing. Games for Change is a pioneering nonprofit organization with a vast global network of game developers that are creating games for social impact. Their archive for games targeted to ages 7 and up is located on the **Games for Change website**. Note that we don't endorse each game on the list, and the quality varies, but adults can prescreen games which can help reinforce lessons and show many creative ways to get excited and involved with the world. More on educational games with meaning can be found at **Playful Learning**, **Games With Purpose**, **BrainPop's GameUp**, **iCivics**, and **GeoGames**.

Learn about **parasites**, **malaria**, and other conditions that challenge life where resources are few through the simple video game Nobel. org site, where Peace, Medicine, and Literature pioneers are the real heroes.

These examples demonstrate how a limited amount of video game play, usually considered a passive activity, can be used actively for a greater good. But don't depend on the game to do all the teaching and processing for the child. Have a conversation around the mechanics of game play and what the game's greater good purpose was (e.g., Was the charity mission built into the game's narrative or was social good/global understanding a benefit that came after the game was over?). Which does the child prefer? Which might create a more lasting impact? Why?

If your kids could create a game that would do some good for someone in the world, how would they set it up? What cause would it benefit? Can they start creating their own game?

For more examples of games with a global education angle in this Toolkit, see Chapter 3, Section 4: Social Studies, under "Online Games, Activities, and Apps."

## Take Your Child to the Meeting—And See What Sticks

We've taken our children to many meetings and nothing immediate came out of the experience, but once in a while, something magical happens—an "aha" moment. That's what occurred when Rachel Wheeler, at age 9, attended a **Food For The Poor** meeting in 2009 with her mom. When Rachel heard about conditions in Haiti, that some kids eat "mud cookies" and live in cardboard houses because they're so poor, she vowed to help make a difference. Partnering with Food For The Poor, an international relief and development organization that feeds hundreds of thousands of people daily, she committed to raising enough money to build 12 homes in a small village near Port-au-Prince the very first year she got involved.

To get started, she organized bake sales, passed a donation can at homecoming games, and sold homemade pot holders at her Deerfield Beach, Florida, school. She turned to her parents' friends and her church, and the local Chamber of Commerce even made substantial contributions.

By the time she was 12 years old, **her fundraising efforts surpassed $250,000**, enough to erect 27 concrete two-room homes, and a year later, she spearheaded fundraising to rebuild a local school that was devastated in the 7.0 magnitude earthquake in 2010, where the school's 250 students were attending classes in a shabby one-room structure that frequently flooded. Wheeler's acts of kindness earned her a nomination in 2012 as one of the top 15 finalists from the United States and Canada in the Huggable Hero program by the Build-A-Bear Workshop, and she hopes to have a career that helps others when she grows up.

## Empty Bowls—Where Art Fights Hunger

Kids in K–5 classes across the country have utilized **The Empty Bowls** Project for over two decades. In this service-learning venture, students in art classes, often with the guidance of local potters, make handcrafted bowls. Guests are invited to a simple meal of soup and bread. In exchange for a cash donation (sometimes it's a set amount, like $5 or $10, and sometimes simply "any donation amount"), guests can keep a bowl as a reminder of all the empty bowls in the world. The money raised is donated to a local food bank, soup kitchen, or global hunger organization.

In one Michigan school, the entire K–8 school community got involved in making bowls, preparing soups, harvesting vegetables from the school garden for their event, and performing a song they wrote for the event. In many other schools, the project may be simpler—revolving around one dinner and the bowls participants will take home with them—but remains meaningful. We were struck by the range of communities holding their own Empty Bowls dinners. A simple search with the terms "empty bowls elementary school" came up with so many examples! See the example of the Stratford Road Elementary School in New York featured in Chapter 2 to learn about their experience.

## Upgrade Your Bike, Help More Kids Get to School, and Engage in Purposeful Work

Bicycles offer a great source of freedom, mobility, exercise, fun, and they're good for the planet. Bikes also allow a tangible way to connect and impact kids around the world, as the model offered by the organization Bikes for the World (BfW) makes clear.

Ted Haynie, a retired school principal from Maryland, shared his experience with us:

> We engaged in many opportunities for our students to develop awareness traits like respect, responsibility, self-discipline, empathy, etc., all the standard stuff but not by just talking to them about it; rather by giving them multiple chances to experience these traits in practice. This led us to Bikes for the World. The idea of expanding students' global awareness of life in developing countries where children are unable to attend school or get to the doctor because of the lack of personal transportation was an important concept. The whole notion of our throw-away society was also something we wanted to convey as well as just simple activism and becoming involved in service to others.

Mr. Haynie described how they created an ambitious campaign:

- They established "team captains" at individual schools, consisting of students and teachers.

- These team captains worked with BfW to create bike drives at each school.

- Individual, school-based collections worked up to a major collection day at four different sites in their community.

- Mr. Haynie, as the "hub" or instigator of the campaign, was ready to visit schools and offer presentations about the impact of donating a bike.

The result: They had set a goal of 500 bikes. In the end, 700 were collected!

Bikes for the World's outreach coordinator, Yvette Hayes, offered many examples of the impact when kids see other kids' lives affected by the donations they make. In one case, she shared this experience:

> *During my last visit [to Colvin Run Elementary in Vienna, Virginia], I shared with the school my experiences from a recent trip to our Bikes for Education program in the Philippines. . . . While in the community of Baclayon, on the island of Bohol, I was able to meet our bike beneficiaries, visit their schools, and ride with them to and from school. I found sharing this experience with Colvin Run students to be exciting and energizing because the faces in front of me looked no different from the ones I saw smiling back at me overseas. I found it easy to put a face on a bike donation for these kids. What I remember most about speaking to this large group of students is one boy standing up and asking me, "What other countries do you serve, and how are those bikes helping them?" Not only did these kids GET it, but they really CARED.*
>
> *In the classroom, teachers are able to pool our resources to integrate this service opportunity with an existing curriculum, making it a more complete education experience. When we know ahead of time where the bikes are going, we can share this with teachers and they are able to put together a lesson on an area, such as Ghana, to teach students geography or another culture.*

BfW programs also have tied in with science lessons on the environment and promoting a greener lifestyle and spurred art activities like producing creative signage for bike donation campaigns. Children and parents work together to raise funds to ship bikes and form work crews to load donated bicycles onto containers that will travel across the world.

Yvette added,

> The kids tend to like the grease and the tools and forget that what they are doing is "work." I've also seen shy kids open up once they are taught how to use a pedal wrench. Girls jump right in once they realize it's not "just for boys." It's a "doing" activity that reaches kids who are sometimes used to being left out because they aren't "athletic enough." One school we worked with was able to bring mainstream kids together with the "high-intensity language training (HILT)" kids, many recent immigrants, who otherwise might be alienated or apart. What I've seen it do here and overseas is give kids confidence where they once had little or none.

## One School's Culture of Service-Learning

A 40-year history of global and local outreach has been woven into the fabric of life at Ohlone Elementary, a public school in Palo Alto, California.

When we reached out for examples for this Toolkit, Ohlone's principal, Bill Overton, responded enthusiastically, reflecting his deep commitment to service and learning going hand in hand. This commitment has resulted in a significant ramp up of community service at the elementary school. As he shared,

> Last year alone, we had over 20 school, classroom, and student-driven projects. Some of the different ways the community participated in community service last year were
>
> - collecting books for the African Library Project,
> - collecting canned food for the Halloween for Hunger project supported by Free the Children,
> - participating in the read-a-thon to raise money for clean water for villages in Kenya,

- *selling student-made beaded animals for another cause,*
- *collecting coats and jackets for people in need,*
- *selling student-made origami (a K–1 endeavor), and*
- *collecting spare change in a change jar to support Free the Children.*

For the past 8 years, they have partnered with **Free the Children (FTC)**, an organization which in turn has provided an abundance of advice, materials, support, and phenomenal speakers, like Spencer West and Mollie Burke. As Bill relates,

> *Spencer's story was about overcoming adversity, since he has been without the lower part of his body since early in his life. (He just climbed Kilimanjaro to raise funds for clean water.) Mollie is a blind person who endured in high school some unbelievable bullying experiences. Other members from FTC have provided leadership training for our Student Council over the years as well as done their own talks to students. They also have been supportive and attended our own Make a Difference Day at Ohlone, spaghetti feed fundraisers and more. We modeled our Make a Difference Day after FTC's We Days (which students are invited to only if they've done something for others). I've been fortunate to attend these for the past several years in Toronto, Vancouver, and Seattle.*

The school also has held an annual Global Awareness Week (GAW) since 2011, which started as a community-wide response to the devastating tsunami in Japan. GAW encompasses creative fundraising and sharing of diverse cultures through food, music, guest speakers, and art with a purpose, like a 1,000-cranes artwork display. A parent volunteer has created a catalog of resources for teachers, and partnerships with the local high school and middle school have been formed to assist elementary schools to be active in community service. Increasingly, individual children and groups, like Ohlone's Girl Scouts, initiate their own service projects.

As Bill concluded in an e-mail, "I could go on and on about the path and commitment Ohlone has to community service. The truth be told, it's as much for others as it is for us."

## Treat the Earth With Care—Together

Join TUNZA, the partnership of children from around the world working with the **United Nations Environment Program**. TUNZA is a word in Kiswahili (a.k.a., Swahili, the common language of most East African countries) that means to "treat with care," referring to caring for our common home, Earth. When you click on the "Actions" tab you will see a world map with icons placed all over the world. Click those and you'll see notes from children and youth describing actions they have taken. Have your school add to those initiatives!

TUNZA's Junior Board consists of children from around the world, ages 10–12, and welcomes the participation of clubs that are working for a cleaner, greener planet. "The key focus areas are awareness building, capacity building, information exchange, and facilitating the involvement of young people in decision making mechanisms." Through TUNZA, you can join the **Plant for the Planet: Billion Tree Campaign**. Plant a tree in your backyard or another approved location, register on the site, and be part of a global movement greening the planet.

## Section 5: 12 Take-Aways From Awesome Kids Changing the World for the Better

The initiatives highlighted in this section bring out key lessons that can be generalized across diverse projects. Here are some of our important take-aways:

- Partner with a successful nonprofit organization so it can offer its expertise on organizational elements like fundraising, donating, communication, and rallying volunteers.

- Start with what you love. When combined with activities kids enjoy, from basketball to chess, baking cookies, or creating art, outreach efforts will stick longer and more meaningfully.

- Listen humbly. Don't assume that your idea to "help beneficiaries" is what others need. You may start with one idea for making a difference, but through effective communication and humble listening, you may emerge with a completely different—and more effective, more needed—initiative.

- Let it sink in. When sharing information with children about serious global needs, from hunger to disaster relief, don't jump right in with solutions. Honor the problem-solving abilities of children and let the issues sink in to their consciousness, then allow some time and space for them to come up with solutions and initiatives. This could take a few minutes or overnight—ask them to sleep on it, to think about it for a day, then continue the conversation. You can help guide their thinking not by offering answers, but instead by asking driving questions which help explore challenging issues more meaningfully and profoundly.

- Set fundraising goals in small, manageable chunks. The primary objective for young children's engagement is rarely the amount of money raised; rather it is the long-term connection, service, and learning that comes out of a project. Groups that sought pennies or a single dollar often emerged with the most funds, largely because the buy-in was wholehearted from their community.

- Service, when integrated into academics, makes the learning stick. Aiming to make a difference in the world and integrating research, implementation, and outreach into math, science, social studies, reading, and writing provides an ideal vehicle for high-quality project-based learning.

- Kids are more resilient than we often give them credit for. Those children who walked longer than they ever had before, or who carried heavy bottles of water across the field, or skipped a meal, or slept in a box to raise awareness on the plight of the homeless came out stronger and more committed to causes that went beyond their own desires, demonstrating that a little hardship (with their parents' blessing) can have a powerful effect.

- Start with tangible gifts and causes. Just like having a home, elementary-aged children can relate to going to school, playing, and eating. So for early outreach efforts, collect items like school supplies, sports equipment, backpacks, and shoes that enable other kids to enjoy these basic rights; then donate through a trusted organization.

- Children who are given space to make mistakes, set ambitious goals then revise them, and commit to serving a cause for a longer period than one school project with a deadline often emerge from high school with a clear mission and purpose for their lives, including clarity on future studies and careers as well as healthier interpersonal relationships.

- When processing the learning from a project, go beyond the material aspects. Yes, discuss the donation and logistics and learn from the experience to organize an even stronger initiative next time, but don't miss out on discussing the intangibles: what virtues or qualities you needed to summon, like empathy, patience, flexibility, and responsibility; how your perspective may have changed over the course of the effort; and what you will continue to work on beyond the project.

- Working together for a cause builds friendships and breaks social barriers.

- Think of the effort like a compound-interest earning bank account: The children who start early will realize the greatest long-term gains and the benefits of their "investment"—of time, energy, courage, and material resources. At first, the small steps may not feel like much, but with consistent, sustained exertion, the impact may seem surprising and significant.

## Concluding Reflection

While the problems of the world seem formidable, solutions and heroes seem to be sprouting up everywhere, every day—with one more innovative than the next. This positive take on often-deteriorating global conditions offers a boundless learning opportunity for young people, as well as an outlook on life: Will they ignore the challenges, feel overwhelmed by them, or tap into an ability to empathize and channel creativity, leading to a search for solutions and ways they can make a difference? This choice can be taught. Among adults living lives of service, we often find this empowered outlook was instilled from a young age, inspired by the example of a particular adult, usually a parent or teacher.

As we began to compile so many inspiring initiatives involving kids, their schools, and their families—most of whom were from unremarkable circumstances, until they began their quest to make a difference—we grew in our astonishment of the impact they were making and also felt more empowered to get ourselves and our children involved in service that was systematic, as well as global in its reach. We hope that by learning about the change that young people with a commitment and limited resources can make, you might also feel inspired to encourage and engage.

When classrooms and clubs embrace global education as a substantive pillar of their 21st century learning, a desire to be of service will grow, naturally. Otherwise, how can global citizenship move from theory to reality, from external to internal? Action, in its myriad forms of making meaningful connections, can be seen as the secret sauce, making global citizenship "stick."

The choice to embark on service-learning with your students or children, however, can take some time, and there is no particular sequence of implementation required to begin a global learning process. Your school culture might be more disposed to start Geography Stars before school, or literature units within the Common Core Standards framework, or a limited global service activity. Each of these efforts can operate independently from each other, and though adapting an integrated approach (where multiple departments support the goal) to building global competency is ideal, it is perfectly fine to begin a new initiative, starting small, doing what you love, perhaps with support from a small circle of like-minded friends or colleagues, to get your feet wet.

If an initiative feels like a "failure," take a cue from Icelanders, where, Eric Wiener found in *The Geography of Bliss,* "failure doesn't carry a stigma." As was explained to him, sometimes failure is even admired if the attempt was made with the best of intentions or if the effort "wasn't ruthless enough." This mindset has cultivated more artists and writers per capita than any other country and a willingness to try new things, "For if you are free to fail, you are free to try."[3]

We recognize the heavy burden on teachers today—where "failure" could cost your job. But if you take on a service-learning project where the first few attempts don't turn out as you hope, this might be a safe place to experiment. Try to foster a culture in your school, classroom, club, or home that celebrates a willingness to try, the curiosity to search for root causes and possible solutions, empathy to put yourselves in someone else's shoes, and patience that problems may not be solved according to your expectations. Such qualities as persistence, patience, flexibility, empathy, looking for root causes/issues/sources, helpfulness, generosity, kindness, and love can form the core values of a learning environment that celebrates effort rather than outcome when the goal is to be of service or to make a difference in the world.

If you decide you're ready to start a make-a-difference activity, we'd love to hear from you. Please contact us to share your experiences, and we hope to continue to feature world-changing kids, teachers, and parents on www.globaledtoolkit.com. You are not alone!

# NOTES

1. RMC Research Corporation for Learn and Serve America's National Service-Learning Clearinghouse. (2009). *K–12 service-learning project planning toolkit* (p. 7). Retrieved from http://www.servicelearning.org/filemanager/download/8542_K–12_SL_Toolkit_UPDATED.pdf

2. At the time of publication, Citizen Effect directors had decided to close the organization; however, we felt this experience remains valuable for readers and are grateful for their service.

3. Wiener, E. (2009). *The geography of bliss: One grump's search for the happiest places in the world* (p. 162). New York, NY: Twelve.

# Additional Resources

www.corwin.com/globaledtoolkit

# Printable Global Citizen Passport Template

Use the Global Citizen Passport template as an interactive keepsake for your next global activity. Print out the internal pages as many times as you need for recording stamps or icons depicting the country you "visit." You might like to use colored paper as the background of your front and back cover page (to look more like a passport from a particular nation) or have students color and decorate the cover to reflect their interests and personality. More detailed instructions follow.

The passport can track the countries visited in a year's worth of reading, in music, art, science, math, and other subject areas. It can be used as a companion to your international day, week, or month activities and can help build excitement around experiential learning and friend making that comes with global learning. It also can serve to record experiences using fabulous online resources. Our friend Sasha Martin, the brilliant and talented founder of **Global Table Adventure**, where she cooks "a meal from every country in the world, A–Z!" teamed up with us to create this Global Citizen Passport. You'll also find the Global Citizen Passport on Global Table Adventure so you can "eat your way around the world." What are you waiting for?! Explore! Have fun!

# INSTRUCTIONS

1. Print off one copy of the "Passport Cover" and "Passport Cover Side 2" files. As indicated by the names, the "Passport Cover Side 2" file should be printed on the back of the Passport Cover file.

2. Print off as many Passport Insides as you'd like. Print them on both sides of your paper.

3. Use scissors or a paper cutter to cut along the dotted line.

4. Fold along the gray lines.

5. Nest the pages in numerical order to make a passport book.

6. Include a photo, self-portrait or your fingerprint in the box under the space for your name inside the passport cover.

7. Enjoy!

 **Gl⬤bal Table Adventure**

GlObal Table
Adventure

# PASSPORT

*Global Citizen*

*Travel the world, expand your mind!*

Entries/Entradas    *Visas*    Departures/Salidas

First Name/Middle Initial/Last Name

Nationality:

Date of Birth:

Place of Birth:

```
<<<<<<<<DOUTXO990<<<<<<<<<
1248097204444-08398188300 0<<<<<<18
```

APPROVED

The ministry of foreign affairs for Global Citizens
invites all nations to allow the bearer of this passport
to learn about their country's culture and traditions.

Place of Issue: _____

Date of Issue: _____

*Entries/Entradas*  *Visas*  *Departures/Salidas*

*Entries/Entradas*  *Visas*  *Departures/Salidas*

*Entries/Entradas*  *Visas*  *Departures/Salidas*

| Entries/Entradas | *Visas* | Departures/Salidas | | Entries/Entradas | *Visas* | Departures/Salidas |

| Entries/Entradas | *Visas* | Departures/Salidas | | Entries/Entradas | *Visas* | Departures/Salidas |

# Printable "Where Are You From?" World Map Activity

Our friends in Devon, Pennsylvania, shared this page that accompanies a giant world map placed in their school hallway. Every child, regardless of actual travel experience, found a way to contribute to embellishing the map, creating something that engaged and belonged to the entire school.

# Where are you from? Where have you been?
# Where do you want to go?
# EXPLORE YOUR WORLD

During "Explore Your World" week, we will display on a **gigantic world map** the places around the world that our children are from (or ancestry), have visited, and places they want to go. Each is shape coded as defined below. Parents, please help your child write the **NAME OF THE PLACE** (city, state, and/or country), **YOUR CHILD'S NAME**, and decorate as desired. Photocopy this sheet if you need more shapes! Cut out each shape and return in a sealed envelope labeled "EXPLORE YOUR WORLD MAP" to the main office no later than _____. Questions? Contact _____.

### THANK YOU and HAVE FUN!

**CIRCLE** = "I/my ancestors are from" **SQUARE** = "I have been to" **HEXAGON** = "I want to go to"

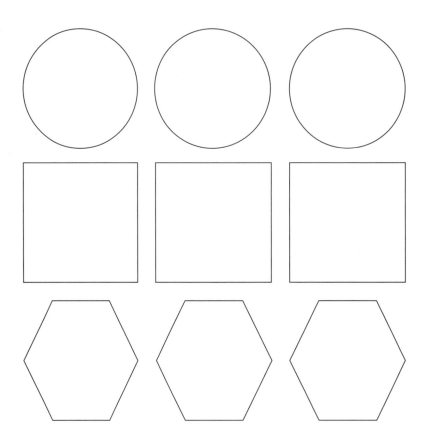

## Geography Stars Sample Flyer

This is the flyer used for the Sugar Land, Texas, club.

# GE◉GRAPHY STARS!

**The International Club is pleased to announce a new 7-week geography experience for all grades, starting (DATE)!**

*Learn more about the world!* Every Tuesday morning for 7 weeks, parent volunteers will be in the cafeteria from 7:30 to 7:45 to test the interested participants on the following questions. You choose the level, and we assign two new countries every week (see attached schedule). The parents will record and keep track of the weekly scores.

All participants will receive a prize at our **International Night on (DATE)**, and the top students in each grade will get special recognition!

---

**LEVEL 1**: Locate the countries on a map

**LEVEL 2**: Identify the continent

**LEVEL 3**: Name the hemisphere (north or south)

**LEVEL 4**: Name one official language spoken

**LEVEL 5**: Tell the capital

---

**Participation details:**

- No registration necessary—just show up between 7:30 and 7:45 am on Tuesday mornings in the cafeteria!

- Every week children can choose to do whichever level they'd like. If they would like Level 2, they should answers questions for Level 1 and 2. For Level 3, they should answer Levels 1, 2, and 3. Level 4 should answers Levels 1, 2, 3, and 4. Level 5 will have to answers all of the questions☺.

- No problem if you miss/skip a week! **This is for FUN and to learn geography!**

**Questions? Would you like to be a parent volunteer?** E-mail (NAME OF SCHOOL) International Club Coordinator: (Name, e-mail address, any other relevant contact info)

# GE⊕GRAPHY STARS!
## at
## (SCHOOL NAME)!

**Week 1: January 22nd**

Russia
Nicaragua

**Week 2: January 29th**

India
Angola

**Week 3: February 5th**

Canada
Peru

**Week 4: February 12th**

The Netherlands
China

**Week 5: February 19th**

Mexico
United Arab Emirates

**Week 6: February 26th**

Brazil
France

**Week 7: March 5th**

Australia
Ethiopia

*For great geography resources, check out these:*

www.cia.gov/library/publications/the-world-factbook/

www.timeforkids.com/around-the-world

nationalgeographic.com/kids/places/find/

kidworldcitizen.org/category/geography

# Multicultural Book List: A Few Hundred of Our Favorites

*"The world was hers for the reading."*
— Betty Smith, *A Tree Grows in Brooklyn*

Like the experience of the character Francie from Betty Smith's classic *A Tree Grows in Brooklyn,* books can become our faithful friends and offer us the world. For teachers, great books can become our companions in illuminating the impact of a different climate, culture, language, or lifestyle and are a means of building empathy, curiosity, joy, and global citizenship.

Yet the choices can be overwhelming. When choosing children's literature to increase global awareness, we look for books that are visually appealing, culturally accurate, and without stereotypes, so they aren't lumping together distinct groups into generic or negative typecasts. Age-appropriate, engaging stories that subtly inform and showcase new traditions and people not only increase cultural awareness but also help grow kindness and respect.

We hope this Multicultural Book List can serve as a companion for your journey around the world. The list is broken into geographical categories and cultural groups used by international and multilateral organizations such as the United Nations. For example, a book about Iraq would be found in "Western Asia," and we have included it in the section on Northern African/Western Asian. At the same time, Afghanistan is considered "Southern Asia" by the United Nations and so is included in the section on Asian/Pacific/Central and Southern Asian/Asian American. Though imperfect, these categories can help teachers and parents locate great books.

In compiling this list, we consulted librarians, educators, academics, and leaders in various ethnic communities. Although we have over 300 excellent multicultural books listed, we surely have missed some of your favorites. Please contact us via e-mail, Twitter, or Facebook and let us know which books you think should be added to future editions! We would love your input as we explore children's literature that showcases varying perspectives and world cultures.

# Lower Elementary (Grades preK–2, ages 4–8)

*African/African American/African Diaspora*

1. Aardema, Verna, & Vidal, Beatriz (1981). *Bringing the Rain to Kapiti Plain: A Nandi Tale.* New York, NY: Dial Press.
2. Atinuke (2007). *Anna Hibiscus.* London, UK: Walker Books.
3. Boelts, Maribeth (2007). *Those Shoes.* Cambridge, MA: Candlewick Press.
4. Cameron, Ann (1981). *The Stories Julian Tells.* New York, NY: Pantheon Books.
5. Chamberlin, Mary, Chamberlin, Rich, & Cairns, Julia (2006). *Mama Panya's Pancakes.* Cambridge, MA: Barefoot Books.
6. Cox, Judy (2003). *My Family Plays Music.* New York, NY: Holiday House.
7. Diakite, Baba Wague (1999). *The Hatseller and the Monkeys: A West African Folktale.* New York, NY: Scholastic.
8. Diakite, Penda (2006). *I Lost My Tooth in Africa.* New York, NY: Scholastic.
9. English, Karen (2007). *Nikki and Deja.* New York, NY: Clarion Books.
10. Gerson, Mary-Joan (1992). *Why the Sky Is Far Away: A Nigerian Folktale.* Hong Kong: Little, Brown.
11. Greenfield, Eloise (1978). *Honey, I Love and Other Love Poems.* New York, NY: HarperCollins.
12. Haley, Gail E. (1970). *A Story, a Story: An African Tale.* New York, NY: Atheneum.
13. Hoffman, Mary (1991). *Amazing Grace.* New York, NY: Dial Books for Young Readers.
14. Hughes, Langston (2009). *My People.* New York, NY: Atheneum Books for Young Readers.
15. Levine, Ellen (2007). *Henry's Freedom Box: A True Story From the Underground Railroad.* New York, NY: Scholastic.
16. Lottridge, Celia Barker (1990). *The Name of the Tree: A Bantu Tale Retold.* New York, NY: M. K. McElderry Books.
17. McKissack, Patricia (1988). *Mirandy and Brother Wind.* New York, NY: Knopf.
18. Myers, Walter Dean (2009). *Looking Like Me.* New York, NY: Egmont USA.
19. Onyefulu, Ifeoma (1997). *A Is for Africa.* New York, NY: Puffin Books.
20. Onyefulu, Ifeoma (2006). *One Big Family: Sharing Life in an African Village.* London, UK: Frances Lincoln.
21. Paye, Won-Ldy, & Lippert, Margaret H. (2002). *Head, Body, Legs: A Story From Liberia.* New York, NY: Henry Holt.
22. Pinkney, Andrea (1993). *Alvin Ailey.* New York, NY: Hyperion Books for Children.
23. Pinkney, Gloria Jean (1994). *The Sunday Outing.* New York, NY: Dial Books for Young Readers.
24. Pinkney, Sandra L. (2000). *Shades of Black: A Celebration of Our Children.* New York, NY: Scholastic.
25. Seeger, Pete (1986). *Abiyoyo: Based on a South African Lullaby and Folk Song.* New York, NY: Macmillan.

26. Tarpley, Natasha Anastasia (1998*). I Love My Hair!* New York, NY: Little, Brown.

27. Zolotow, Charlotte (1958). *Do You Know What I'll Do?* New York, NY: Harper & Row.

### American Indian/Native American/First Nations

28. Ata, Te, & adapted by Moroney, Lynn (1995). *Baby Rattlesnake.* San Francisco, CA: Children's Book Press.

29. Bruchac, Joseph, & Ross, Gayle (1995). *The Story of the Milky Way, a Cherokee Tale.* New York, NY: Dial Books for Young Readers.

30. Campbell, Nicola I. (2005). *Shi-Shi-Etko.* Toronto, Canada: Groundwood Books.

31. Campbell, Nicola I. (2008). *Shin-Chi's Canoe.* Toronto, Canada: Groundwood Books.

32. Confederated Salish & Kootenai Tribes (2005). *Beaver Steals Fire: A Salish Coyote Story.* Lincoln: University of Nebraska Press.

33. Griese, Arnold (1995). *Anna's Athabaskan Summer.* Honesdale, PA: Boyds Mills Press.

34. Harjo, Joy (2000). *The Good Luck Cat.* San Diego, CA: Harcourt Brace.

35. Landon, Jonathan, & Pinola, Lanny (1993). *Fire Race: A Karuk Coyote Tale of How Fire Came to the People.* San Francisco, CA: Chronicle Books.

36. Messinger, Carla, & Katz, Susan (2007). *When the Shadbush Blooms.* Berkeley, CA: Tricycle Press.

37. Smith, Cynthia Leitich (2000). *Jingle Dancer.* New York, NY: Morrow Junior Books.

38. Sockabasin, Allen (2005). *Thanks to the Animals.* Gardiner, ME: Tilbury House.

39. Swamp, Chief Jake (1995). *Giving Thanks: A Native American Good Morning Message.* New York, NY: Lee & Low Books.

40. Tingle, Tim (2006). *When Turtle Grew Feathers: A Folktale From the Choctaw Nation.* Atlanta, GA: August House.

41. Van Camp, Richard (1997). *A Man Called Raven.* San Francisco, CA: Children's Book Press.

42. Van Laan, Nancy (1995). *In a Circle Long Ago: A Treasury of Native Lore From North America.* New York, NY: Apple Soup Books.

43. Waboose, Jan Bourdeau (1997). *Morning on the Lake.* Toronto, Canada: Kids Can Press.

44. Waboose, Jan Bourdeau (2002). *SkySisters.* Toronto, Canada: Kids Can Press.

45. Wheeler, Bernelda (1986). *Where Did You Get Your Moccasins?* Winnipeg, Canada: Pemmican.

### Asian/Pacific/Central and Southern Asian/Asian American

46. Cheng, Andrea (2000). *Grandfather Counts.* New York, NY: Lee & Low Books.

47. Choi, Sook Nyul (1993). *Halmoni and the Picnic.* Boston, MA: Houghton Mifflin.

48. Choi, Yangsook (2001). *The Name Jar*. New York, NY: Knopf.
49. Compestine, Ying Cheng (2011). *Crouching Tiger*. Somerville, MA: Candlewick.
50. Demi (1995). *The Stonecutter*. New York, NY: Knopf.
51. Heo, Yumi (1994). *One Afternoon*. New York, NY: Orchard Books.
52. Heo, Yumi (1995). *Father's Rubber Shoes*. New York, NY: Orchard Books.
53. Ho, Minfong (1996). *Hush! A Thai Lullaby*. New York, NY: Orchard Books.
54. Krishnaswami, Uma (2000). *Out of the Way*. Chennai, India: Tulika.
55. Jaffe, Nina (1995). *Older Brother, Younger Brother*. New York, NY: Viking.
56. Lin, Grace (2010). *Ling & Ting: Not Exactly the Same!* New York, NY: Little, Brown.
57. Look, Lenore (2006). *Uncle Peter's Amazing Chinese Wedding*. New York, NY: Atheneum Books for Young Readers.
58. Paek, Min (1978) *Aekyung's Dream*. San Francisco, CA: Children's Book Press.
59. Pak, Soyung (2001). *Dear Juno*. New York, NY: Viking.
60. Park, Linda Sue (2003). *The Firekeeper's Son*. New York, NY: Clarion Books.
61. Park, Linda Sue (2005). *Bee-Bim Bop!* New York, NY: Clarion Books.
62. Say, Allen (1993). *Grandfather's Journey*. Boston, MA: Houghton Mifflin.
63. Surat, Michele Maria (1983). *Angel Child, Dragon Child*. Milwaukee, WI: Raintree.
64. Thong, Roseanne (2000). *Round Is a Mooncake: A Book of Shapes*. San Francisco, CA: Chronicle Books.
65. Uegaki, Chieri (2003). *Suki's Kimono*. Toronto, Canada: Kids Can Press.
66. Wells, Rosemary (2009). *Yoko's Paper Cranes*. New York, NY: Hyperion Book for Children.
67. Wong, Janet S. (2002). *Apple Pie 4th of July*. San Diego, CA: Harcourt.
68. Yamate, Sandra S. (1992). *Ashok by Any Other Name*. Chicago, IL: Polychrome.
69. Zia, F. (2011). *Hot, Hot Roti for Dada-Ji*. New York, NY: Lee & Low Books.

## *Latino/Hispanic American/Latin American*

70. Aardema, Verna (1991). *Borreguita and the Coyote: Tale From Ayutia*. New York, NY: Knopf.
71. Alvarez, Julia (2000). *The Secret Footprints*. New York, NY: Knopf.
72. Cisneros, Sandra (1994). *Hairs/Pelitos*. New York, NY: Knopf.
73. Dorros, Arthur (1991). *Abuela*. New York, NY: Dutton Children's Books.
74. Ets, Marie Hall, & Labastida, Aurora (1959). *Nine Days to Christmas: A Story of Mexico*. New York, NY: Viking Press.
75. Figueredo, D. H. (1999). *When This World Was New*. New York, NY: Lee & Low Books.
76. Gonzalez, Lucia M. (1997). *Señor Cat's Romance: And Other Favorite Stories From Latin America*. New York, NY: Scholastic.
77. Johnston, Tony (1994). *The Tale of Rabbit and Coyote*. New York, NY: Putnam.

78. Jules, Jacqueline (2011). *Freddie Ramos Takes Off (Zapato Power)*. Park Ridge, IL: Albert Whitman.

79. Lopez, Loretta (1997). *The Birthday Swap*. New York, NY: Lee & Low Books.

80. Mohr, Nicholasa (1996). *Old Letivia and the Mountain of Sorrows*. New York, NY: Viking.

81. Mora, Pat (1994). *The Desert Is My Mother/El Desierto Es Mi Madre*. Houston, TX: Piñata Books.

82. Mora, Pat (1996). *Confetti: Poems for Children*. New York, NY: Lee & Low Books.

83. Mora, Pat (2000). *Tomás and the Library Lady*. Decorah, IA: Dragonfly Books.

84. Morales, Yuyi (2003). *Just a Minute! A Trickster Tale and Counting Book*. San Francisco, CA: Chronicle Books.

85. Orozco, Jose-Luis (1994). *De Colores and Other Latin American Folksongs for Children*. New York, NY: Dutton Children's Books.

86. Palacio Jaramillo, Nelly (1994). *Las Nanas de Abuelita/Grandmother's Nursery Rhymes*. New York, NY: Henry Holt.

87. Paulsen, Gary (1995). *The Tortilla Factory*. San Diego, CA: Harcourt Brace.

88. Reiser, Lynn (1993). *Margaret and Margarita/Margarita y Margaret*. New York, NY: Greenwillow Books.

89. Shute, Linda (1995). *Rabbit Wishes: Cuban Folktales*. New York, NY: Lothrop, Lee & Shepard Books.

90. Soto, Gary (1993). *Too Many Tamales*. New York, NY: Putnam.

91. Soto, Gary (1995). *Chato's Kitchen*. New York, NY: Putnam.

92. Tafolia, Carmen (2009). *What Can You Do With a Paleta?* Berkeley, CA: Tricycle Press.

93. Tonatiuh, Duncan (2011). *Diego Rivera: His World and Ours*. New York, NY: Abrams Books for Young Readers.

94. Zepeda, Gwendolyn (2008). *Growing Up With Tamales/Los Tamales de Ana*. Houston, TX: Piñata Books.

*Northern African/Western Asian*

95. Alalou, Elizabeth, & Alalou, Ali (2008). *The Butter Man*. Watertown, MA: Charlesbridge.

96. Gilani-Williams, Fawzia (2010). *Nabeel's New Pants: An Eid Tale*. Tarrytown, NY: Marshall Cavendish Children.

97. Heide, Florence Parry (1990). *The Day of Ahmed's Secret*. New York, NY: Lothrop, Lee & Shepard Books.

98. Jahanforuz, Rita (2013). *The Girl With a Brave Heart: A Story From Tehran*. Cambridge, MA: Barefoot Books.

99. Johnson, Julia (2005). *A Is for Arabia*. London, UK: Stacey International.

100. MacDonald, Margaret Read, & Taibah, Nadia Jamil (2009). *How Many Donkeys: An Arabic Counting Tale*. Morton Grove, IL: Albert Whitman.

101. Nye, Naomi Shihab (1994). *Sitti's Secrets*. New York, NY: Four Winds Press.
102. Rania, Queen, consort of Abdullah II, King of Jordan, & DiPucchio, Kelly (2010). *The Sandwich Swap*. New York, NY: Disney-Hyperion Books.
103. Rumford, James (2008). *Silent Music: A Story of Baghdad*. New York, NY: Roaring Brook Press.

## Upper Elementary (Grades 3–6, ages 8–12)

*African/African American/African Diaspora*

104. Barnes, Derrick (2008). *Ruby and the Brand-New School, Brave New Ruby*. New York, NY: Scholastic.
105. Bridges, Ruby (1999). *Through My Eyes*. New York, NY: Scholastic.
106. Bryan, Ashley (2009). *Ashley Bryan: Words to My Life's Song*. New York, NY: Atheneum Books for Young Readers.
107. Cameron, Ann (2002). *Gloria Rising*. New York, NY: Frances Foster Books/Farrar, Straus and Giroux.
108. Curtis, Christopher Paul (2005). *Bud, Not Buddy*. New York, NY: Yearling.
109. Ferris, Jeri (1989). *Arctic Explorer: The Story of Matthew Henson*. Minneapolis, MN: Carolrhoda Books.
110. Grimes, Nikki (2010). *Make Way for Dyamonde Daniel*. New York, NY: G. P. Putnam's Sons/Penguin Young Readers Group.
111. King, Casey (1997). *Oh, Freedom! Kids Talk About the Civil Rights Movement With the People Who Made It Happen*. New York, NY: Knopf.
112. Lester, Julius (1994). *John Henry*. New York, NY: Dial Books.
113. Lester, Julius (1999). *Uncle Remus: The Complete Tales*. New York, NY: Phyllis Fogelman Books.
114. McKissack, Patricia C., & Fredrick (1994). *Christmas in the Big House, Christmas in the Quarters*. New York, NY: Scholastic.
115. Mead, Alice (1995). *Junebug*. New York, NY: Farrar, Straus and Giroux.
116. Merrill, Jean (1974). *The Toothpaste Millionaire*. Boston, MA: Houghton Mifflin.
117. Nelson, Vaunda Micheaux (2009). *Bad News for Outlaws: The Remarkable Life of Bass Reeves, Deputy U.S. Marshall*. Minneapolis, MN: Carolrhoda Books.
118. Pearsall, Shelley (2006). *All of the Above*. New York, NY: Little, Brown.
119. Polacco, Patricia (1994). *Pink and Say*. New York, NY: Philomel Books.
120. Shange, Ntozake (2004). *Ellington Was Not a Street*. New York, NY: Simon & Schuster Books for Young Readers.
121. Tarshis, Lauren (2013). *I Survived the Battle of Gettysburg*. New York, NY: Scholastic.
122. Taylor, Mildred D. (1976). *Roll of Thunder, Hear My Cry*. New York, NY: Dial Press.

123. Williams-Garcia, Rita (2010). *One Crazy Summer*. New York, NY: Amistad.

124. Woodson, Jacqueline (2003). *Locomotion*. New York, NY: G. P. Putnam's Sons.


*American Indian/Native American/First Nations*

125. Bird, E. J., & Hoyt-Goldsmith, Diane (1992). *Arctic Hunter*. New York, NY: Holiday House.

126. Braine, Susan (1995). *Drumbeat . . . Heartbeat: A Celebration of the Powwow (We Are Still Here)*. Minneapolis, MN: Lerner.

127. Bruchac, Joseph (1995). *Gluskabe and the Four Wishes*. New York, NY: Cobblehill Books/Dutton.

128. Bruchac, Joseph (1997). *Eagle Song*. New York, NY: Dial Books for Young Readers.

129. Dorris, Michael (1997). *The Window*. New York, NY: Hyperion Books for Children.

130. Erdich, Louise (1999). *The Birchbark House*. New York, NY: Hyperion Books for Children.

131. Freedman, Russell (1992). *An Indian Winter*. New York, NY: Holiday House.

132. Monture, Joel (1996). *Cloudwalker: Contemporary Native American Stories*. Golden, CO: Fulcrum.

133. Ortiz, Simon J. (1977). *The People Shall Continue*. San Francisco, CA: Children's Book Press.

134. Ortiz, Simon J., & Lacapa, Michael (2004). *The Good Rainbow Road/ Rawa 'Kashtyaa'tsi Hiyaani: A Native American Tale*. Tucson: University of Arizona Press.

135. Savageau, Cheryl (1996). *Muskrat Will Be Swimming*. Flagstaff, AZ: Northland.

136. Smith, Cynthia Leitich (2001). *Rain Is Not My Indian Name*. New York, NY: HarperCollins.

137. Smith, Cynthia Leitich (2002). *Indian Shoes*. New York, NY: HarperCollins.

138. Tingle, Tim (2010). *Saltypie*. El Paso, TX: Cinco Puntos Press.

139. Thomson, Peggy (1995). *Katie Henio: Navajo Sheepherder*. New York, NY: Cobblehill Books/Dutton.


*Asian/Pacific/Central and Southern Asian/Asian American*

140. Cha, Dia (1996). *Dia's Story Cloth*. New York, NY: Lee & Low Books.

141. Chari, Sheela (2011). *Vanished*. New York, NY: Disney-Hyperion Books.

142. Cheng, Andrea (2012). *The Year of the Book*. Boston, MA: Houghton Mifflin.

143. Clements, Andrew (2009). *Extra Credit*. New York, NY: Atheneum Books for Young Readers.

144. Edmonds, I. G. (1961). *Ooka the Wise: Tales of Old Japan*. Indianapolis, IN: Bobbs-Merrill.

145. Hamanaka, Sheila (1990). *The Journey: Japanese Americans, Racism and Renewal*. New York, NY: Orchard Books.

146. Han, Jenny (2011). *Clarla Lee and the Apple Pie Dream*. New York, NY: Little, Brown Books for Young Readers.

147. Ho, Minfong (1996). *Maples in the Mist: Poems for Children From the Tang Dynasty*. New York, NY: Lothrop, Lee & Shepard.

148. Kadohata, Cynthia (2006). *Weedflower*. New York, NY: Atheneum Books for Young Readers.

149. Kent, Rose (2010). *Kimchi & Calamari*. New York, NY: Atheneum Books for Young Readers.

150. Krishnaswami, Uma (2011). *The Grand Plan to Fix Everything*. New York, NY: Atheneum Books for Young Readers.

151. Lai, Thanhha (2011). *Inside Out and Back Again*. New York, NY: HarperCollins.

152. Lin, Grace (2006). *The Year of the Dog*. New York, NY: Little, Brown Books for Young Readers.

153. Lin, Grace (2011). *Where the Mountain Meets the Moon*. New York, NY: Little, Brown.

154. Lord, Bette Bao (1984). *In the Year of the Boar and Jackie Robinson*. New York, NY: Harper & Row.

155. Lorenzi, Natalie Dias (2010). *Flying the Dragon*. Watertown, MA: Charlesbridge.

156. Marsden, Carolyn, & Niem, Thay Phap (2010). *The Buddha's Diamonds*. Cambridge, MA: Candlewick.

157. Namioka, Lensey (1992). *Yang the Youngest and His Terrible Ear*. Boston, MA: Joy Street Books.

158. Park, Linda Sue (2011). *A Single Shard*. Boston, MA: Sandpiper.

159. Perkins, Mitali (2007). *Rickshaw Girl*. Watertown, MA: Charlesbridge.

160. Shang, Wendy Wan-Long (2013). *The Great Wall of Lucy Wu*. New York, NY: Scholastic.

161. Sheth, Kashmira (2010). *Boys Without Names*. New York, NY: Balzer & Bray.

162. Yang, Gene Luen (2006). *American Born Chinese*. New York, NY: First Second.

163. Yee, Lisa (2003). *Millicent Min, Girl Genius*. New York, NY: Arthur A. Levine Books.

164. Yep, Laurence (1989). *The Rainbow People*. New York, NY: Harper & Row.

165. Yep, Laurence (1995). *Hiroshima*. New York, NY: Scholastic.

166. Yumoto, Kazumi (1996). *The Friends*. New York, NY: Farrar, Straus and Giroux.

*Latino/Hispanic American/Latin American*

167. Ada, Alma Flor (1993). *My Name Is Maria Isabel*. New York, NY: Atheneum.

168. Alvarez, Julia (2009). *Return to Sender*. New York, NY: Knopf.

169. Davila, Claudia (2012). *Luz Makes a Splash.* Toronto, Canada: Kids Can Press.

170. Delacre, Lulu (1996). *Golden Tales: Myths, Legends, and Folktales From Latin America.* New York, NY: Scholastic.

171. Jaffe, Nina (1996). *The Golden Flower: A Taino Myth From Puerto Rico.* New York, NY: Simon & Schuster Books for Young Readers.

172. Mohr, Nicholasa (1993). *All for the Better: The Story of El Barrio.* Austin, TX: Raintree Steck-Vaughn.

173. Munoz Ryan, Pam (2000). *Esperanza Rising.* New York, NY: Scholastic.

174. Myers, Walter Dean (1988). *Scorpions.* New York, NY: Harper & Row.

175. Nye, Naomi Shihab (1995). *The Tree Is Older Than You Are: A Bilingual Gathering of Poems & Stories From Mexico With Paintings by Mexican Artists.* New York, NY: Simon & Schuster Books for Young Readers.

176. Ortiz Cofer, Judith (2004). *Call Me María.* New York, NY: Orchard Books.

177. Palacios, Argentina (1993). *Viva Mexico! The Story of Benito Juarez and Cinco de Mayo.* Austin, TX: Raintree Steck-Vaughn.

178. Resau, Laura (2010). *Star in the Forest.* New York, NY: Delacorte Press.

179. Soto, Gary (1992). *Taking Sides.* Orlando, FL: Harcourt.

180. Skarmeta, Antonio (2003). *The Composition.* Toronto, Canada: Groundwood Books.

181. Taylor, Theodore (1973). *The Maldonado Miracle.* Garden City, NY: Doubleday.

*Northern African/Western Asian*

182. Abdel-Fattah, Randa (2010). *Where the Streets Had a Name.* New York, NY: Scholastic.

183. Azzoubi, Rana (2007). *Through a Mud Wall.* Jordan: Book Surge.

184. Azzoubi, Rana (2009). *Million Star Hotel.* Jordan: RaMa for EduCulture.

185. Ellis, Deborah (2001). *The Breadwinner.* Toronto, Canada: Douglas & McIntyre.

186. Englar, Mary (2009). *Queen Rania of Jordan.* Mankato, MN: Capstone Press.

187. Farmer, Nancy (2006). *Clever Ali.* New York, NY: Orchard Books.

188. Halls, Kelly Milner (2010). *Saving the Baghdad Zoo.* New York, NY: Greenwillow Books.

189. Johnson, Julia (2003). *The Pearl Diver.* London, UK: Stacey International.

190. Laird, Elizabeth (1992). *Kiss the Dust.* New York, NY: Dutton Children's Books.

191. Marston, Elsa (2005). *Figs and Fate: Stories About Growing Up in the Arab World Today.* New York, NY: George Braziller.

192. Maydell, Natalie, & Riahi, Sep (2008). *Extraordinary Women From the Muslim World.* New York, NY: Global Content.

193. National Geographic (2012). *1001 Inventions and Awesome Facts From Muslim Civilization.* Washington, DC: National Geographic Children's Books.

194. Nye, Naomi Shihab (1995). *19 Varieties of Gazelle: Poems From the Middle East.* New York, NY: HarperCollins.

195. Nye, Naomi Shihab (1999). *Habibi.* New York, NY: Simon & Schuster Books for Young Readers.

# All Elementary (Grades preK-6, ages 4-12)

### *African/African American/African Diaspora*

196. Aardema, Verna (1975). *Why Mosquitos Buzz in People's Ears: A West African Tale.* New York, NY: Dial Press.

197. Aardema, Verna (1977). *Who's in Rabbit's House?* New York, NY: Dial Press.

198. Agard, John, & Nichols, Grace (1994). *A Caribbean Dozen: Poems From 13 Caribbean Poets.* Cambridge, MA: Candlewick Press.

199. English, Karen (2004). *Speak to Me (and I Will Listen Between the Lines).* New York, NY: Farrar, Straus and Giroux.

200. Grimes, Nikki (1999). *Meet Danitra Brown.* New York, NY: Dial Books for Young Readers.

201. Hamilton, Virginia (1985). *The People Could Fly: American Black Folktales.* New York, NY: Knopf.

202. Johnson, James Weldon (1993). *Lift Ev'ry Voice and Sing.* New York, NY: Walker.

203. McBrier, Page (2001). *Beatrice's Goat.* New York, NY: Atheneum Books for Young Readers.

204. Milway, Katie Smith (2008). *One Hen—How One Small Loan Made a Big Difference.* Toronto, Canada: Kids Can Press.

205. Myers, Christopher (2000). *Wings.* New York, NY: Scholastic.

206. Ringgold, Faith (1991). *Tar Beach.* New York, NY: Crown.

207. Stuve-Bodeen, Stephanie (2003). *Babu's Song.* New York, NY: Lee & Low Books.

208. Winter, Jeanette (2008). *Wangari's Trees of Peace: A True Story From Africa.* New York, NY: HMH Books for Young Readers.

209. Yarbrough, Camille (1979). *Cornrows.* New York, NY: Coward, McCann & Geoghegan.

### *American Indian/Native American/First Nations*

210. Bruchac, Joseph (1992). *Native American Animal Stories.* Golden, CO: Fulcrum.

211. Bruchac, Joseph (1993). *Fox Song.* New York, NY: Philomel Books.

212. Goble, Paul (1989). *Beyond the Ridge.* New York, NY: Bradbury Press.

213. Grace, Catherine O'Neill (2001). *1621: A New Look at Thanksgiving.* Washington, DC: National Geographic Society.

214. Sneve, Virginia Driving Hawk (1994). *The Nez Perce (First Americans Book).* New York, NY: Holiday House.

215. Sneve, Virginia Driving Hawk (2011). *The Christmas Coat: Memories of My Sioux Childhood.* New York, NY: Holiday House.

216. Van Camp, Richard (1998). *What's the Most Beautiful Thing You Know About Horses?* New York, NY: Children's Book Press.

## Asian/Pacific/Central and Southern Asian/Asian American

217. Casey, Dawn (2006). *The Great Race: The Story of the Chinese Zodiac.* Cambridge, MA: Barefoot Books.

218. Cheng, Andrea (2012). *The Year of the Book.* New York, NY: HMH Books for Young Readers.

219. Garland, Sherry (1997). *The Lotus Seed.* Orlando, FL: HMH Books for Young Readers.

220. Howard, Ginger (2002). *A Basket of Bangles: How a Business Begins.* Brookfield, CT: Millbrook Press.

221. King, Dedie, & Inglese, Judith (2010). *I See the Sun in China.* Hardwick, MA: Satya House.

222. King, Dedie, & Inglese, Judith (2010). *I See the Sun in Nepal.* Hardwick, MA: Satya House.

223. King, Dedie, & Inglese, Judith (2011). *I See the Sun in Afghanistan.* Hardwick, MA: Satya House.

224. Landowne, Youme (2010). *Mali Under the Night Sky.* El Paso, TX: Cinco Puntos Press.

225. Lipp, Frederick (2001). *The Caged Birds of Phnom Penh.* New York, NY: Holiday House.

226. Lipp, Frederick (2003). *Tea Leaves.* New York, NY: Mondo.

227. McCully, Emily Arnold (1998). *The Beautiful Warrior: The Legend of the Nun's Kung Fu.* New York, NY: Arthur A. Levine Books.

228. Mochizuki, Ken (1993). *Baseball Saved Us.* New York, NY: Lee & Low Books.

229. Mortenson, Greg (2009). *Listen to the Wind: The Story of Dr. Greg & Three Cups of Tea.* New York, NY: Dial Books for Young Readers.

## Latino/Hispanic American/Latin American

230. Ada, Alma Flor (1997). *Gathering the Sun: An Alphabet in Spanish and English.* New York, NY: HarperCollins.

231. Alarcon, Francisco X. (1997). *Laughing Tomatoes: And Other Spring Poems/Jitomates Risueños: Y Otros Poemas de Primavera.* San Francisco, CA: Children's Book Press.

232. Alarcon, Francisco X. (1998). *From the Bellybutton of the Moon: And Other Summer Poems/Del Ombligo de la Luna: Y Otros Poemas de Verano.* San Francisco, CA: Children's Book Press.

233. Alarcon, Francisco X. (1999). *Angels Ride Bikes and Other Fall Poems/Los Ángeles Andan en Bicicleta y Otros Poemas de Otoño.* San Francisco, CA: Children's Book Press.

234. Anzaldua, Gloria (1993). *Friends From the Other Side/Amigos del Otro Lado.* San Francisco, CA: Children's Book Press.

235. Brusca, Maria Cristina (1991). *On the Pampas.* New York, NY: Henry Holt.

236. dePaola, Tomie (1980). *The Lady of Guadalupe.* New York, NY: Holiday House.

237. dePaola, Tomie (1994). *The Legend of the Poinsettia.* New York, NY: Putnam.

238. Gollub, Matthew (1994). *The Moon Was at a Fiesta.* New York, NY: Tambourine Books.

239. Lomas Garza, Carmen (1990). *Family Pictures/Cuadros de Familia.* San Francisco, CA: Children's Book Press.

240. Mora, Pat (1997). *Tomás and the Library Lady.* New York, NY: Dragonfly Books.

241. Perez, Amada Irma (2002). *My Diary From Here to There; Mi Diario de aquí hasta allá.* San Francisco, CA: Children's Book Press.

## Northern African/Western Asian

242. Al Redha, Ahmad AbdulGhani (2008). *The Sifrah Glider.* Dubai, United Arab Emirates: Jerboa Books.

243. Devine, Barbara (2001). *Elvis the Camel.* London, UK: Stacey International.

244. Heide, Florence Parry, & Gillilan, Judith Heide (1992). *Sami and the Time of the Troubles.* New York, NY: Clarion Books.

245. Johnson, Julia (2004). *A Gift of the Sands.* London, UK: Stacey International.

246. Johnson, Julia (2012). *Saluki: Hound of the Beduoin.* London, UK: Stacey International.

247. Rumford, James (2008). *Silent Music: A Story of Baghdad.* New York, NY: Roaring Brook Press.

248. Winter, Jeanette (2004). *The Librarian of Basra: A True Story From Iraq.* Orlando, FL: Harcourt.

249. Winter, Jeanette (2009). *Nasreen's Secret School.* San Diego, CA: Beach Lane Books.

## Multicultural/Relationships With Multiethnic Characters

250. Ajmera, Maya, & Ivanko, John (2001). *Back to School (It's a Kids' World).* Watertown, MA: Charlesbridge.

251. Braman, Arlette (2002). *Kids Around the World Play! The Best Fun and Games From Many Lands.* New York, NY: John Wiley & Sons.

252. Conkling, Winifred (2011). *Sylvia and Aki.* Berkeley, CA: Tricycle Press.

253. Dooley, Norah (1996). *Everybody Bakes Bread.* Minneapolis, MN: Carolrhoda Books.

254. Dooley, Norah (1991). *Everybody Cooks Rice.* Minneapolis, MN: Carolrhoda Books.

255. Dooley, Norah (2000). *Everybody Serves Soup*. Minneapolis, MN: Carolrhoda Books.

256. Dooley, Norah (2002). *Everybody Brings Noodles*. Minneapolis, MN: Carolrhoda Books.

257. Erlbach, Arlene (1997). *Sidewalk Games Around the World*. Brookfield, CT: Millbrook Press.

258. Fox, Mem (1997). *Whoever You Are*. San Diego, CA: Harcourt Brace.

259. Hamanaka, Sheila (2003). *Grandparents Song*. New York, NY: HarperCollins.

260. Hausherr, Rosemarie (1997). *Celebrating Families*. New York, NY: Scholastic.

261. Hollyer, Beatrice (1999). *Wake Up, World! A Day in the Life of Children Around the World*. New York, NY: Henry Holt.

262. Ichikawa, Satomi (2006). *My Father's Shop*. La Jolla, CA: Kane/Miller.

263. Katz, Karen (1999). *The Colors of Us*. New York, NY: Henry Holt.

264. Kindersley, Anabel, & Kindersley, Barnabas (1995). UNICEF. *Children Just Like Me: A Unique Celebration of Children Around the World*. New York, NY: DK.

265. Kindersley, Anabel, & Kindersley, Barnabas (1997). *Children Just Like Me: Celebrations!* New York, NY: DK.

266. Kissinger, Katie (1994). *All the Colors We Are: Todos los Colores de Nuestra Piel/The Story of How We Get Our Skin Color*. St. Paul, MN: Redleaf Press.

267. Kostecki-Shaw, Jenny Sue (2011). *Same, Same But Different*. New York, NY: Henry Holt.

268. Lester, Julius (2005). *Let's Talk About Race*. New York, NY: HarperCollins.

269. Menzel, Peter, & D'Aluisio, Faith (1994). *Material World: A Global Family Portrait*. San Francisco, CA: Sierra Club Books.

270. Menzel, Peter, & D'Aluisio, Faith (2005). *Hungry Planet*. Berkeley, CA: Ten Speed Press.

271. Morris, Ann (1992). *Houses and Homes (Around the World Series)*. New York, NY: Lothrop, Lee & Shepard Books.

272. Parr, Todd (2001). *It's Okay to Be Different*. Boston, MA: Little, Brown.

273. Polacco, Patricia (2001). *Mr. Lincoln's Way*. New York, NY: Philomel Books.

274. Schuett, Stacey (1995). *Somewhere in the World Right Now*. New York, NY: Knopf.

275. Smith, David J. (2011). *If the World Were a Village: A Book About the World's People*. Toronto, Canada: Kids Can Press.

276. Smith, Peggy, & Shaley, Zahavit (2007). *A School Like Mine*. New York, NY: DK.

277. Soto, Gary (1992). *Pacific Crossing*. San Diego, CA: Harcourt Brace Jovanovich.

278. Spier, Peter (1980). *People*. Garden City, NY: Doubleday.

279. Tingle, Tim (2006). *Crossing Bok Chitto*. El Paso, TX: Cinco Puntos Press.

280. UNICEF (United Nations Children's Fund), & Belafonte, Harry (foreword), Amanda Rayner (Editor) (2006). *A Life Like Mine: How Children Live Around the World*. New York, NY: DK.
281. Veitch, Catherine (2012). *Farms Around the World*. Chicago, IL: Heinemann Library.
282. Vyner, Tim (2006). *World Team*. Brookfield, CT: Roaring Brook Press.
283. Weiss, George David (2001). *What a Wonderful World*. Milwaukee, WI: Hal Leonard.

*Empathy/Respect/Diversity*

284. Boelts, Maribeth (2007). *Those Shoes*. Cambridge, MA: Candlewick.
285. Bunting, Eve (2006). *One Green Apple*. New York, NY: Clarion Books.
286. Coerr, Eleanor (1977). *Sadako and a Thousand Paper Cranes*. New York, NY: Putnam.
287. Derolf, Shane (1997). *The Crayon Box That Talked*. New York, NY: Random House.
288. Kerley, Barbara (2002). *A Cool Drink of Water*. Washington, DC: National Geographic Society.
289. Kerley, Barbara (2005). *You and Me Together: Moms, Dads, and Kids Around the World*. Washington, DC: National Geographic Children's Books.
290. Kerley, Barbara (2007). *A Little Peace*. Washington, DC: National Geographic Children's Books.
291. Kerley, Barbara (2009). *One World, One Day*. Washington, DC: National Geographic Children's Books.
292. Kim, Joung Un, & Pak, Soyung (2003). *Sumi's First Day of School Ever*. New York, NY: Viking Juvenile.
293. Moss, Peggy (2004). *Say Something*. Gardiner, ME: Tilbury House.
294. Reitano, John (1998). *What if the Zebras Lost Their Stripes?* New York, NY: Paulist Press.
295. Soros, Barbara (2003). *Tenzin's Deer*. Cambridge, MA: Barefoot Books.
296. Williams, Karen Lynn, & Mohammed, Khadra (2007). *Four Feet, Two Sandals*. Grand Rapids, MI: Eerdmans Books for Young Readers.

*World Religions/Holidays/Diverse Perspectives*

297. Addasi, Maha (2008). *The White Nights of Ramadan*. Honesdale, PA: Boyds Mills Press.
298. Addasi, Maha (2010). *Time to Pray*. Honesdale, PA: Boyds Mills Press.
299. Buller, Laura (2005). *A Faith Like Mine: A Celebration of the World's Religions Through the Eyes of Children*. New York, NY: DK.
300. Cohen, Barbara (1983). *Molly's Pilgrim*. New York, NY: HarperCollins.
301. Demi (1997). *Buddha Stories*. New York, NY: Henry Holt.
302. (Also see: *The Dalai Lama. The Fantastic Adventures of Krishna. Jesus. Muhammad. St. Francis of Assisi. Lao Tzu. Mary.*)

303. Glossop, Jennifer, & Mantha, John (2003). *The Kids Book of World Religions*. Toronto, Canada: Kids Can Press.

304. Gross, Judith (1992). *Celebrate: A Book of Jewish Holidays*. New York, NY: Grosset & Dunlap.

305. Hesse, Karen (1992). *Letters From Rifka*. New York, NY: Puffin Books.

306. Jalali, Reza (2010). *Moon Watchers: Shirin's Ramadan Miracle*. Gardiner, ME: Tilbury House.

307. Khan, Hena (2008). *Night of the Moon: A Muslim Holiday Story*. San Francisco, CA: Chronicle Books.

308. Khan, Hena (2012). *Golden Domes and Silver Lanterns: A Muslim Book of Colors*. San Francisco, CA: Chronicle Books.

309. Kimmel, Eric A. (1989). *Hershel and the Hanukkah Goblins*. New York, NY: Holiday House.

310. Lankford, Mary (1995). *Christmas Around the World*. New York, NY: HarperCollins.

311. Medearis, Angela S. (2000). *Seven Spools of Thread: A Kwanzaa Story*. Morton Grove, IL: Albert Whitman.

312. Mobin-Uddin, Asma (2007). *The Best Eid Ever*. Honesdale, PA: Boyds Mills Press.

313. Mobin-Uddin, Asma (2009). *A Party in Ramadan*. Honesdale, PA: Boyds Mills Press.

314. Muth, Jon J. (2002). *The Three Questions*. Singapore: Scholastic.

315. Muth, Jon J. (2005). *Zen Shorts*. New York, NY: Scholastic.

316. Neale, John (2005). *Good King Wenceslas*. Grand Rapids, MI: Eerdmans Books for Young Readers.

317. Osborne, Mary Pope (1996). *One World, Many Religions: The Ways We Worship*. New York, NY: Knopf Books for Young Readers.

318. Polacco, Patricia (1992). *Mrs. Katz and Tush*. New York, NY: Dragonfly Books.

319. Renberg, Dalia Hardof (1994). *King Solomon and the Bee*. New York, NY: HarperCollins.

320. Robinson, Gary (2007). *Native American Night Before Christmas*. Santa Fe, NM: Clear Light.

321. Schwartz, Howard, & Rush, Barbara (1991). *The Diamond Tree: Jewish Tales From Around the World*. New York, NY: HarperCollins.

322. Silver, Gail (2009). *Anh's Anger*. Berkeley, CA: Plum Blossom Books.

323. Strom, Yale (1996). *Quilted Landscape: Conversations With Young Immigrants*. New York, NY: Simon & Schuster Children's.

324. Wayland, April Halprin (2009). *New Year at the Pier: A Rosh Hashanah Story*. New York, NY: Dial Books/Penguin Group.

325. Whitman, Sylvia (2008). *Under the Ramadan Moon*. Morton Grove, IL: Albert Whitman.

326. Yolen, Jane (2004). *The Devil's Arithmetic*. New York, NY: Puffin Books.

# Index

*Note: In page references, f indicates figures, t indicates tables and w indicates websites.*

National Association of
Independent Schools
(NAIS), 125
NAIS Challenge 20/20
program, 97
National Chinese Language
Conference, 146
National Endowment for the
Humanities Summer
programs, 152w
National Geographic, 94w
e-mail-based collaborative
projects from, 124
ePals and, 54–55
geographic learning and, 134
YouTube and, 137
*National Geographic:*
geography and, xxiii
for global photography, 136w
National Geographic Bee,
13–14, 58w
National Geographic's
Education, 92w
National Museum of the
American Indian, 102w
National Resource Centers, 149w
National Service-Learning
Clearinghouse, 159w
Natural resources:
children as tomorrow's leaders
and, xviii
power of pictures and, 72
theme ideas for, 5
Navajo rug patterns, 87w
Ndonyo-Wasin Primary
School, 128
NetGenEd Project, 141w
News outlets, 138–139
Newspaper articles, 139
Newspaper Map, 139w
Newspapers, online, 139w
New Year, 5
*New York Times,* 136
Nings, 140–141
Nippon News, 139w
Nobel Peace Prize winners,
28, 80
Noon Day Project, 88w
Nothing But Nets, 178w
November, A., 138

O'Brien, A. S., 81
Ohlone Elementary, 183–184
*Oliver!,* 49
Olympics, 25, 28, 54, 84, 88

Omprakash Volunteer Abroad
Grants, 152w
One Hen, 90w
One To World, 61w
*One Well: The Story of Water on
Earth,* 81w
Online courses, 147
Online newspapers, 139w
*Our World of Water,* 81w
Out of Eden Walk, 76–77w
Outreach World, 149w
Overton, B., 183–184
Oxfam, 99t, 133w
America Hunger Banquet and,
33–34, 33w
Oxford University, 107

Packer Collegiate Institute, 128
Paper dolls, 24
Parents:
Facebook and, 118
gaining support from,
6, 9–11, 13–14
as guest speakers, 60
incorporating food with, 31
planning global-themed events
and, 4
planning international events
and, 16
Twitter and, 117
Parent volunteers, 10–11, 13–14
e-mail and, 10, 11, 12
geography education by, 64–65
holiday bulletin board and,
29–30
immigrants and, 10–11
*See also* Volunteers
Pariser, E., 143
Parry, F. H., 80
Partnership for 21st Century
Skills, 113–114w
Passport Club, 65w
Passport Day, 51–52
Passport template, 192–196
PBS Kids, 100–101w
PBS Learning Media, 132w
Peace Corps, 55
guest speakers and, 62
lesson plans by, 133
Peace Corps Challenge Online
Game, 93w
Peace Corps Education
Portal, 100t
Peace Corps World Wise Schools,
55w, 62w, 92w

## CORWIN

A SAGE Company

The Corwin logo—a raven striding across an open book—represents the union of courage and learning. Corwin is committed to improving education for all learners by publishing books and other professional development resources for those serving the field of PreK–12 education. By providing practical, hands-on materials, Corwin continues to carry out the promise of its motto: **"Helping Educators Do Their Work Better."**